THE SECOND WORLD WAR

An Illustrated History

THE SECOND WORLD WAR

An Illustrated History

JAMES HOLLAND

Illustrated by Keith Burns

MICHAEL JOSEPH

For Lucas and
Sebastian Lambourne.

JAMES HOLLAND

Dedicated to Claire, James
and Edith, thanks to Stu Steele.

KEITH BURNS

CONTENTS

Opposite: British tanks mass for Operation VERITABLE.

Frontispiece: HMS Hood leads HMS Rodney and HMS Renown on manoeuvres on the High Seas.

1: BLITZKRIEG

On Monday, 21 August 1939, Nazi Germany signed a non-aggression pact with the Soviet Union. Politically and ideologically, the two countries were natural enemies, but the USSR was not ready for war, and Adolf Hitler, the German leader, wanted to invade Poland without risk of being attacked from the east in turn. Both countries understood this was a temporary treaty of convenience. It did, however, pave the way for the outbreak of the Second World War.

The following day, Tuesday, 22 August, Hitler called together his senior commanders to the Berghof, his house near Berchtesgaden in the Bavarian Alps, and outlined his plans for war against Poland. Since 1919, the enclave of East Prussia, still part of Germany, had been cut off by a narrow strip of land known as the Danzig Corridor. It was time, he told them, to take it back, and to test German military strength. 'We are faced,' he said, with his usual black-and-white world-view, 'with the harsh alternatives of striking or of certain annihilation sooner or later.' The only choice remaining was to crush Poland.

A day later, Hitler announced that the invasion would be launched in a matter of days. Curiously, that evening the Northern Lights were showing over the Alps and a shroud of deep red was cast over the Untersberg. The Führer and his followers were watching from the terrace as the same red light now bathed their faces and hands.

Hitler turned to one of his military adjutants and said, 'Looks like a great deal of blood.'

Britain and France, two of the world's most powerful nations, had vowed to defend Poland's sovereignty. This meant that if Germany invaded, then they would both declare war. Many senior commanders in the Wehrmacht, the German armed services, believed this threat, but Hitler thought they were bluffing. After all, in 1936 he had marched back into the Rhineland, ceded from Germany after the end of the First World War, and the French and British had done nothing. Then, in spring 1938, his forces had poured into Austria and brought that country into the Third Reich without a shot being fired; and that autumn, German troops had occupied the Sudetenland of Czechoslovakia, then six months later had taken control of the entire country. Once again, the rest of the world had sat back and watched. Now, in the late summer of 1939, he could not imagine Britain or France risking war over Poland.

Opposite: Hitler and his senior commanders meet at the Berghof.

In Germany, Hitler's popularity had never been higher. He had created jobs, grown the armed forces, given the German people back their pride, and had taken back all the German-speaking territories, and more besides, without any opposition.

Most Germans also believed that much of Poland was rightfully theirs. Certainly, much of the western part of the country had been within Germany until Poland had been recreated following the end of the First World War. Many there spoke German rather than Polish. Nazi propaganda also told the world that Poles had been carrying out atrocities against Germans.

Propaganda had been a key component of Nazi strategy from the outset. To a large degree, this was due to Dr Josef Goebbels, the Reich Minister for Popular Enlightenment and Propaganda. It was Goebbels who whipped up hatred of Jews – anti-Semitism – and Communists, as well as convincing the German people of the rightness of Hitler's ambitions. Key to this was repetition and the new media of radio and film.

Goebbels recognized that radios, especially, were an ideal way to get a message across. Germany lagged behind other leading nations in many innovations of the age, but not when it came to radios,

which were made in large numbers and cheaply, too. By 1939, almost 70 per cent of the population owned radios, and most were the DKE, or *Deutscher Kleinempfänger*, the 'German Little Radio'. Small and affordable, this ensured there were more people with a radio in Germany than in any other country in the world, including the USA. Public squares, restaurants and bars were also fitted with speakers from which the radio could be heard. 'Repeat, repeat, repeat,' was Goebbels' mantra. Over the airways, on film and in newspapers, the state-controlled media were able to bombard the German people with the same messages: Hitler's genius, the rightness of German territorial ambitions, the growing strength and invincibility of the German armed forces, as well as virulent anti-Semitism and anti-Communism.

And it worked. 'The anger that I felt inside at their unreasonableness,' Lieutenant Hajo Herrmann, a young bomber pilot, said of the Poles, 'matched my sacred conviction: that of German rightness.'

Hajo Herrmann was one of the many bomber pilots in the Luftwaffe – the German Air Force – flying over to attack Polish targets in the early hours of Friday, 1 September 1939. On the ground, troops poured over the border. Artillery boomed, panzers – tanks – rumbled forward, while Stuka dive-bombers screamed down, sirens wailing, to drop their bombs. Two days later, on 3 September, Britain and France honoured their pledge to Poland and declared war on Germany.

The German plan was to use the Luftwaffe as aerial artillery, hitting at cities, communications, military targets and also airfields and aircraft on the ground, and so effectively paralyse the Polish defence. The Polish Air Force was much smaller in size and for the most part lacked modern aircraft. Hajo Herrmann and his colleagues were able to destroy much of it in a matter of days.

The German Army attacked in three separate thrusts, all of them driving towards Warsaw, the

Polish capital. Despite some stoic Polish defence, the Germans were closing in on the city just eight days after the campaign had begun, with the Poles falling back to the south-east.

On 17 September, Soviet forces invaded from the east, as earlier agreed with Germany, and Poland's fate was sealed. With Warsaw and other towns in ruins, the last resistance capitulated on 28 September. Even so, sweeping aside a militarily weak country like Poland was one thing, but beating two super-powers like Britain and France would be another altogether.

On 27 September, with Poland destroyed, Hitler called together all his senior commanders and told them to get ready for an immediate attack in the west against France and the Low Countries. No one said a word in protest, but there were many among them, not least General Franz Halder, the chief of staff of the army, who understood that Germany's armed forces were nothing like as strong as they needed to be to take on Britain and France.

Propaganda had depicted Germany as a giant, modern, mechanized force, better trained and equipped than any other on earth. The reality, however, was rather different. It was true that, in the

Luftwaffe, Germany had the largest and best-equipped air force of any country, but France alone had a larger army, with better and greater numbers of tanks, and considerably more artillery. Britain, meanwhile, had the largest navy and merchant shipping fleet, with access to more than 80 per cent of the world's merchant shipping. Its empire was also the biggest that had ever been known. Both Britain and France had ready access to the world's oceans and with it to the kind of resources needed for war.

Germany, on the other hand, lay at the heart of Europe. Her limited access to the world's sea lanes lay in a small strip into the North Sea, now blockaded by the Royal Navy, and ports on the Baltic Sea. It had no direct access to any ocean.

Despite these clear advantages and despite the fact that the vast majority of Germany's military forces had been ploughed into the Polish campaign, neither Britain nor France had ever had much intention of taking the offensive on behalf of the Poles. Britain had a small army, which meant that France would have to take the primary role in any land operation across the border into western Germany. In any case, the British Army was still in Britain when war was declared.

General Maurice Gamelin, the Commander-in-Chief of the French Armed Forces, had, however, promised back in May that French forces would come to Poland's rescue. It was one of the reasons the Poles had earlier resisted any diplomatic solution. Now that war had been declared, Gamelin ordered what he called an 'offensive reconnaissance' into the Saar region of Germany. Nothing happened very quickly, however, and when the French did move, they rumbled just 5 miles across the border, then stopped. By this time, Soviet troops had invaded Poland from the east and the country had been all but destroyed. The French then pulled back behind the Maginot Line, the massive fixed defences that lined the Franco-German border.

Left: Hitler shocks General Franz Halder by demanding an immediate attack on the West.

Opposite: French troops move into the Saar.

A golden opportunity to hit the Germans at their weakest had gone begging. Instead, Britain and France planned to play for time. However, German geographical isolation and economic limitations suggested they would opt for a rapid and decisive attack in the west before too long. The Allied strategy was to withstand this initial attack, continue to build strength, then strike back.

Insecurity lay at the heart of the French military leadership, and they certainly believed Germany to be far stronger than was the reality. In August 1938, for example, General Joseph Vuillemin, the head of the French Air Force, had been invited to Germany to inspect the Luftwaffe. He was shown lines of bombers and fighters and watched them take off and land again, then was driven to another air base, where, unbeknown to him, the same aircraft had arrived just ahead of him. Returning to France, he told the French Prime Minister that, if it came to war, the French Air Force would be annihilated in days. In fact, Britain and France together had more aircraft than the Luftwaffe.

Nor was Germany anything like as mechanized as propaganda suggested. On the eve of war, there was one motorized vehicle for every forty-seven people in Germany, but one for every fourteen in Britain and one for every nine in France. For the invasion of Poland, just fifteen German divisions of the fifty-four used were mechanized. The rest had been dependent on horses, carts and the soldiers' own two feet, which was how German troops had moved for centuries.

Nor was this about to change any time soon, because there were not enough factories, spare parts, mechanics or drivers. Perhaps most importantly, nor was there enough fuel. Germany was, and would remain, extremely short of oil and, without access to the world's oceans, there were limited ways of getting hold of it.

The shortcomings of the German Army were all too apparent to many of its senior commanders, including General Halder, who was now supposed to devise a plan of attack against the West in a matter of weeks. The vehicles they did have had taken a battering on the rough Polish roads, but, even worse, the army had almost entirely run out of ammunition. Furthermore, the fighting in Poland had shown shortcomings in training in many of the German divisions. The division was the military unit by which most armies were judged and tended to contain around 15,000 men, including infantry, artillery and support troops.

By producing a succession of highly unimaginative plans of attack, Halder incurred the wrath of Hitler, but did ensure there could be no immediate assault on the West. It was true that British and French factories would be continuing to produce arms over the winter, but Germany needed to do

Right: The Messerschmitt 108 carrying Halder's plan crash lands near Mechelen in Belgium.

Opposite: The German Army still relied heavily on horses in 1939.

the same. Only with replenished stocks of ammunition and more trained troops could the Germans have a hope of success.

They also needed a plan of attack that might give them a chance of victory, and Halder knew his current proposal to march into the Low Countries as they had in 1914 was not the answer. Then, in January, two German officers made a forced landing at Mechelen in Belgium and were promptly captured, along with Halder's current plans. This changed everything.

The Allies responded by carrying out extensive troop movements along the Belgian border, all of which were watched by Luftwaffe reconnaissance planes. What at first had seemed an intelligence disaster now looked like giving Germany a glimmer of hope.

Not only did the Allies clearly expect an attack through the Low Countries, but French troop movements had been very slow. This suggested that if German forces could move with greater speed, and in a way the Allies were not expecting, they might be able to catch them by surprise.

Halder now reconsidered a different plan that had been proposed by General Erich von Manstein, but which he had earlier rejected. This was to launch a feint attack into the Low Countries, which would draw the Allies north. Meanwhile, the bulk of the few precious panzer divisions would sweep through the hilly and wooded Ardennes Forest, then drive in behind the advancing Allies in a giant encirclement (see map on page 324).

As it happened, von Manstein's plans had also reached Hitler, who had embraced them immediately. Even better, as far as Halder was concerned, the Führer was now talking about attacking Denmark and Norway first. This meant the attack in the west would be launched even later, with better weather and longer days, which would make moving through the Ardennes easier. It was still an enormous gamble, but it was the only plan that Halder could see having even the slightest chance of success. Furthermore, while British and French rearmament had continued, the German Army was now in much better shape, with ammunition stocks replenished and more men properly trained.

In actual fact, a drive through the Ardennes was hardly original. The Prussians had passed through the same area in 1870 in the war against France, and again in 1914. Furthermore, the German way of war was always to try to strike hard and fast, knock their enemy off balance and then complete a rapid encirclement before the opposition forces had recovered. This approach went back to the early eighteenth century and was because of the fundamental vulnerability of the country's geographical position in central Europe and because of its shortage of natural resources.

Although the principles of striking hard and fast have come to be termed 'Blitzkrieg' – lightning war – it was not a conscious doctrine for the Germans. Rather, they called it *Bewegungskrieg*: war of rapid manoeuvre.

What was different in 1940 was the machinery and equipment they were using. Germany now had the Luftwaffe to help the spearhead of any attack and provide aerial artillery. They also had tanks. And, perhaps most importantly of all, they had radios: small and easy-to-manufacture radios that could be fitted inside a panzer or even on a motorcycle sidecar.

Despite these advantages, the senior command of the German Army was mostly filled with men who secretly believed Germany had little chance in any battle against the Allies and who had little understanding of how this new technology might be applied. But there were a few exceptions, and one of those was a dynamic panzer general called Heinz Guderian.

Opposite: The German doctrine of 'war of rapid manoeuvre'.

Von Manstein's plan might not have been so very original, but just how it was to be carried out most certainly was, and for that the man responsible above all others was General Guderian. Aged fifty-one, he was a deep thinker on military matters and had even published a book, *Achtung Panzer!*, about the use of tanks in modern warfare. He was breathing new life into the old principles of *Bewegungskrieg*.

It was widely accepted, though, in the German Army and in other countries too, that tanks could not be used without the support of the infantry. Britain and France had developed armoured divisions made up almost entirely of tank units, which would then operate alongside infantry divisions. Guderian, however, was creating something quite different. A panzer division included not just tanks but also motorized infantry and motorized artillery. In other words, it was a mechanized formation of all arms. Tanks, infantry and artillery could then move together and operate together, offering mutual support in one self-contained unit. What's more, they could keep in communication by radio, liberally spread throughout every part of the division. It was this ability to communicate with each component that was so crucial. Radios gave the division enormous flexibility and, with it, speed of manoeuvre.

Training together was also crucial, but it was this speed of operations that Guderian thought would give them a significant edge because he knew from intelligence that the French operated far more slowly.

Even so, the numbers of mechanized divisions available for the spearhead was small. In fact, just sixteen of the 135 earmarked for the attack in the west were motorized, of which only ten were panzer. None the less, Guderian reckoned these sixteen elite divisions would be enough to create

the vital breakthrough. The key, he believed, was for the leading divisions to get through the Ardennes and reach the River Meuse, the principal French defensive position along that part of the front, in just three days, and cross it in four.

If they could achieve that, then he knew they could break through the main French line of defence and get in behind them before the enemy could organize itself into a coordinated counter-attack. They could round up and defeat the French bit by bit and so ensure that at the point of attack they would have superior numbers. The crucial thing was to ensure the French were unable to mass their reserves together.

Senior commanders in the German Army who both understood and believed in the kind of panzer tactics Guderian was advocating were few and far between. However, as Halder now realized, this plan was the only one

Right: General Halder, right, considers von Manstein and Guderian's plan.

Opposite: General Guderian in his command vehicle standing over radio and Enigma code-machine operators.

offering even a chance of a decisive victory, and because it was also supported by the Führer it was the one adopted. Even so, it remained a massive all-or-nothing gamble and its chances of success depended on a great deal that could very easily go wrong.

In the meantime, though, Hitler also announced plans to attack Denmark and Norway, and to do so before an attack in the west. This made little sense. Far more logical would be to attack France and the Low Countries first. If they were successful, then they would be able to walk into Norway almost unopposed: France would already have been vanquished and Britain at the very least in no position to fight. But by attacking Denmark and Norway first, Hitler risked losing precious men and materiel just before the greatest clash of arms yet faced by the Wehrmacht.

As it happened, since the previous autumn Britain and France had been debating the possibility of a pre-emptive strike on Norway and Sweden. Nearly all Germany's iron ore came from northern Sweden and was mostly shipped out through the northern Norwegian port of Narvik. However, the Allies could not agree on the right plan, nor were they willing to risk Scandinavian hostility. Not until early April did they finally decide to mine the Leads, the waters off Narvik.

By coincidence, Allied warships were sailing towards the Leads at exactly the same time as the Germans were launching their invasion of Denmark and Norway. German naval forces were spotted steaming up the Norwegian coast on 7 April, prompting frantic recalculations from the British. Next day, HMS *Glowworm*, a British destroyer, intercepted the German heavy cruiser *Admiral Hipper* and four destroyers. After being repeatedly hit, and with her decks on fire, *Glowworm* in an heroic final act rammed the *Admiral Hipper*, shearing off 40 metres of the cruiser's prow. Moments later, *Glowworm* rolled, then blew up.

Then, early on 9 April, Germany invaded both Denmark and southern Norway simultaneously, using air and naval forces, and both ground and airborne troops.

Despite the questionable strategy, the German invasion of Denmark and Norway was none the less brilliantly planned and executed. Denmark fell in a matter of hours as German *Fallschirmjäger* dropped from the sky in what was the first ever use of paratroopers in action. At the same time, ground troops stormed ashore in five simultaneous landings. In Norway, further airborne troops and landings, supported by large numbers of air forces, also quickly overwhelmed any resistance. Oslo, the capital, fell that day, 9 April.

Left: German destroyers sink at Narvik.

Opposite: HMS Glowworm *rams the* Admiral Hipper.

Britain hurriedly sent reinforcements, but they lacked support from the air as well as any heavy firepower, and, despite trying to meet the German drive northwards, were soon pushed back. Only at Narvik, in the far north, was a joint British and French force successful. Eventually, however, in June, they were compelled to evacuate even this small foothold. On the ground, and with much shorter lines of supply than the Allies, the Germans swiftly swept over most of the country.

At sea, however, it was a very different story. The size and training of the Royal Navy soon inflicted a hammer-blow on the German Navy, the Kriegsmarine: half the German destroyer force was sunk, as were one of two heavy cruisers, two of six light cruisers and six U-boats. Other vessels were badly damaged, leaving Germany with a much-depleted navy capable of achieving little. On top of that, the Luftwaffe lost 242 aircraft in the campaign – machines and crew that would be needed in the summer to come.

The Germans finally launched their attack on the West early on Friday, 10 May 1940. The bulk of the Luftwaffe attacked targets in support of the northern thrust of Army Group B through the Netherlands and Belgium, while airborne troops parachuted down to capture key bridges and, in the first-ever glider-borne operation, the important Belgian fort of Eben-Emael was swiftly taken too.

As the Germans had hoped, the French and British immediately started moving from their positions in northern France into Belgium to meet the attack. Belgium had been neutral and had refused to allow French and British troops on to their soil before Germany made any attack. This meant these troops now had to travel up to 80 miles to the River Dyle, where they planned to link up with Dutch and Belgian forces and make their main stand. In all, twenty-five French and five British divisions began moving north, albeit slowly. The first British troops did not cross into Belgium until 10.20 a.m., nearly four hours after first being ordered to do so. Furthermore, the roads were already beginning to clog with fleeing civilians heading in the opposite direction. This was something none of the Allied war leaders had considered beforehand. It was already looking like quite a bad oversight.

Meanwhile, across the Channel in London, the British Prime Minister, Neville Chamberlain, had been forced to resign over Britain's failure in Norway. At this moment of extreme crisis, Winston Churchill, seen by many as a dangerous maverick with poor judgement, took over the reins.

While British and French troops moved into the Low Countries, the main German thrust by Army Group A began its drive through the Ardennes. Leading the advance was Guderian's panzer corps of three divisions, heading to Sedan. To help them reach the Meuse in only three days, the troops were given an amphetamine called Pervitin to keep them awake and were told to keep going at all costs. They had 100 miles and six major obstacles to overcome: the Luxembourg border, two lines of Belgian defences, then the River Semois, the French border posts, and finally the River Meuse, the French main line of defence.

Meanwhile, following behind Guderian was a second panzer corps, under General Georg-Hans Reinhardt, which was to cross the Meuse 25 miles to the north at Monthermé, while a further 20 miles north from there, two more panzer divisions were to get across the Meuse at Dinant. Once over, these three thrusts were to advance rapidly and link up, then wait for the infantry to catch up. Then, with the bulk of the northern Allied forces facing Army Group B, the southern thrust would sweep west behind them and catch them in an enormous encirclement. There remained, however, much that could go wrong.

In fact, the plan was already beginning to unravel because behind Guderian's troops were almost 40,000 of Army Group A's vehicles, as well as infantry divisions now cutting across Panzer Corps Reinhardt's advance. The roads were narrow and few and far between. Gridlock ensued.

Tragically for the Allies, although aerial reconnaissance spotted this vast traffic jam, the information was dismissed by the French 9th Army intelligence section as impossible. As a result, the opportunity to mass-bomb much of Army Group A while they were sitting ducks was not taken.

Meanwhile, Guderian's lead troops reached Sedan, as planned, on the afternoon of 12 May. Sedan lay on the hinge of the French defences. To the south, along the Franco-German border, were the forts, tunnels and bunkers of the Maginot Line. To the north-west, however, was the Belgian border and from here French and British troops were swinging north towards the Dyle. Sedan had been crossed by German troops in 1870 and again in 1914, and in 1917 it had been in German hands and the site of a war school, which Guderian had attended. He knew the area well.

His troops attacked across the Meuse in three places on 13 May. French defences were weak, the Luftwaffe struck in force, and Guderian's infantry were able to storm the river and smash the French bunkers. By nightfall on the 13th, Sedan had fallen and the French were on the run. French tanks waiting in reserve were slow to move and by the following morning, with the first panzers now across the river, they were caught in a trap and destroyed.

Meanwhile, at Monthermé, just enough of Reinhardt's troops had miraculously reached the Meuse and crossed on the 13th too, while at Dinant, Major-General Erwin Rommel's 7th Panzer and the 5th Panzer Division also attacked successfully across the river.

These attacking troops were the best-trained and most motivated in the German Army and, although they were by no means representative of the whole – only around 38 per cent of the army was fully trained – the achievement of this spearhead was extraordinary and a masterpiece example of *Bewegungskrieg*. None the less, the French defenders should have been able to stop them. The trouble was, many of the French senior commanders were too old and too stuck in the doctrine of the past, and so believed this new war would be much like the last, with little movement. They had believed it would take the Germans two weeks to reach their main line of defence, not three days. And although the French were bristling with double the number of guns and bigger, better tanks than the Germans, they lacked radios. Communications depended on land lines, which were all too

Left: A half-track of the 1st Panzer Division advancing through Sedan.

Opposite: A German armoured column advances through the Ardennes.

quickly cut by bombing, and dispatch riders who got nowhere on roads now choked with refugees.

The inability of the French to move swiftly was demonstrated horribly on 15 May when the 1st Armoured Division came up against Rommel's 7th Panzer and the 5th Panzer Division. The French 1st Armoured began the day with 176 tanks, but by nightfall had just thirty-six left. By the following morning there were only sixteen. Although French tanks were superior, the Germans, using radio, were able to lure them into hidden screens of high-velocity anti-tank guns. In this way, the crème de la crème of the French Army was destroyed.

The entire French front along the Meuse had collapsed. French troops had been trained to hold a fixed position. They had not been encouraged to use their initiative and so now did not know what to do. Many simply put their hands in the air and surrendered.

The French leaders were caught like rabbits in headlights. Panic set in as the scale of the catastrophe swiftly sank in. General Alphonse Georges, the French commander in the north, visited British headquarters and burst into tears. It did little to help matters.

In the north, the Dutch surrendered on 15 May. That same day, the French Prime Minister, Paul Reynaud, called Churchill and said, 'We have been defeated.' Then he paused and added, 'We have been beaten; we have lost the battle.' He was quite right. Momentum was with the Germans and the French were unable to respond swiftly enough to mount the kind of rapid and concentrated counter-attack needed. How could they when orders were taking up to twelve hours to get through and sometimes even longer?

Meanwhile, the panzer divisions were ignoring the orders of their senior commanders to wait for the infantry and instead continued their drive west. 'Keep going, don't look left or right,' Rommel told his men. 'The enemy is confused. We must take advantage of it.' Guderian was urging his men to do the same: 'Hit hard, not softly!'

On 20 May, just ten days after setting out from the German border, the first of Guderian's troops reached the Atlantic coast near Abbeville.

The great gamble had paid off.

Following the Dutch surrender, Belgian, British and French troops began falling back to the next defensive line along the River Escaut, 40 miles to the west, along roads heaving with refugees. The Luftwaffe bombed and machine-gunned at will, and also hit Allied airfields, where, without radar or any early-warning system, many aircraft were destroyed on the ground.

Right: French troops surrender.

Opposite: Knocked-out Char Bs of the French 1st Armoured Division.

The bulk of the Allied forces were now trapped in a large, narrow corridor and the danger was that all too soon German troops would encircle them entirely and cut them off from the Channel coast.

On 19 May, General Maurice Gamelin was sacked as commander-in-chief, but replaced with an even older man, General Maxime

Weygand, aged seventy-three. Meanwhile, the British had demanded a major joint Anglo-French counter-attack with simultaneous strikes from south and north in an effort to drive a wedge through the advancing panzers. On 21 May, the British attacked Rommel's troops southwards to the west of Arras, but only a handful of French joined them and none at all attacked from the south. The Arras counter-attack proved to be little more than a demonstration in force.

Even so, Rommel himself had thought the situation so desperate that he took personal command of some anti-tank guns. It suggested a major blow might have been achieved had the French been able to organize themselves more quickly. As it was, the failure of the counter-attack signalled the last hope for the northern Allied armies.

The Allied troops were still corralled in a long, narrow wedge of Flanders, which had become a corridor of military failure and civilian misery. General Weygand now ordered a second major counter-attack, but General Lord John Gort, the commander of the British Expeditionary Force, had already decided there was only one option left: to try to evacuate as many troops as possible from the Channel ports while they still had the chance.

At this point, the British were offered an unexpected lifeline. Field Marshal Gerd von Rundstedt, the commander of Army Group A, had been shocked by the Arras counter-attack and now ordered his panzer divisions to halt to allow the infantry to catch up. Halder, realizing they had a golden chance to neatly trap all the northern Allied armies, immediately countermanded this. When Hitler found out what Halder had done, however, he chose to berate the army chief of staff and sided with von Rundstedt. Thus the panzers remained halted, although by this time both Boulogne and Calais had fallen. Only Dunkirk remained in Allied hands.

When Gort learned about this order, he immediately called on the Royal Navy to put Operation DYNAMO, the naval evacuation of the BEF, into effect, although he did so with little optimism; he suspected only a fraction would be successfully brought home.

Back in Britain, on Sunday 26, May, King George VI called a National Day of Prayer. Few could believe the scale of the defeat.

Sunday 26 May was also the first day of the evacuation and a mere 7,669 men were safely lifted from the beaches. None the less, while some units were ordered to make for Dunkirk, others were fiercely defending a rapidly shrinking corridor. It was these actions that enabled the bulk of the BEF to fall behind a defensive perimeter of canals around Dunkirk.

It was Hitler's determination to show the army command who was boss, rather than any good military sense, that made him insist on the halt order. By the time it was lifted and the panzers began moving again on the morning of 27 May, the Royal Navy had discovered that a narrow wooden mole, or jetty, at the end of the wrecked Dunkirk harbour could support ships. What's more, the weather had turned and the low cloud, combined with thick plumes of smoke from burning fuel stores, made it very difficult for the Luftwaffe successfully to attack the evacuation below. Also now helping were RAF Fighter Command's Spitfires and Hurricanes, flying over from southern England.

On 28 May, Belgium surrendered, leaving a dangerous gap in the northern part of the line. In a daring and brilliantly executed night march, however, General Bernard Montgomery's 4th Division moved overnight to plug the hole and a crisis was prevented. At the same time, Churchill managed

Opposite: Rommel directs the fire of a battery of 88mm guns during the British counter-attack at Arras.

to avert a major argument in his War Cabinet. There would be no suing for peace, as Lord Halifax had suggested. Britain would fight on.

With dykes broken, fields waterlogged and determined resistance from British and French troops around the Dunkirk perimeter, the Germans found progress much harder. All the while, more and more men were being evacuated: by naval vessels, civilian cross-Channel steamers and even a mass of 'little boats' that answered the call and hurried across the Channel to help.

On 29 May, 53,823 men were lifted; the next day, 68,014 made it home. By 2 June, all British troops had been successfully picked up and then French troops were taken to England too. By 4 June, when Dunkirk finally fell, an incredible 338,226 men had been evacuated. Most of the equipment was left behind, along with some 70,000 casualties, but the bulk of the BEF's troops had been saved.

The same could not be said for the French, who were now resigned to their fate. The Germans swept southwards. Paris, the capital, fell on 14 June, by which time Paul Reynaud had lost the support of his government and his senior commanders. Both Weygand and Marshal Philippe Pétain, the hero of the great French defensive victory at Verdun back in 1916, had given up and were demanding an armistice. Churchill and his senior advisors urged the French to fight on, but Reynaud had been right: the battle had been all but lost the moment the Meuse front had collapsed.

The French, who had shed so much blood and fought with such iron determination a generation earlier, no longer had the heart to do so again.

The French armistice was signed on 22 June in the same railway carriage in Compiègne in which the Germans had surrendered in 1918. For Hitler, who was there to witness France's humiliation, there could be no sweeter moment of victory.

Their success, however, was as much about French failures as it was about German brilliance, and the facts remained that German losses in the air had been high and the bulk of the damage had been accomplished by a very small proportion of the army. If Germany could continue to defeat her enemies in campaigns of only a few weeks, then their lack of resources would not matter very much.

Right: Hitler poses for photographs in Paris with architect Albert Speer (left) and artist Arno Breker.

Opposite: British troops trying to escape to HMS Icarus from the beaches of Dunkirk.

On the other hand, Britain was still in the war and had been given a lifeline by Hitler's own ego and incompetence. Without the halt order, it is hard to see how so many could possibly have escaped. What's more, Britain lay across the sea, with her mighty navy and merchant fleet and with a growing air force protected by the world's only fully coordinated air defence system. *Bewegungskrieg* – which was now becoming known as 'Blitzkrieg' – would not work on water or in the air alone. Thus, for all the brilliance of the German victory in the west, the war was not over yet, not while Britain fought on. Despite its successes, in its failure to defeat Britain the Blitzkrieg had fallen short.

2: THE BATTLE OF BRITAIN

On 6 July 1940, Adolf Hitler returned in triumph to Berlin after his astonishing victory against France. Millions lined the streets to get a glimpse of their Führer, most of them believing the war had already been won. Half of Europe now lay in the hands of Nazi Germany, including once-mighty France, which had been defeated in just six weeks. Britain's army had also been smashed, and forced to retreat across the English Channel. In so doing, nearly all its arms and equipment had been left behind.

Hitler had always seen Britain as Germany's most dangerous enemy. Britain had the world's largest empire, and was the centre of a global trading network bigger than that of any other country. Her access to the kind of resources needed to wage war was far better than that of Germany, whose location in the heart of Europe offered few outlets to the world's oceans. At a time when the sea remained the best way of moving goods around the world, this was a great disadvantage.

Another concern was the United States. Although neutral, the USA backed Britain and was no friend of Nazi Germany. If Britain was no longer a belligerent, the potential threat from America would be less.

Germany could not afford a long drawn-out conflict like the last one of 1914–1918. Hitler knew he had to force Britain out of the war, and on that July day he was confident the British would soon sue for peace. After all, they no longer had much of an army left with which to fight.

Six weeks earlier in Britain, the shock of defeat on the Continent had been enormous. Most had been confident that the combined armed forces of Britain and France, not to mention Belgium and the Netherlands, would halt German ambitions. Few had imagined France would be so swiftly overrun and, to many, the image the Nazis had projected before the war of unparalleled might had been borne out. The spearhead of this military juggernaut was the Luftwaffe, the German Air Force. It was now expected that massed formations of German bombers would soon appear over the skies of Britain and that their raids would be followed by terrifying numbers of enemy paratroopers.

On 27 May 1940, Britain's future had hung in the balance. Winston Churchill had been Prime Minister for only seventeen days and there was heated debate between him and his Foreign Secretary, the widely respected Lord Halifax. Churchill believed Britain should not even consider sending out peace feelers to Germany. Halifax felt the situation was so bleak that Britain should at least make moves in that direction and threatened to resign over the matter, an act likely to have brought down Churchill's new government.

Opposite: Hitler returns to Berlin in triumph

Fortunately, Churchill was able both to dissuade Halifax and to convince his wider cabinet colleagues that Britain should never surrender.

In the following days, the evacuation of the British Expeditionary Force from France was more successful than anyone had hoped and the question of making peace with Hitler was never mentioned again. Britain would fight on.

One of the reasons the British Expeditionary Force had been so successfully rescued from Dunkirk was because the Luftwaffe had failed to halt the evacuation. After its successes in Poland and Norway, and now in the Low Countries and France, the Luftwaffe had seemed unstoppable, and Field Marshal Hermann Göring, its commander-in-chief, had boasted to Hitler that his air force alone could destroy the BEF as they tried to escape.

Over the beaches, low cloud and smoke from bombed and burning oil depots protected the troops, while, above, the Luftwaffe crews suddenly found themselves up against RAF Fighter Command for the first time. From 23 May, when Fighter Command initially flew over the French coast, to the end of the evacuation on 5 June, the Luftwaffe lost 326 aircraft against Fighter Command's 121. This was no small number, but the Luftwaffe had discovered that hitting moving vessels was extremely difficult, and that their bombers, and the much-feared Stuka dive-bombers especially, were very vulnerable to the RAF's Spitfires and Hurricanes waiting to pounce on them.

RAF Fighter Command was created and designed to defend Britain, and first did so over Dunkirk. In many ways, the Battle of Britain really began during that period at the end of May. It is the time the country probably came closest to losing the war.

Britain has often been portrayed as David to Germany's Goliath, but this was not really the case. Despite the shock and scale of the defeat on the Continent, there were good reasons for Churchill's decision to continue the war. Britain was separated from the rest of Europe by the English Channel and the North Sea. Any invasion force would have to cross one or the other, which history had shown was no easy operation. Britain's army might have been defeated, but it had been tiny in comparison with that of France and Germany. Rather, Britain's military strength lay primarily in her Royal Navy, which was the world's largest and known as the 'Senior Service' for a very good reason. The Royal Air Force was also growing in size. Additionally, Britain could call on the resources and armed forces of her empire. Men from Canada, South Africa, New Zealand, Australia, India

Above left: Churchill and Halifax arguing in the Cabinet Room.

Opposite: The Dunkirk evacuation from the air.

and elsewhere were preparing to fight for the mother country, while large numbers of immigrants arriving from Nazi-occupied territory were also eager to join the cause – among them Poles, Czechs, Frenchmen, Belgians and Norwegians.

Britain also had the world's largest merchant navy and around 80 per cent of the world's cargo shipping was operating or prepared to operate on her behalf. This gave Britain the kind of strength in depth of which Nazi Germany could only dream.

If the war continued, Britain therefore had reason to feel confident that in the battle for resources, upon which the warring sides so heavily depended, she had the upper hand.

After the fall of France, Göring began moving his air forces up to new airfields closer to the Channel coast. Fighter aircraft, especially, had limited range, and so for an aerial assault on Britain they needed to be based as near to their targets as possible. Building new airfields took time, however, as did moving up supplies and personnel. None the less, from 18 June, the day the French asked for an armistice with Germany, the Luftwaffe attacked targets in Britain every single night, mostly RAF airfields. The first time German planes flew over England in daylight was on 2 July. None of these raids was very effective or large in scale, and certainly went against well-worn German principles of concentration of force, but the air fighting had begun.

On Tuesday, 9 July, for example, a flight of Spitfires from 609 Squadron, based at Middle Wallop in Wiltshire, was patrolling over Portland on the south coast at around 7.15 p.m. when they spotted Stuka dive-bombers attacking shipping below. The Spitfires sped towards them, only to be dived upon in turn by Messerschmitt 110 twin-engined fighters. Among those in 609 Squadron was Pilot Officer David Crook, who spotted the Messerschmitts in time to warn his colleagues, and together they hurtled into cloud cover. For a few minutes the German and British pilots played cat-and-mouse in and out of the clouds, but Crook was successfully able to stalk a Stuka, open fire and see the burning dive-bomber roll over and then plunge into the sea.

Lieutenant Siegfried Bethke was a Messerschmitt 109 pilot in Jagdgeschwader 2 – Fighter Group 2 – who, with his colleagues, reached a new airfield in Normandy on 25 June and was immediately ordered on to the defensive. He spent most of the following days sitting in his cockpit, waiting to be scrambled in case any British bombers came over to attack their airfields. He and his comrades found this frustrating. 'General situation,' he wrote in his diary, 'no-one knows anything!'

Meanwhile, Hitler had retreated to his mountain home in Bavaria, the Berghof, where he received

Above: HMS Hood leads the Royal Navy's Force H.

Opposite: Pilot Officer David Crook downs a Stuka over Portland.

his navy, army and air force commanders in turn and grilled them about their plans for the attack against Britain. All had different ideas. No combined-services planning team had been formed.

The truth was Hitler still hoped Britain would sue for peace. The army was his strongest force and the Luftwaffe had been designed to support ground operations; it was not intended to operate on its own as an attacking force, and no one had given much thought to how best to subdue Britain. Hitler was in a quandary.

On 19 July, he returned to Berlin to make a speech, in which he made an appeal to Britain to 'see reason' and stop the war. It fell on deaf ears and so he left for the annual Wagner Festival at Bayreuth. Meanwhile, Göring spent much of his time plundering art and treasures from the newly occupied territories in Europe.

Göring, like Hitler, had been hoping Britain would see sense and negotiate peace terms. When those hopes faded, he decided to wait for Hitler to issue his directive for air operations against Britain. Because the Führer was in a lather of indecision and busy watching Wagner, this did not happen until 1 August. Only then did Göring start drawing up his own plans for the all-out air attacks on the RAF. As it was, these plans were based on an intelligence report given on 16 July by Colonel Josef 'Beppo' Schmid, most of which was based on very little reliable intelligence. He was not the most senior Luftwaffe intelligence officer, but as a member of Göring's personal staff and a good Nazi party man, he had learned it was always best to tell his boss what he wanted to hear.

His report erroneously suggested the RAF's Hurricane was inferior to Göring's favourite fighter, the twin-engined Messerschmitt 110; he had no idea the RAF was divided into three commands; he entirely discounted the ability of the British to repair damaged aircraft very efficiently and quickly and he massively underestimated the speed and scale of new aircraft production. Later, he reported that Britain had built only 133 new fighters in July. In fact, 496 were produced, twice as many as were supplied to the Luftwaffe.

In a totalitarian state like Nazi Germany knowledge was power, and so the various intelligence bodies were reluctant to pool their information, regarding each other as rivals rather than colleagues working towards a common cause. This often led to a very faulty intelligence picture, which was certainly the case with the Luftwaffe in the summer of 1940.

Right: Göring visiting the Goudstikker Gallery in Amsterdam.

Opposite: A Bristol Blenheim approaching a German airfield as two Me109s take off.

In contrast, Britain was a democracy where intelligence gathered from different bodies was swiftly collated and shared. As a result, Air Chief Marshal Sir Hugh Dowding, the commander-in-chief of Fighter Command, had a pretty clear picture of the enemy. However, British intelligence wrongly assumed German squadrons to be the same size as those in Fighter Command. Each RAF squadron had around two dozen planes and pilots, with no more than twelve airborne at any one time. German squadrons were supposed to have a dozen of each but rarely had more than nine aircraft

ready to fly. It was, however, not necessarily a bad thing for Dowding to overestimate the strength of the Luftwaffe.

Conversely, Colonel Schmid's report overlooked entirely the air defence system that had been created over the four years since Dowding became the first head of RAF Fighter Command.

Key to this was the chain of radar stations that covered eastern and southern Britain (see map on page 324). The first was set up in 1935, and by 1940 the system was using two types of detection: Chain Home, which had a range of around 120 miles but was not especially accurate, and Chain Home Low, which could pick up greater detail and at lower heights than Chain Home, but within a shorter range. Enemy raids were displayed as a mass of light moving across a cathode ray screen. The bigger the mass, the more planes there were, although the actual number was hard to determine.

Information from the radar stations was fed to the Filter Room at Bentley Priory in north-west London, the headquarters of Fighter Command. This was repeatedly updated as plots of enemy raids evolved and the filtered information was then passed on to the operations rooms.

Fighter Command was divided into four operational groups. London and the south-east, for example, came under 11 Group, commanded by Air Vice-Marshal Keith Park. Each group was then further divided into sectors. Each sector had two or three airfields, of which one would be designated the sector station. Headquarters and each group and sector station had its own operations room, all of which looked much the same.

At the centre of each was a large map on which both enemy raids and RAF squadrons could be plotted. Overlooking this was a dais on which the controller sat. On the wall opposite was the 'tote' board, where each sector and squadron was listed with lights that showed their state of readiness or activity. Below were charts monitoring cloud levels and other information. This meant that, at a glance, controllers could obtain a very clear picture of what was happening in the air.

Also covering much of the country, including all of southern and eastern England, were posts of the 30,000-strong Observer Corps. Each post was provided with equipment to assess height and numbers of enemy aircraft and a telephone. Each post passed on information to their own group headquarters, who in turn passed it up the chain to Fighter Command HQ.

Since British radar was static and looked out to sea, once enemy aircraft crossed the coast the Observer Corps took over and were able to provide more detailed information. Over a million reports from radar stations and observer posts might be telephoned in over a twenty-four-hour period, but this information could reach the ground controllers and pilots in the air in a matter of minutes.

Opposite:
The different
elements of
Dowding's air
defence system,
run from HQ
at RAF Bentley
Priory (bottom
of page).

Ground controllers were in radio contact with the pilots and used technology such as High Frequency Direction Finding – HF/DF or 'huff-duff' – to monitor the movements of friendly squadrons via cockpit-transmitted signals known as 'pip-squeak'. This meant they could accurately direct, or 'vector', squadrons towards the enemy. British planes were also equipped with a homing device called Identification Friend or Foe, or IFF, which gave a distinctive blip if the aircraft flew near the coast and were picked up by radar.

Every operations room was duplicated with a second fully functioning room a few miles away that could be used at a moment's notice, while the Defence Teleprinter Network, or DTN, acted as an extra back-up network in case telephone lines were disabled.

Dowding's air defence system was not perfect, but it was the only one of its kind in the world. Collectively, the various cogs in the system added up to considerably more than the sum of their parts. And the more experienced those running the system became, the more efficiently it worked.

By the end of July Hitler was back at the Berghof, the Wagner Festival finished and his appeal to reason to Britain rebuffed. He briefed his senior commanders on the thirty-first. The aim was to bludgeon Britain into submission, starting with the air assault. The commanders of the German navy, the Kriegsmarine, reckoned mid-September was probably the earliest they would be ready for a seaborne invasion, code-named 'Sealion'. Timing was crucial for, soon after that, shorter days and worsening weather would make it impossible until the following spring. However, even Hitler realized it would be suicidal to attempt a Channel crossing without command of the skies and sea lanes secure.

Britain's access to global resources, and the enormous economic and military might of the United States waiting in the wings, meant Hitler simply had to knock Britain out of the war. By contrast, Germany was short of the supplies necessary for sustained warfare, especially oil and food.

Hitler hoped to resolve this by invading the Soviet Union, currently an uneasy ally. But that was some way off and he knew that Britain had to be defeated first. Fighting on two fronts was to be avoided at all costs.

Back on 18 June, Prime Minister Winston Churchill had made a broadcast, saying, 'Hitler knows he will have to break us in this island or lose the war.' That was nothing less than the truth.

The stakes for the monumental air battle about to begin could not have been higher.

On 6 August, Göring briefed his commanders at Carinhall, his large country house in the forests north of Berlin, for the all-out attack against the RAF. He knew by now that the radar masts along Britain's coastline were some kind of radio signal system and ordered them to be destroyed as a priority along with the RAF's fighters, both on the ground and in the air.

That day, he had a combat-ready strength of 2,156 aircraft with which to do the job, of which 823 were bombers, 343 were dive-bombers, 760 were single-engined Messerschmitt 109Es and 230 were twin-engined Messerschmitt 110s. The RAF had around 1,400 combat-ready aircraft, of which some 750 were fighters. Against Fighter Command, that gave the Luftwaffe a superiority of around 3:1, which, as a military rule of thumb, was about the minimum numerical advantage needed for an attacking force.

In the Me109E, however, it did have the best fighter in the world that summer. The Me109 could climb faster than any other, had 55 seconds' worth of machine-gun ammunition as well as 20mm high-explosive and armour-piercing cannons. These cannons were far more destructive than the much smaller-calibre machine guns of the Spitfires and Hurricanes, which carried only 14.7 seconds' worth of ammunition. The Me109 could also dive faster than any other plane. These were significant advantages.

Above left: Hitler with his commanders at the Berghof.

Opposite: A squadron of Messerschmitt 109s in flight.

As well as their airborne advantage, the men of the Luftwaffe had plenty of experience and were full of confidence. So too was Göring, even though he secretly hoped Britain might still concede defeat. He told his commanders that destruction of the RAF would take three days but, to be on the safe side, he wanted four clear days of weather. Favourable skies were due from 10 August. He called his assault 'Adlerangriff – Attack of the Eagles – and the launch 'Adlertag': Eagle Day.

Clear weather finally arrived on the twelfth, and Göring ordered preliminary strikes that day to knock out British radar. A number of sites were hit and Luftwaffe crews returned to their bases reporting success. However, by mid-afternoon, Luftwaffe signals intelligence was picking up pulses from nearly all the British radar stations. In fact, only one, Ventnor on the Isle of Wight, had been knocked out for more than a couple of hours, and from there pulses were being sent out from a mobile transmitter instead to make the Germans believe it had been repaired.

Ironically, the Germans had far more advanced radar than Britain, but it was operated by the Kriegsmarine and not available for the Luftwaffe, which was why men like Siegfried Bethke had to spend so much time strapped into their Messerschmitts waiting to intercept British bombers coming over. Nor did the Luftwaffe have ground controllers and, once airborne, pilots could communicate only with their own squadrons.

Eagle Day was 13 August. It turned into something of a fiasco. Bombers headed across the Channel that morning, unescorted by fighters because of a communication error, and attacked Eastchurch, an RAF Coastal Command airfield. They destroyed no fighters and the airfield was fully operational again by the end of the day.

A large formation of Stukas attempted to attack Middle Wallop in the afternoon but were intercepted by four squadrons of Spitfires and Hurricanes, including 609 Squadron. David Crook and his colleagues were at 20,000 feet with the sun behind them when they attacked. A large battle followed to the north of Weymouth, in which Crook shot down an Me109 and the squadron twelve other enemy planes; thirteen proved a lucky number for them that day.

Despite the forecast, the weather was poor the next day so it was not until the fifteenth that any further large-scale attacks took place. Several RAF airfields were heavily bombed and above there were ferocious battles. The Luftwaffe lost seventy-six aircraft that day and Fighter Command thirty-five. It was to be the most costly day for the Luftwaffe in the entire battle.

The next day, Göring called another conference of his commanders. He was not happy and now ordered his fighters to close-escort the Stukas all the way to the target and back. He was forgetting his fighters could not dive with the Stukas and that his order risked losing their advantages in speed and height. Göring also cancelled further attacks on radar stations. 'It is doubtful whether there is any point,' he said.

There were still heavy Luftwaffe raids that day, 16 August. Over Southampton, James Nicolson of 249 Squadron was hit by four cannon shells in his Hurricane. Badly wounded, and with flames erupting, he flew on and shot down an Me110 before finally baling out. He survived and was awarded the battle's only Victoria Cross.

The weather was once again poor on the seventeenth but a glorious sunny day dawned on Sunday, 18 August. The Luftwaffe came over in droves, attacking airfields and clashing with Fighter Command in the air. Those on the ground below, in the countryside and in the cities, were able to watch a mass of swirling contrails, white against the deep blue sky, and hear the distant chatter of guns. Sometimes a plane would plummet downwards, trailing thick smoke. In all, Fighter Command had thirty-three aircraft shot down that day. The Luftwaffe lost sixty-seven, among them Julius Neumann of JG 27.

After shooting down a Spitfire, his Me109 had also been hit – in the radiator. His engine was overheating and he knew he had no chance of making it back across the Channel. He eventually crash-landed in a field on the Isle of Wight, still in one piece, and was soon after taken prisoner by the local Home Guard.

Once again, poor weather followed. Göring was not getting his four clear days. When they could fly, however, his Stukas were being decimated. He blamed the fighters for the losses.

Göring was wrong. In truth, the shortcomings of the dive-bomber, first exposed over Dunkirk, combined with the effectiveness of Dowding's system were to blame. The Luftwaffe had not faced an enemy that could anticipate their arrival or be vectored from the ground. By 24 August, Göring had withdrawn his entire Stuka force from the battle.

The staff of RAF Bomber Command are usually omitted from the story of the Battle of Britain, yet both day and night, whenever the weather allowed, they were flying over German-occupied territory, bombing airfields, ports and even targets within Germany. The threat from British bombers was why a proportion of the Luftwaffe's fighter force had to remain in France on guard duty. It was also why Germany spent so much time and effort building anti-aircraft defences.

British bombing raids in Germany had not been especially accurate or damaging, but they had unsettled the Nazi high command and proved to the German people that the war was still far from over.

Despite the attacks by Bomber Command, Hitler had forbidden the Luftwaffe from attacking civilian targets. Then, on the night of 24 August, the Luftwaffe bombed north London by mistake. The British War Cabinet demanded retaliation, and so the following night some fifty RAF bombers flew all the way to Berlin. Only a handful of bombs actually fell on the German capital, but they returned again on the night of 28 August, a second gesture of defiance that angered and goaded Hitler and the German high command.

Left: British bombers – Hampdens and Wellingtons – attacking Berlin by night.

Opposite: 609 Squadron attacking a large formation of Stukas.

Meanwhile, the Luftwaffe continued to bomb British airfields and now the aircraft industry as well. They were most accurate when they came in low, under the radar, and often singly or in small numbers. A lone raider caused huge damage at Middle Wallop, for example, but was then promptly shot down and the crew killed. The price for accuracy was extreme high risk to those doing the bombing.

Göring was repeatedly tinkering with tactics and blaming his fighters, but this was born of frustration and desperation: the battle was not going at all to plan. Nor had he had four consecutive days of clear weather. In truth, he simply did not possess enough bombers to do the job required. The alternative to low-level bombing was mass bombing, but to destroy a 100-acre grass airfield, such as those used by Fighter Command, required a much larger force than he had available. So far, only one airfield, Manston in Kent, had been knocked out for more than twenty-four hours.

None the less, by 1 September a number of British airfields were in a parlous state with hangars, buildings and stores destroyed and the ground pockmarked by hastily filled-in bomb craters. Both Dowding and Park were also very worried about pilot shortages. Already, the final process in training – converting to Spitfires and Hurricanes at an Operational Training Unit – had been shortened, which risked making these new pilots lambs to the slaughter. Despite this, many of 11 Group's squadrons were now operating at just 75 per cent strength.

Squadron life was exhausting for all of its members, which meant ground crew and staff officers as well as pilots. Ground crew would be up earliest, but the pilots would also be woken before dawn, and would then make their way to dispersal. Here there would be a building, hut or tent which was their base for the day. Their aircraft would be nearby. Each pilot had a fitter and rigger assigned to help them look after their aircraft, who would carry out checks and make sure the plane was ready to fly.

British pilots would fly at most four times a day, but usually not more than twice, which meant in between there was a lot of waiting at dispersal. Pilots had different ways of passing the time: reading, napping, playing cards. Pete Brothers of 32 Squadron would spend the time filing down the rivets of his Hurricane. He reckoned it gave him a couple of extra miles per hour.

When scrambled for action, pilots would run to their aircraft, which would be started up immediately by the fitter. Grabbing their parachutes, they would clamber in, attach oxygen and radio leads and move off. A squadron of twelve was split into two flights of six, and again into sections of three. Usually a section, or even a flight, would take off together. They would expect to be airborne in a matter of minutes.

They would be stood down in the evening, usually at dusk.

Squadrons had differing cultures. Some were known to party and drink hard while others were more sober. Dowding insisted his pilots were not pushed to breaking point. Each was given twenty-four hours off each week and forty-eight hours every three. This was why squadrons were supposed to have around two dozen pilots to keep twelve planes airborne.

In contrast, German pilots had no regular leave. Siegfried Bethke, for example, had had no leave at all since May. And while RAF pilots were encouraged not to talk 'shop' once stood down, the same was not the case for their German counterparts, who would be expected to write reports and discuss tactics long after the last flight of the day. Nor were they being patted on the back

Opposite:
A lone Junkers
88 attacks RAF
Middle Wallop.

by a grateful native population. Most French understandably resented their presence. They were certainly not being given free drinks in the local bar.

German fighter pilots also had further to fly to engage the RAF and the Channel to cross. This might have looked like a river from 20,000 feet but seemed vast if a pilot was unfortunate enough to bale out into it. The chances of being rescued were slim. Many pilots feared drowning above all. 'Our conversations now revolve almost solely on the Channel and all that water,' wrote Bethke in his diary, a theme he returned to repeatedly. 'It is so terribly disagreeable to all of us.' The Luftwaffe pilots had a name for this fear: *Kanalkrank*.

For many British pilots, the biggest fear was burning alive. Hurricanes, especially, were prone to catch fire. There were fuel tanks in the wing roots and, if hit, wind coming through the gun ports would fan the flames into the cockpit. In such cases, pilots had around three seconds to bale out.

As August gave way to September, however, the biggest fear for Dowding and Park remained the shortage of combat-ready pilots. On Saturday, 7 September, both men met with other senior officers to discuss the problem. Park suggested a new system of squadron categorization. New pilots straight from OTUs could be sent to squadrons away from the front line. These squadrons would have a few experienced pilots who could teach the new boys the ropes and help them build up flying hours. These would be called Category C squadrons.

Those in the front line, such as Park's 11 Group, would be Category A and all experienced pilots. Category B squadrons would be a mixture of both and would be closer to the action but still not in the front line. It was a simple and ingenious plan that meant raw pilots were no longer being sent straight into the thick of the battle.

Also entering the fray were new Polish and Czech squadrons – made up from mostly experienced pilots. Their contribution would prove invaluable. Moreover, Park's squadrons might have been at 75 per cent strength, but that still meant sixteen to eighteen pilots, considerably more than were available in Luftwaffe squadrons.

Britain was producing between two and three times the number of aircraft being built in Germany. By 2 September Siegfried Bethke's squadron had only five planes and four days later just three. It was the same for other fighter groups. Göring was still expecting all his bombers to be continuously protected by fighters, however, which meant those who did still have planes had to fly more and more often, sometimes up to seven times a day. The physical and mental stress of so much combat flying was immense. 'The strain of unrelenting front-line flying,' said Ulrich Steinhilper, a pilot in JG 52, 'was beginning to show.' Dowding and Park might have been less worried had they known the Luftwaffe's true state of affairs by this stage of the battle.

Above left: Park, Dowding and Deputy Chief of the Air Staff, Air Vice-Marshal Sholto Douglas discussing squadron classification.

Opposite: British pilots waiting at dispersal.

However, on that Saturday, 7 September, as Park devised his A-B-C plan, Dowding was handed what proved to be another lifeline. By this time, Bomber Command had hit Berlin four times and Hitler wanted revenge. London was bombed heavily that day and night. There was widespread concern across Britain, and when photographs of massed river barges stacked up in the Channel ports were published, it was feared the invasion was imminent.

In fact, the Germans were still far from ready to invade. Rather, Hitler now hoped to bomb Britain into submission instead. London was hit again and again over the next week, though how the Luftwaffe was supposed to destroy the RAF by dropping bombs on the capital was not clear.

This change of tactics, however, did give the badly knocked-about airfields a chance to recover and also enabled Park to hone his own tactics. Even with radar and the Observer Corps, it was hard to counter a mass of raids on different targets launched simultaneously. But now that much larger formations of aircraft appeared to be heading to London, it was easier to intercept more effectively. Park's plan was to harry the enemy from the moment they crossed the Kent coast and for squadrons to operate in pairs.

British pilots were usually massively outnumbered at the point of attack, and to be one of twelve Spitfires attacking a formation of over two hundred bombers and fighters required incredible courage. Overall, however, it was not always so one-sided. The air battles over south-east England and London on Sunday, 15 September are a case in point.

The first raid peaked around midday, when some 25 Dorniers, escorted by 50 fighters, were attacked variously by 24 squadrons amounting to over 280 fighter aircraft. The second and larger raid was of around 100 bombers and 200 fighters and was attacked and harried constantly by 330 RAF fighters, including the new 'Big Wing' of five squadrons from Duxford in 12 Group.

Millions below saw the dramatic air battles that took place that fine late-summer day and it has since become commemorated as Battle of Britain Day.

Fighter Command lost 31 planes that day and 16 pilots, but the Luftwaffe suffered losses of 61 aircraft and 156 aircrew. British pilots who baled out could fly again, but Luftwaffe aircrew were taken prisoners. It was an important home advantage for the RAF.

These prisoners were kept together and their conversations secretly monitored. Analysis by Air

Left: RAF fighters were often hugely outnumbered.

Opposite: German bombers attack the East End of London.

Intelligence revealed a growing loss of confidence and criticism of the Luftwaffe high command. Hitler was beginning to doubt the Luftwaffe's ability to destroy the RAF too. He still referred to Britain as the 'most dangerous enemy' and knew full well how vital it was to defeat her. But to launch an invasion and fail would be catastrophic.

Now, in mid-September, time was running short. The nights were drawing in. On 17 September, the Führer delayed the invasion, and then, on 12 October, postponed it once again, this time until the following spring. It would never be seriously considered again.

There was no let-up in the Luftwaffe's attacks, however. On 23 September, more than two hundred Me109 fighters flew over on a 'free hunt' – a far more effective use of these machines than close-escort missions. There were very heavy raids on the last day of the month too. David Crook and Siegfried Bethke found themselves fighting in the same action over southern England that day. Crook shot down two confirmed Me109s and a probable third. He reckoned it was one of the best days he had ever had in the squadron.

Certainly, the RAF were not at breaking point, as Göring continued to claim. Fighter Command now had over seven hundred aircraft, more than when they had started the battle.

Rather, by the middle of October, it was the Luftwaffe that was at breaking point. Throughout the war, no British bomber crew would be expected to fly more than fifty missions. By 18 October Lieutenant Hajo Herrmann, a pilot in Kampfgeschwader 4 – Bomber Group 4 – had flown over ninety since the start of the war, and twenty-one against London alone. He was utterly exhausted.

The Luftwaffe had been the spearhead of Hitler's stunning victories, but had been created to support ground operations. During the Battle of Britain it had proved ill-suited to operate independently: tactically, it had failed; operationally, in terms of aircraft shortage and a lack of support such as radar and ground equipment, it had failed; and strategically, in its inability to fulfil Hitler's aims, it had also failed.

Officially, the Battle of Britain ended on 31 October, but the night attacks continued. The Blitz on Britain's cities would last until the following May, but British morale was not broken nor her industry destroyed. Fighter Command struggled to find an effective means of attacking bombers by night, but Britain's sovereignty was no longer under threat. It had been a decisive victory, and one that ensured there would be no early British defeat or swift total victory for Hitler's Nazi Germany.

3: THE BATTLE OF THE ATLANTIC

The Atlantic battle began just a few hours after war was declared by Britain and France on 3 September 1939. Some 370 miles north-west of Ireland, a German submarine, or U-boat, *U-30*, spotted a large vessel steaming west. Lieutenant Fritz Lemp, *U-30*'s commander, was convinced it was an armed merchant cruiser and so opened fire with two torpedoes. These struck at 7.40 p.m., and just after midnight the ship finally sank along with 128 men, women and children. Tragically, the boat was not armed at all, but had been a small transatlantic liner, the SS *Athenia*, heading to America from Britain with civilians fleeing the war.

It was the start of the longest battle of the entire Second World War, in which ships, submarines and aircraft fought a bitter war of attrition that saw the deaths of over 100,000 servicemen and civilians. Those fighting across these brutal grey seas also fought an ongoing battle with the ocean itself. The Atlantic is a vast and unforgiving place. This was also, in the context of six years of war, possibly the most important battle of them all, because without supplies, warring nations cannot fight. For the Axis forces to defeat the Allies, those supply lines across the ocean had to be severed.

Right: Passengers aboard the SS Athenia as U-30 attacks at dusk.

Opposite: Hitler launches the mighty battleship Bismarck.

Sinking the *Athenia* was against 'Prize' rules, which forbade the sinking of civilian passenger vessels during armed conflict and to which Germany had agreed. For Britain, that the ship was sunk by a U-boat also had worrying echoes of the First World War, when German submarines had severely affected the flow of transatlantic supplies. Britain was utterly dependent on seaborne trade, so severing those sea lanes was an overwhelming priority for Germany's war.

At the same time, the Germans also knew that, the moment war was declared, Britain's vastly superior navy would impose an economic blockade against Germany – which was precisely what they did. This was comparatively easy for

the Royal Navy to do because Germany was stuck in central Europe with only a comparatively short coastline, so access to the world's oceans was very limited.

The most obvious way to break through such a blockade was by submarine. Technology in U-boats had advanced significantly since the last war, and with Germany's poor natural resources and geographical isolation, combined with demands for a large army and air force, it made sense for its navy, the Kriegsmarine, to focus almost entirely on developing as sizeable a U-boat fleet as possible. U-boats were also smaller, easier and cheaper in every regard to build and keep in fuel than a large surface fleet.

Despite this obvious logic, however, Hitler, the German Führer, had backed the so-called 'Z Plan' to build a fleet of battleships, aircraft carriers, cruisers and destroyers. Only a fraction of these had been constructed by September 1939.

The British responded to the sinking of *Athenia* by immediately imposing the convoy system, whereby a mass of merchant ships sailed together protected by escorting warships. These were mostly destroyers: fast, manoeuvrable vessels that were much smaller than the larger cruisers and battleships known as 'capital ships'. Destroyers were equipped with depth-charges – mines that sank beneath the surface and then exploded – as well as with guns and torpedoes. The theory was that these escorts would provide a protective screen, while the merchant ships would also benefit from safety in numbers. It was very hard to protect a lone vessel sailing across the Atlantic.

Convoys did cause problems, however, because they meant a mass of ships departed and arrived at port at the same time, and needed loading and unloading all at once too. In between, dockworkers had little to do. It was not an efficient use of port facilities, but unquestionably made the ships' passage safer.

As German troops swarmed over Poland, the Kriegsmarine's new surface fleet was largely stuck behind the British blockade. Not so the U-boats, however. In September, one of the Royal Navy's precious aircraft carriers, HMS *Courageous*, was sunk. Then, in October, in one of the most daring and skilled attacks of the war, Lieutenant Günther Prien of *U-47* managed to slip into the narrow and heavily protected British base at Scapa Flow in the Orkneys and sink the mighty battleship *Royal Oak*, with the loss of 833 men. It was a severe shock not just to the navy but to Britain as a whole.

These attacks showed all too clearly what a potent force U-boats could be, yet at the war's start Admiral Karl Dönitz, the commander of the BdU, the U-boat arm, had just 57 rather than the 300 for which he had been pleading. Even this small number looked more impressive on paper than it was in reality, because submarines operated to the rule of thirds: one third at sea, one third heading to and from their hunting grounds, and one third undergoing re-equipping and repairs. In all, there were only 3,000 men in the entire BdU and few more than 50 U-boat commanders. Training took time, as did building up the necessary skill and experience. Should Dönitz ever have the chance to increase the size of his force significantly, the pool of manpower for such an expansion was very slight indeed.

The trouble was, Hitler was a continentalist and understood naval power even less than he did land warfare. Building a surface fleet was more about his monstrous ego than anything. Certainly, the mighty battleship *Bismarck* looked a lot more impressive than a Mk VII U-boat, the mainstay of the BdU. Just a handful of U-boats were operating in the Atlantic in the opening months of the war and yet these few were demonstrating all too clearly the potential they possessed. A hundred U-boats operating together, rather than fewer than ten, would certainly have greatly hindered Britain and France's ongoing war effort.

Germany was keenly aware that it was short of resources, which was why the Prussian and then, after 1871, the German approach to war was always to try to win as quickly as possible and to avoid a long, drawn-out conflict at all costs. The four-year attrition of the First World War had shown only too clearly these fundamental shortcomings. Back then, the Royal Navy's blockade had crippled the country, and it now threatened to do so again.

Britain, by contrast, not only had the largest empire the world had ever known, but also possessions beyond her empire. Much of Argentina, for example, from cattle farms and meat factories to the railway system, was owned by British companies. Britain also had the world's largest navy and merchant navy, and access to more than 80 per cent of the world's merchant shipping. These tens of thousands of ships were delivering supplies from all around the globe.

Furthermore, the world's largest oil producers, and by some margin, were the USA and Venezuela, both in the west. And whether timber and rubber from the Far East, copper and bauxite from Africa, or oil and food from the Americas, all this shipping reached Britain via the Atlantic.

Britain's navy was the country's Senior Service and its pre-war size ensured there was now a greater pool of experience and skill to spread during rapid wartime expansion. There were also the shipyards and shipbuilding skills to continue the flow of new vessels, while on the other side of the Atlantic lay Canada, a British dominion. The Canadians were to play a crucial part in this battle.

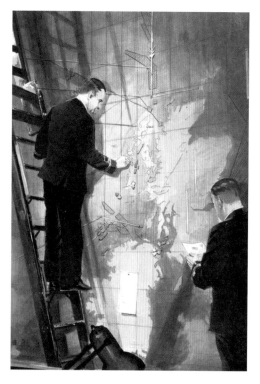

Despite the loss of *Royal Oak* and *Courageous*, the British were not especially worried by the U-boat threat in the early months of the war. Britain alone had over 10,000 merchant vessels, while there were barely ten U-boats ever operating at one time in the entire expanse of the Atlantic.

The British also had good intelligence and infrastructure, which included a global organization called the Naval Control of Shipping, which tracked the movements, cargoes and destinations of almost all Allied shipping. Naval intelligence was overseen by the Operational Intelligence Centre, which in turn drew on a number of sources of intelligence, including the Government Code and Cypher School at Bletchley Park, where civilian mathematicians and scientists were working on cracking enemy signal codes. It was also served by a network of Radio Intercept Stations and reports from around the world sent via secure underwater telegraph cables known as the VESCA system.

Left: The Operations Room at the HQ of the Royal Navy's Western Approaches Command.

Opposite: The Graf Spee under attack from the Royal Navy.

A further source of intelligence came from the crews of the Royal Air Force's Coastal Command. U-boats were not proper submarines, but rather 'submersibles', and could only fully submerge for a short period of time and at much reduced speed. This meant they mostly travelled on the surface and so, as convoys entered the Western Approaches – the part of the Atlantic off the west coast of the British Isles – aircraft could scan the waters around them and, if they spotted a U-boat, drive it under the surface where it would immediately lose speed.

These systems collectively ensured that it was, in theory at any rate, possible to know exactly where any ship was at any moment of any given day. The challenge now was to work out where the U-boats were as well.

While the tiny U-boat force attempted to form itself into 'Wolfpacks' of six at a time operating together off the west coast of Ireland, the German surface fleet remained in port, hardly daring to venture out. In October, the battle-cruiser *Gneisenau* headed into the North Sea, but as soon as she learned the British Home Fleet had picked up her movement, she hurried back again.

Meanwhile, three U-boats were sunk in October alone and nine by the end of the year – a significant number considering the size of the BdU. In December, the small 'pocket' battleship *Graf Spee* managed to break through the British blockade and sink three Allied freighters, but was then chased all the way south across the Atlantic to the River Plate in Argentina. Cornered, the *Graf Spee* was then scuttled to avoid being captured. Her demise rather underlined the folly of taking on a much larger and more proficient navy with lesser capital ships.

On the other hand, the small U-boat force continued to sink significant numbers of Allied merchant ships – albeit mostly independents operating outside the convoys. Fifty-six ships were sunk in February 1940, for example. Little was happening in the war on the land, but there could be no doubting that the war at sea was now well under way.

In April, the war at sea shifted to the waters around Norway, where the Germans had invaded, and then, at the end of May, came the evacuation of British and Allied troops from Dunkirk and elsewhere in France. With the fall of France in the third week of June and the end of the Norwegian campaign, the U-boats were sent back to the Atlantic, while fast German torpedo boats – *Schnellboote* – together with the Luftwaffe, the German air force, turned their attention to British coastal shipping. Many supplies, particularly coal, travelled in small convoys down the east and along the south coasts. They were now pummelled by the Germans.

At the same time, Britain was preparing for a possible German invasion and so Admiral Sir Dudley Pound, the First Sea Lord – the head of the Royal Navy – insisted the Home Fleet should concentrate in the south and south-east in case the Germans attempted a seaborne crossing of the Channel. Admiral Sir Charles Forbes, commander-in-chief of the Home Fleet, believed this concentration of force was overly cautious. He rightly argued that, so long as the RAF was still flying, the Germans would never be able to launch an invasion in secret and that there would always be time to send warships from the Western Approaches to the Channel. He also pointed out there were now large numbers of trawlers and lighters, newly armed, which were part of the Royal Navy Patrol Service. Better known as 'Harry Tate's Navy', these tough trawlermen were sweeping German mines in the Channel, laying their own and keeping watch for an invasion.

Opposite: German torpedo boats – Schnellboote – speed across the Channel.

Forbes' arguments fell on deaf ears, much to Britain's cost. The convoys crossing the Atlantic were now doing so with almost no escorts. Most were entering port on the west coast, at Liverpool, or Greenock in Scotland, and so, despite the vast size of the ocean, U-boats could safely lie in wait in the Western Approaches and know they were likely to intercept them. Convoys at this stage of the war never exceeded 35 ships but were spaced in columns around 600 metres apart, with each vessel roughly 400 metres behind the other, so they covered a sizeable area. The smoke from their stacks could be seen for miles around. Intercepting them was still no simple matter, but certainly the U-boats had never had easier prey than these unprotected convoys.

Throughout 1940, there were never more than 14 U-boats operating in the Atlantic at one time, but in June they sank 134 boats, in July 102 and in August 91, amounting to more than a million tons of shipping. One of those relishing the slaughter was Lieutenant Teddy Suhren, the torpedo officer on *U-48*. By 20 June, they had been on patrol for more than three weeks and had already sunk seven ships. Suhren then spotted a tanker and, a little after 5.30 p.m., having made the calculations of distance, course and speed, he fired a torpedo from 5,000 metres. This was a massive distance. 'No one believed it would hit,' recorded Suhren. But it did, and the Dutch tanker *Moordrecht* exploded in a massive fireball and sank.

While the Battle of Britain raged over southern England, out in the Atlantic the high number of sinkings continued. This period became known as the 'Happy Time' by the U-boat crews, yet despite this, not once did Admiral Dönitz's U-boat fleet sink anything like the half million tons in one month he reckoned was needed to bring Britain to its knees – the most had been 375,000 tons in June. As it was, the magic 500,000-ton monthly total was based on the assumption that Britain would have to continue to import more than 80 per cent of its food, as had been the case before the war.

Already, though, Britain had begun to turn that around with a major revolution in agriculture. Much open grassland had been ploughed up for crops and the number of livestock reduced. Limited rationing – far less severe than in Germany, for example – was introduced, which ensured everyone was provided with a balanced diet. At the same time, the increased food production on British farms meant more shipping space was freed up for the resources needed to build weapons. Bad though the losses in the Atlantic were, they were nothing like enough to prevent Britain carrying on the fight, let alone force her to end the war.

At the same time, German imports were down as much as 80 per cent on pre-war figures as a

Right: A Land Girl ploughs a field.

Opposite: German U-boat crews became expert at hitting moving targets at distance.

direct consequence of the British blockade. That was a problem because it meant Germany had to look elsewhere for those all-important resources.

None the less, just a handful of U-boats had sunk a huge amount of Allied shipping, including, on 14 December, the unescorted *Western Prince*, carrying cargo and passengers. One of those rescued was Cyril Thompson, a ship designer from Sunderland who had been in the USA to try to get the Americans to start building a new type of easy-to-construct merchant ship he had designed. A deal had been struck with the US government and an entrepreneur called Henry Kaiser, who promised to construct two new shipyards specially for the task. Thompson made it back safely and continued to build his first such boat in Sunderland. It would be called *Empire Liberty*, and from this all such vessels became known as 'Liberty ships'. Henry Kaiser pledged to produce each in just over 200 days. British and American shipbuilders were now joining forces.

Time was working against Germany. The 'Happy Time' had shown all too clearly what might have been achieved had Admiral Dönitz had the kind of numbers of U-boats he'd demanded. Instead, the mighty battleships lay idle in port, doing very little, although a lone pocket battleship, *Admiral Scheer*, did manage to slip unseen into the Atlantic, sink five ships and hurry back again.

With the failure to bring Britain to heel, Hitler had begun preparing for the invasion of the Soviet Union far earlier than he had originally intended. This was now Germany's main focus rather than the Atlantic, where, in January 1941, just six U-boats were operating. What's more, Allied convoys already had much increased numbers of escorts, and from shipyards in America, Britain and Canada more were arriving too.

On 3 February 1941, the German cruisers *Gneisenau* and *Scharnhorst* managed to slip through the Royal Navy's blockade and head out into the Atlantic, where they continued to evade the British Home Fleet. It was a dent to British pride and Prime Minister Winston Churchill, for one, was set on revenge. The Battle of the Atlantic, he declared, was to receive top priority.

And so it was. Before the war, Britain had very sensibly focused on building and upgrading larger ships, but now most warship construction was of destroyers and even smaller corvettes. By the start of 1941, the Royal Navy could call on 126 destroyers, 39 sloops and 89 corvettes for Western Approaches Command alone. RAF Coastal Command was now using longer-range aircraft, and both aircraft and ships were starting to be equipped with small onboard radar sets. This was possible because of the British invention of the cavity magnetron, a device that dramatically reduced the size needed for effective radar detection. The cavity magnetron was not known about by the Germans.

Western Approaches HQ in Liverpool was also re-equipped and developed, and by February 1941 was a much-improved new operations centre, while escort groups of destroyers and corvettes were introduced to protect the precious convoys. 'The U-boat at sea must be hunted,' Churchill had declared, and 'the U-boat in the building-yard or dock must be bombed.'

The results were not long in coming.

Above left: Cyril Thompson shows the Americans blueprints for his 'Liberty' ship design.

Opposite: An RAF Sunderland – known as the 'Flying Porcupine' – circles a U-boat.

In March, *U-47*, commanded by Günther Prien, was sunk with the loss of all hands, as was Joachim Schepke's *U-100*, while Otto Kreschmer's *U-99* was also sunk and the crew captured. These were three of the U-boat arm's most skilled, successful and celebrated aces and, because of the BdU's small size, were blows from which it would not easily recover. In all, five U-boats were sunk in March 1941.

Further setbacks followed for the Germans. That same month, German naval cypher materials were captured by British commandos during an attack on the Norwegian Lofoten Islands. Then, in May, *U-110* was captured in the Atlantic along with its Enigma coding machine and, crucially, its code books. The Germans did not know about the capture of either. British cryptanalysts at Bletchley Park could use these prizes to start deciphering German naval signal traffic. The benefits of this breakthrough were potentially enormous.

Also in May 1941, the mighty battleship *Bismarck* and heavy cruiser *Prinz Eugen* escaped the blockade and headed into the Atlantic. The Home Fleet hurried after them and in the first exchange of fire *Bismarck* sank the battlecruiser HMS *Hood*. It was a short-lived victory, however, as Royal Navy aircraft torpedoed the battleship, jamming her rudder and leaving her circling helplessly. British battleships and cruisers closed in for the kill and soon after *Bismarck* was sent to the bottom. *Prinz Eugen* managed to escape back to Brest, but not one German capital ship ever dipped into the grey, bitter seas of the Atlantic again.

In the opening eighteen months of the war, a lack of mid-Atlantic refuelling bases, combined with a shortage of escorts, had meant there was a large section in the middle of the ocean where the convoys were on their own and vulnerable. In April 1941, however, Allied naval and air bases finally opened in Iceland, which meant the British could now escort convoys as far as 35° west – a huge improvement. Then, in May, the rapidly growing Royal Canadian Navy agreed to close the final gap all the way to Newfoundland. It was another crucial marker in Canada's huge commitment to the war, and one that was out of all proportion to the small size of its population of just over 10 million.

There were now some eighty Canadian corvettes in service, or nearly so. The crews lacked the training and experience of the Royal Navy, but this was hardly surprising considering their navy had grown from just 3,000 personnel at the war's start. In the vicious seas of the north-west Atlantic they would soon learn, however. At any rate, from now on the Canadians, volunteers all, would escort transatlantic convoys to what was

Right: Corvettes in the mid-Atlantic.

Opposite: A torpedo-carrying Royal Navy Fairey Swordfish attacks the Bismarck.

called the Mid-Ocean Meeting Point, then head to Iceland for refuelling before escorting another convoy back.

There were also now over 200 aircraft operating from Iceland. For the aircrews, anti-U-boat patrols were thankless: long hours scanning a vast and often empty sea. But they were making a difference, pushing Dönitz's U-boats further west to the one part of the ocean aircraft still could not reach: the mid-Atlantic.

In August 1941, Winston Churchill and the US President, Franklin D. Roosevelt, along with their respective chiefs of staff – senior military commanders – met at Placentia Bay off the Canadian coast for what became known as the Atlantic Conference. By this time, American factories were just starting to produce significant amounts of war materiel, much of which was heading to Britain, while Henry Kaiser's new shipyards were already constructing the new Liberty ships. America was still not in the war, but during these meetings Roosevelt did agree that the US Navy should now join the Battle of the Atlantic and play a part in protecting Allied shipping.

A month later, the US Navy's Atlantic Fleet, although still officially neutral, was out at sea, escorting convoys as far as the Mid-Ocean Meeting Point with the Canadians now under their command. Among those Americans serving in the Atlantic was Hollywood star Douglas Fairbanks Jr. 'What the hell had I got myself into?' he wondered as he first headed out on to the ocean.

Meanwhile, cryptanalysts at Bletchley Park were now able to decode Enigma signals traffic with greater speed, enabling convoys to avoid the U-boats and giving the RAF a narrower area to search. This intelligence, combined with improved escorts, meant shipping losses had fallen dramatically. Dönitz now sent his U-boats deeper into the mid-Atlantic and on 9 September they found and struck Convoy SC42. Although protected by the Canadians, the escorts lacked both modern anti-submarine warfare equipment (ASW) and experience. Fifteen freighters were lost in two days.

Bad though those losses were, Dönitz's U-boats were by this time sinking just 66 tons of shipping per U-boat per day, a figure that had been 727 tons a year earlier. At the same time, Dönitz now reckoned his U-boats needed to sink a massive 800,000 tons of Allied shipping per month, up 300,000 tons from his estimation at the start of the war. So far, they had yet to achieve half that. Well over 80 per cent of all convoys were getting through unscathed. Escort group commanders like Lieutenant-Commander Donald Macintyre, who had captured U-boat ace Otto Kretschmer back in May 1941, had a mass of experience and were sailing aboard destroyers equipped with the latest radar; Macintyre barely had a single loss on his watch. With every passing month, more Allied ships were being upgraded.

On 31 October 1941, the Germans suffered another setback when *U-552* sank an American destroyer, *Reuben James*, not realizing it was a neutral vessel. The American public were shocked and outraged by the news; the United States' entry into the war had been brought a step closer. For the U-boat's commander, Erich Topp, it was a long journey back to base after he realized what he had done. 'The tension a man endures when he thinks he is making history,' he noted, 'however unintentional, is indeed enormous.'

As it turned out, Topp need not have worried unduly, because just over a month later the Japanese attacked the US Pacific Fleet at Pearl Harbor in Hawaii, and the United States was suddenly in the war for good.

At the start of 1942, Dönitz had 91 operational U-boats, although 23 were in the Mediterranean on Hitler's direct orders – and against Dönitz's wishes – and 60 per cent were undergoing repairs, which left only a dozen for patrols in the Atlantic. The British had also introduced escort carriers – ships hastily converted to carry a flight deck. Among those flying US-built Martlets on the escort carrier *Audacity* was Lieutenant Eric 'Winkle' Brown. The flight deck was just 100 metres long, but Brown quickly mastered the technique of taking off and landing back again. During escort duty to and from Gibraltar, he managed to shoot down two of the Luftwaffe's precious Focke-Wulf Condors, four-engine transports converted to become maritime bombers and operating from airfields along the Biscay coast. Brown's technique was to fly directly towards the Condor, firing at the cockpit.

Audacity's luck soon ran out, however, when on 21 December she was hit by three torpedoes fired from *U-751*. 'Literally,' said Brown, 'the bows fell off the ship.' He himself was very lucky to survive and was eventually picked up from the water.

Two and a half years into the battle, another shift was now about to take place. The British were no longer cracking Enigma codes as quickly, while American entry into the war had actually made the Allied position in the Atlantic weaker, because the US Navy immediately sent most of its warships to the Pacific to combat the Japanese threat. What's more, the shipping lanes off the coast of America, into the Gulf of Mexico and down through the Caribbean to Brazil and Argentina were some of the most congested in the world. Here, American coastal shipping was sailing independently, unescorted and through a series of narrow straits between strings of islands. For the U-boats these represented rich pickings. Another slaughter swiftly began to unfold.

Crossing the width of the Atlantic meant much longer patrols for the U-boat crews. Now patrolling off the American coast was Teddy Suhren, commanding his own boat, *U-564*. He and his crew sank two of seventy-one ships sent to the bottom in February. In March, ninety-two were sunk. The answer was to increase air patrols and establish a convoy system, but this could not be done overnight, and so the carnage off America continued.

Life at sea was tough enough to break any man, physically and mentally. The crew of a U-boat lived in cramped, primitive conditions. Water had to be very carefully rationed, so no one could wash or shave. A U-boat soon stank of sweat, oil, mildew and rotten food. Long periods of boredom were followed by moments of high tension and fear. Being stalked by a destroyer was terrifying: under the surface it was impossible to see their enemy, but around them depth-charges would explode, causing the U-boat to shake and roll. Any moment might be their last.

Merchant crews were extremely vulnerable and had to depend on others for their safety. Just like the crew of a hunted U-boat, merchant sailors never knew when they might be struck by an enemy torpedo. Luck played a huge part. Those lost at sea were rarely recovered, and most faced a lonely death.

Conditions were often brutal. Even in summer, crews could find themselves in the middle of a storm with waves crashing over them. In winter, it was also frequently freezing cold, especially in the northern Atlantic. Out on deck or on the ship's bridge, they were exposed to wind, rain, sea spray and thunderous waves. Once soaked, it was hard to get dry again. Donald Macintyre reckoned that on one winter escort patrol he had not been dry once. Not for nothing was the Atlantic known as the cruel sea.

Opposite:
Lt Eric 'Winkle'
Brown shoots
down a Condor
by attacking
head-on.

Left: Conditions aboard the U-boats were cramped, primitive, filthy and often brutal.

The first US coastal convoy sailed in May 1942, but it was still a while longer before the whole East Coast shipping system was put into convoy and, with increased numbers of U-boats finally reaching Dönitz's force, the slaughter continued, with 125 ships sunk in May and a staggering 144 in June, of which 121 had still been sailing independently.

Even so, this second 'Happy Time' for the U-boats was largely a false resurgence: it was a self-inflicted wound by the Americans rather than a leap forward in technology. A potentially game-changing new U-boat had been successfully tested back in 1940 – one that was a proper submarine rather than a submersible, and which could travel at 23 knots under water, faster than any freighter. But investment lagged and it was still not in production. Otherwise, the most common U-boat, the Type VII, had barely moved forward at all. Nor had torpedoes much improved. There had been some signals developments, but not at a pace that was outstripping the Allies.

Meanwhile, Allied technology most definitely was improving. There were now many more 'Very Long Range' aircraft flying over the Atlantic, equipped not only with radar but also with powerful spotlights so they could operate at night. In July, Teddy Suhren and his crew on *U-564* were on patrol once more and were repeatedly spotted and forced to dive. 'Up and down the whole time,' he wrote. 'It's like being in a lift! These fiendish air patrols of the Allies!'

In Britain the harvest of 1942 was a bumper one. British farmers had produced 46 million tons of grain in 1939, but that had now almost doubled. In contrast, in Germany each harvest had been down on those before the war. Dönitz's U-boats had sunk 636,926 tons of Allied shipping in June, mostly off America, but total imports to Britain had barely dipped: 2,006,000 tons had arrived in January, and an increased 2,214,000 in May, despite the carnage off America.

In July, with increased air cover and convoys, plus the drain of such huge distances to contend with, Dönitz sent his U-boats back to the mid-Atlantic, where their pickings dropped dramatically. Donald Macintyre was commanding a new ship equipped with the latest radar and also 'Huff-Duff' – high-frequency direction finding – which picked up radio signals from U-boats. These interceptions enabled the destroyers to work out the location from where the signals were being sent. Armed with this, an escort or aircraft could then go hunting for the U-boat. It was almost certainly down to Huff-Duff that Teddy Suhren's July patrol was so frequently interrupted.

Above right: A B-24 Liberator attacks a U-boat.

Opposite: A Royal Navy 'Huff-Duff' operator.

What's more, this improved technology was being harnessed to increased experience and, with it, skill, amongst both British and Canadian crews. U-boats had concentrated on sinking merchant ships rather than escorts, so the number of Allied naval losses in the Atlantic was slight. Dönitz, meanwhile, at long last had over 200 operational U-boats, and even more on their way, but most of his experienced crews had gone.

The hunters were increasingly becoming the hunted.

In January 1943, Churchill, Roosevelt and the British and American chiefs of staff met at the Casablanca Conference in Morocco, where they agreed that defeating the U-boat menace was their top priority. Both Britain and America wanted to win the war as quickly as possible and at the least cost, and by using machinery and technology so that the number of men risking their lives at the front line could be kept to a minimum. At the time of the conference, Anglo-US forces were battling in North Africa, but they intended to invade Sicily in the summer and France the following year, in 1944. The foundation of that strategy and of all long-term planning, however, was shipping, because everything, from fuel to tanks, food, ammunition and medical supplies, was brought overseas by ship. But with ever more U-boats now massing in the Atlantic, that smooth flow of supplies was under threat. The Allied war chiefs agreed it was one that had to be destroyed.

Fortunately, the Allies had once again cracked the German naval Enigma codes. What's more, they were continuing to win the technological battle. New weapons were rapidly being thrown into the fight, from acoustic homing torpedoes to rockets with armour-piercing warheads, and superb new American 10cm wavelength radar. Donald Macintyre's ship and other escorts were being equipped with 'Hedgehog'. This new piece of weaponry threw out a pattern of twenty-four contact-fused bombs ahead of a ship hunting a U-boat. It was more accurate than firing off depth-charges.

At the same time, Dönitz was still waiting for his new generation U-boat. He was rapidly running out of time.

Meanwhile, shipyards in Britain and America were continuing to build ever more Liberty ships, and in the United States these were now being launched at an astonishing rate. The first had been constructed in over 200 days, but by July 1942 one had been built in just 43 days and by August another in just 24 days. Then, in September, the *Joseph N. Teal* had been finished in a staggering 10 days. Two months later, the *Robert E. Peary* was completed in just 4 days, 15 hours and 26 minutes.

How could the U-boats, with their still-failing torpedoes and lack of sufficient air cover, possibly compete? The answer, of course, was that they could not.

More ships than ever were now sailing across the Atlantic in larger convoys with greater numbers of escorts with improved weaponry, and with more air protection. New support groups were also being thrown into the battle: fast, well-equipped destroyers whose job was not to protect convoys but to hunt U-boats.

The only downturn the Allies had to overcome was the change in Enigma codes, which meant they were taking too long to crack to have any effect. By March, there were some seventy U-boats

Above left: Roosevelt and Churchill in Casablanca.

Opposite: A Liberty ship under construction.

in the Atlantic, and with their own improved signals intelligence they were getting the highest interception rates of the war. Two convoys, HX229 and SC122, were particularly hard hit when forty U-boats attacked them. The mid-Atlantic was awash with flotsam and debris as one merchant ship after another went down.

March 1943 may have looked like a bad month for the Allies as 633,731 tons of shipping was lost, but the U-boats were now largely corralled into the mid-Atlantic while increased air operations over the Bay of Biscay harried their movement to and from their bases. In May, forty-one U-boats were destroyed, and among the young German submariners gone for ever was Dönitz's only son. Meanwhile, of the 370 merchantmen that sailed, only six were sunk. The U-boat threat had been neutralized. 'Wolfpack operations against convoys in the North Atlantic, the main theatre of operations,' recorded Dönitz, 'were no longer possible.' On 24 May, he ordered them all to withdraw, and with the utmost caution. 'We had lost the Battle of the Atlantic.'

Dönitz was right: the battle had been lost, but that was not the end of the U-boats. Not yet. Over the summer of 1943, he deployed most of them west and south of the Azores, hoping they would snare Allied convoys heading to the Mediterranean. He also sent some to the south Atlantic. New weapons and shipping detectors had been promised. Perhaps they would help him yet turn the tables.

At the same time, the Allies were coordinating efforts even more fully and effectively. The Canadians had massively grown in strength and experience, while the US re-entered the Atlantic battle with the formation of the Tenth Fleet at the end of April. Intelligence efforts were also coordinated and properly shared. Good intelligence, combined with massively superior forces and weaponry, ensured the U-boats would soon be crushed once and for all.

This superiority was demonstrated on 8 July 1943 when a newly equipped Very Long Range RAF Liberator spotted *U-514* off the Spanish coast and so turned in to attack, first with eight armour-piercing rockets, then with eight depth-charges which exploded all around the stricken U-boat. Finally, as *U-514* began to sink, the crew released their homing torpedo. A huge underwater explosion erupted and the U-boat disappeared for ever.

This was the kind of sophisticated weaponry the inexperienced U-boat crews now had to contend with. Only latterly had Hitler accepted the need for a much larger fleet of U-boats. New weapons were also arriving in the summer of 1943, but by then it was too little too late. The novice crews were getting slaughtered. By the autumn, Allied victory over the U-boats was complete.

U-boats continued to patrol until the end of the war, and still achieved some successes, but the losses continued to mount. In the final weeks, Dönitz even managed to launch the new generation Type XXI U-boats. By then, almost three-quarters of all U-boat men had been killed.

In truth, the U-boats had never come close to winning. Just 1.4 per cent of all Allied sailings across the Atlantic had been sunk. Even during the 'Happy Times', the U-boats had fallen well short of their monthly targets, which in turn had never been enough. Greater industrial output and far greater prioritization by the Allies had ensured that in this most crucial of theatres, they had won a crushing victory.

From the outset, the Allies had understood the vital importance of the Atlantic. The same could not be said for Nazi Germany. It cost them the war.

Opposite:
The oily remains of another U-boat sent to the bottom.

*Left: The attack
on the U-514.*

4: THE DESERT WAR

At 6 p.m. on 10 June 1940, Benito Mussolini, the Fascist dictator of Italy, appeared on the balcony of the Palazzo Venezia in Rome and declared war against Britain and France. Crowds had gathered below but, although a few rabble-rousers had been planted there, for the most part the people remained silent. 'People of Italy,' he shouted, 'rush to arms and show your tenacity, your courage, your valour!' Although plenty of young Italians were filled with excitement, they were the minority. 'The news of war,' noted Mussolini's son-in-law and Foreign Minister, Count Galeazzo Ciano, in his diary, 'does not arouse much enthusiasm. I am sad, very sad. The adventure begins. May God help Italy.'

This was a huge gamble by Mussolini. Italy lacked natural resources and geographically was locked into the Mediterranean. Its industry was underdeveloped, far more so than that of Britain, France or Germany, and nor was it anything like as wealthy. On the other hand, its population was growing, although 47 per cent of the Italian workforce was employed in agriculture, which was also backward.

In May 1939, Mussolini had signed the Pact of Steel with Germany, which began the Axis alliance, even though Italy was dependent on Britain and France for 80 per cent of her seaborne imports. Clearly, Nazi Germany had her own expansionist aims, but so too had Mussolini: he hoped to create a new Roman Empire across the Mediterranean and into Africa; Abyssinia in East Africa, for example, had already been conquered. Overseas expansion offered a solution to his country's lack of resources, while an alliance with Hitler and the Nazis ensured Germany would not become Italy's enemy again as she had been during the last war.

Mussolini had chosen the timing of his declaration of war carefully. His armed forces were weak, but he feared that Germany could dominate all Europe and take on all France's – and Britain's – overseas possessions in Africa. Italy's influence would rapidly dwindle to the point where she became little more than a vassal state.

Therefore he felt he had no choice but to enter the war before the fighting was over. By 10 June, France was all but finished and, as far as Mussolini was concerned, Britain looked likely to follow. In other words, there was now a good chance Italy could gain much for not a huge amount, and the number-one target was Egypt, not directly part of the British Empire but a 'protectorate' in which British armed forces were able to base themselves and control the vital Suez Canal that linked the Mediterranean to the Indian Ocean.

The trouble was, for all Fascist Italy's military parades and chest-puffing, any impression of military strength was a charade. The lack of wealth and resources was a big problem, but so too

Opposite: When Italy declared war in 1940 her Army, Navy and Air Force were all ill-equipped to fight.

was excessive bureaucracy and the low calibre of senior leadership. The Regio Esercito – Royal Army, as Italy still had a king, despite Fascism – was short of tanks, artillery, vehicles, rifles and just about everything needed for modern warfare. The Regia Aeronautica – Royal Air Force – was also filled with outmoded aircraft and inept commanders, while the Regia Marina – Royal Navy – the most modern arm, lacked any aircraft carriers or any kind of radar and, most of all, experience.

There was also a pointed lack of enthusiasm for war from Italy's military commanders. Only Mussolini himself, it seemed, had much appetite for a scrap with the British.

From 11 June onwards, Italian bombers began half-heartedly attacking the tiny but strategically vital British island of Malta in the very heart of the Mediterranean. The island was woefully under-defended with just a handful of Gloster Gladiator biplanes and almost no anti-aircraft guns, but the Italians never pressed home their advantage. The British swiftly reinforced the island. Within ten days, Hurricanes had begun arriving and by the end of the year it was bristling with anti-aircraft guns as well as bombers and submarines. Malta had become a major thorn in the Italians' side and an offensive base from which the British could attack Axis convoys heading to Libya.

Then, in July 1940, the Regia Marina ventured out of port and clashed with the British Mediterranean Fleet, receiving a bloody nose for its trouble. Finally, on Friday, 13 September, after continual pressing from Mussolini, Marshal Rodolfo Graziani reluctantly ordered the Italian Tenth Army to cross the Libyan border into Egypt. It advanced 40 miles to Sidi Barrani then halted.

The armed forces were mired in labyrinthine bureaucracy. On the outbreak of war, the Ministry Secretariat, the mechanism of government, had agreed to extend its working day to 4 p.m., but by July a return to the old time of 2 p.m. had been proposed and agreed. Marshal Pietro Badoglio, the Chief of Staff and most senior Italian soldier, was sixty-eight years old and rooted in the past. When handed a perceptive analysis of German tactics, he said, 'We'll study it when the war is over.' Command was top-heavy, training rigid and initiative stifled from top to bottom. 'The tank is a powerful tool,' said General Ettore Bastico, another senior commander, 'but let us not idolize it. Let us reserve our reverence for the infantryman and the mule.'

Britain's determination to keep fighting and her victory in the Battle of Britain was throwing Mussolini's war plans awry. The Italian Navy was proving feckless, so too was Graziani's Tenth Army in Egypt, and Italy was already running short of food. A mass demobilization of some 750,000 men was ordered because many of the peasant soldiers were urgently needed back on the land.

Above left:
Mussolini on the balcony of the Palazzo Venezia.

Opposite: An Italian SM-79 Sparviero being shot down by RAF Spitfires over Malta.

Despite this, on 12 October German troops moved into Romania, fuelling Il Duce's paranoia about German domination in what he considered his own patch. Mussolini was incensed. He had a bullying, dominant ally with a string of victories under its belt, while Britain, supposed to be dead and buried, was getting stronger by the day. So far nothing had gone to plan, but a quick and easy victory over the Greeks could change all that and reassert Italian dominance in the Mediterranean.

On 28 October, Italian forces invaded Greece from Albania and from across the sea. Poorly equipped and without their supply chain properly thought through, the Italians struggled in the mountainous interior and against a determined Greek Army that was ten times the size Mussolini had thought. Within a week, the campaign was unravelling and the Italians falling back.

On 11 November, they suffered a further humiliation when Royal Navy Fleet Air Arm Swordfish attacked the Italian Fleet at harbour in Taranto. Malta-based RAF reconnaissance aircraft had accurately spotted six battleships there. In the night-time attack two were sunk and a third severely damaged, along with a cruiser and destroyer. Half the Italian battle fleet had been put out of action in one brilliantly executed attack.

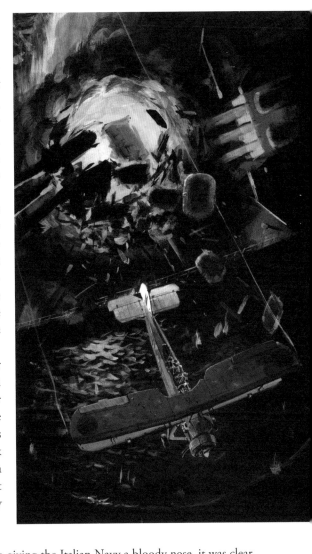

While the British Mediterranean Fleet had been giving the Italian Navy a bloody nose, it was clear there was now a chance to blunt Mussolini's ambitions in Africa too and make the Italians even more of a liability to Germany. Winston Churchill, the British Prime Minister, had been urging General Sir Archibald Wavell, the Commander-in-Chief Middle East, to go on the offensive in Egypt. Since October, the British Western Desert Force, only 36,000 strong and commanded by General Dick O'Connor, had been harrying Italian positions. Among those carrying out raids to capture prisoners and harass the Italians was Albert Martin, a young rifleman in 2nd Rifle Brigade. Beetling about the desert in their six-man trucks, he and his mates were able to lie up their truck then easily creep up on the Italians by night. 'We had total freedom of movement,' he noted, 'the Italians preferring to stay in their defensive enclaves.'

On the night of 8 December, the British attacked in force in what was called Operation COMPASS. They achieved complete surprise, and just three days later the Italian positions had

Above right: Operation JUDGEMENT, the Royal Navy's night attack on Taranto.

Opposite: A six-man section in a 15-cwt truck crossing the desert.

been overrun, Sidi Barrani retaken and 38,300 prisoners captured along with 237 guns and 73 tanks. Rarely had a battle gone so completely to plan.

By 20 December, the Italians had been swept out of Egypt and were on the run, with Albert Martin and the rest of the Western Desert Force in hot pursuit, led by the 6th Australian Division. Mussolini hadn't taken on just Britain but her Dominion countries too.

Now fearing complete Italian collapse, which would have left his southern flank vulnerable, Hitler ordered reinforcements to Africa to shore up his allies. To ensure they crossed the Mediterranean safely, however, an entire Luftwaffe air corps, Fliegerkorps X, was posted to Sicily in order to attack and neutralize the British Mediterranean Fleet. After severely damaging the aircraft carrier *Illustrious*, the Luftwaffe then pounded Malta, where the ship had limped for repairs. The damage to the island was unlike anything experienced at the hands of the Regia Aeronautica, but *Illustrious* did successfully get away from the island and make for Alexandria.

Malta had been blunted as an offensive base, however, and two German divisions under Major-General Erwin Rommel reached Tripoli in February 1941. By this time, the Western Desert Force had smashed the Italians. The Libyan towns of Bardia, Tobruk and Benghazi had all fallen, with the British using the same tactics the Germans had used in France the previous May: enemy airfields were hammered in advance, then mobile troops surged forward and encircled their enemy. On 12 February, the day Rommel reached Tripoli, the British took a further 20,000 Italian POWs, 200 guns and 120 tanks. The Italian Tenth Army had been destroyed and some 130,000 troops captured. 'Never has so much been surrendered to so few,' joked Anthony Eden, the British Foreign Secretary.

Meanwhile, Hitler had also decided to come to the Italians' rescue in Greece. His biggest concern was the possible loss of the vital Romanian oilfields at Ploeşti. With the Balkans and Aegean under Axis control, these would be secure.

The British, meanwhile, were also being drawn into Greece. They had promised to guarantee Greek independence back in April 1939, and had already sent naval and air support and had pledged troops too should Germany ever intervene. Troops for Greece would mean reducing those in Libya as British forces were also now attacking the Italians in East Africa. On the other hand, with the Italians cut off in East Africa, in retreat in Greece and already badly mauled in North Africa, the British felt they were ripe for the plucking. Another attack was launched to drive them even further west in North Africa and once again, Mussolini's men were soon in retreat.

The Italian Navy was also further hammered when the fleet ventured from port to try to stop British shipping to Greece. After a brief chase, the British Mediterranean Fleet closed in on the night of 28/29 March to around 4,000 yards of the Italians – effectively point-blank range. The British commander, Admiral Andrew Browne Cunningham, known to all as 'ABC', gave the order for his fleet to engage the enemy for the first time since Nelson's day. 'Never,' he wrote, 'have I experienced a more thrilling moment.' It was a massacre. All three Italian cruisers were sunk. The Battle of Cape Matapan ensured the Italian Fleet would never threaten British naval supremacy in the Mediterranean again.

While Matapan was raging, Yugoslavia was in turmoil. First the country joined the Axis, then there was a coup and the decision reversed. Hitler's revenge was swift. On 6 April 1941, the Germans invaded both Yugoslavia and Greece simultaneously.

Opposite: The Mediterranean Fleet opening fire at the start of the night action off Cape Matapan.

General Rommel had been told to stabilize the front in Libya and under no circumstances go on the attack, but he ignored this order. With the Western Desert Force now weakened by the Greek venture, he swiftly advanced back across Cyrenaica in Libya, retaking Benghazi and Bardia and besieging Tobruk. He also managed to capture the British commander, General O'Connor.

On 17 April, Yugoslavia surrendered, while the Germans swiftly advanced in Greece, where the Italians had so badly failed. Britain had sent four divisions, which had been hastily brought into battle, although without enough coordination with their Greek allies. It was too little too late, while in the air the Luftwaffe reigned supreme. The future novelist Roald Dahl was one of the few RAF fighter pilots trying to stem the flow, but he and his fellows were horribly outnumbered. Soon both the British and Greeks were in full retreat. Fortunately, the majority of British troops were successfully evacuated, but next on Germany's list was the large island of Crete. There were now some 32,000 British, Australian and New Zealand troops there, as well as 10,000 Greek troops, which should have been enough to hold the island from the Germans.

Operation MERCURY was launched by the Germans with wave after wave of *Fallschirmjäger* – paratroopers – dropping at dawn on 20 May. They suffered catastrophic losses and the invasion should have stalled there and then. However, due to a tragic and terrible oversight, German defeat was all too swiftly turned into a stunning victory.

Crete should never have fallen. General Bernard Freyberg, the New Zealander commander, was convinced a seaborne attack was also likely and so failed to reinforce the key airfield of Maleme in the west of the island. The brigade commander there also prematurely pulled his men back from the airfield and, as a result, Maleme was swiftly captured by the Germans then hurriedly reinforced with *Gebirgsjäger* – mountain troops – flown in directly. The die had been cast and the Germans were able to rapidly build up strength and push the defenders back. By 27 May, another British evacuation had begun and, although the vast majority were successfully lifted, the island was surrendered on 1 July. It was a humiliating defeat, but a costly victory for the Germans. The elite *Fallschirmjäger* units had lost more than 6,000 men, as well as 143 precious transport planes and a further 120 severely damaged. With the invasion of the Soviet Union a few weeks away, these were disastrous losses – and for little strategic gain.

The British Royal Navy suffered badly too: three cruisers and six destroyers were lost during the evacuation. The vital importance of air power and close air support had become ever more obvious during the Greek and Cretan ventures.

On the plus side, the Italians were, by the end of May, all but defeated in Abyssinia, and the island fortress of Malta was once more proving a vital offensive base. On 24 May, the British submarine HMS *Upholder* broke into an Italian destroyer screen and sank the massive 18,000-ton troopship *Conte Rosso* – for which *Upholder*'s captain, Lieutenant-Commander David Wanklyn, was awarded a VC. The Malta submarines were starting to prove a major scourge for Axis shipping. Capturing Malta would have proved a more profitable target for Hitler than Crete.

In much the same way that Germany swept into the Balkans and Greece to prevent the British from doing the same, so the British now became determined to stop German interference in the Middle East. The first objective was Syria, currently held by Vichy – pro-Axis – France. RAF possession of Syrian airfields would counteract any Luftwaffe presence on Crete. Churchill instructed General

Wavell to mount a joint attack with General Charles de Gaulle's small Free French forces in early June.

At the same time, Wavell was anxious to push back Rommel and relieve the port of Tobruk, where the mostly Australian troops were still holding out. Just to make life even harder for Wavell, Rashid Ali al-Gaylani had mounted a pro-Axis coup in Iraq. Britain controlled a vast swathe of territory from Palestine to India and having an openly hostile political leader in Iraq at this time was intolerable. Troops were sent from India and air forces from RAF Middle East, and the rising was quickly quelled, but after the defeats of Greece and Crete, Wavell's Middle East Command was horribly overstretched. Operation EXPORTER, the battle for Syria, was launched on 8 June, while Operation BATTLEAXE, in the Western Desert in Egypt, began a week later, on the 15th. As was now so often proving the way for the British in the Mediterranean and Middle East, fortunes ebbed and flowed.

After three days of intense and blisteringly hot battle with little progress being made, Wavell was forced to call off BATTLEAXE with Tobruk still out of reach. There was better news in Syria, however. On 21 June, Damascus fell, and three weeks later, on 11 July, the Vichy French surrendered. The Eastern Mediterranean was now secure.

Germany invaded the Soviet Union on 21 June 1941. At the same time, German spies were agitating dissent against the British in Iran, which threatened Britain's aid route to Russia through the Persian Gulf. When the British and Soviets jointly demanded the expulsion of all German nationals, the Tehran government refused. On 25 August a joint Anglo-Russian force invaded Iran, occupied Tehran, and the Persian Gulf was secured. East Africa was now almost entirely in British hands; the Middle East all the way to India was secure; and, despite the defeats in Crete and Greece, the British command in the Mediterranean and Middle East theatre was now finally free to concentrate its efforts on North Africa.

Right: Rommel in his command car passing troops of the Afrikakorps.

Opposite: HMS Upholder *arrives back in Malta after another successful patrol.*

General Wavell, however, had been sacked as British C-in-C. His had been a thankless task and he had been horribly overstretched, but Churchill correctly sensed that he lacked the people skills and dynamic flair that was needed. Wavell was replaced by General Claude Auchinleck, who had been C-in-C India. 'The Auk', as he was known, arrived as more reinforcements were reaching Egypt and strength growing. In September, his forces were entirely reorganized. Tenth Army was formed in Iraq,

RAF Beaufighters
attacking an Axis
merchant vessel.

Ninth Army in Palestine and Eighth Army in Egypt under command of Lieutenant-General Alan Cunningham, brother of the admiral and fresh from victory in Abyssinia.

Meanwhile, the Germans continued to boss their Axis ally in Libya. Rommel now took command of the Panzer Group Afrika, which included both German and Italian forces. He was supposed to be answerable to the Italians, but paid them scant regard.

Rommel's men were still trying to bludgeon Tobruk into submission, but the besieged outpost held firm. Both sides were now preparing for a major offensive. For Eighth Army, the first objective was the relief of Tobruk. For the Axis forces, it was breaking the stubborn siege and pushing the British out of Egypt. Of vital importance was the smooth flow of supplies to both sides. While British shipping had the longer route, it was arriving largely untroubled. The same could not be said for Axis shipping across the Mediterranean, which was now being pummelled by Malta-based aircraft, ships and submarines in particular.

In November 1941, for example, submarines, ships and aircraft operating from the island destroyed 77 per cent of all Axis convoys heading across the Mediterranean. Malta's submarines, such as HMS *Upholder*, were sinking not only huge amounts of enemy shipping but also some of the largest supply vessels in the Axis arsenal – ships that could not be replaced. Force K, a group of fast cruisers and destroyers, managed to annihilate one Axis convoy of ten merchant vessels and six Italian destroyers; all but three destroyers were sunk. Malta's aircraft also bombed and torpedoed enemy shipping. Hitler was so incensed that he ordered U-boats to be diverted from the critical Atlantic and into the Mediterranean instead.

It was Eighth Army who struck first in North Africa, on 18 November in what was called Operation CRUSADER. By this time, the British had three times as many tanks and double the number of aircraft as their opponents. What followed was three hard weeks of bloody and confusing battle.

'In all directions came the noise of battle,' noted Albert Martin of 2nd Rifle Brigade, 'twenty-five pounders crashing away just yards off, a cluster of tanks in the distance firing at something, but whether they were friend or foe was difficult to make out; neither could I work out what the target was.' Martin and his comrades were in lightly armoured tracked carriers, but this was a battle of tanks and guns. At one point some panzers rumbled past amid clouds of swirling dust but didn't shoot at the riflemen. Only at dusk did the fighting die down.

Rommel had been caught off guard by the attack and, misreading the

situation, had sent his panzer divisions towards Bardia. In fact, most of the British tanks were further to the south and so were then able to drive up towards Tobruk. Rommel realized his mistake, ordered an about-turn and the two sides clashed at Sidi Rezegh, 10 miles to the south-east of the town, in what was the biggest tank battle of the North African campaign so far. 'Dust, smoke, burning oil, exploding shell and debris filled the air,' wrote Australian journalist Alan Moorehead. 'From a distance, it was merely noise and confusion.'

Over the next couple of days it was high-velocity German anti-tank guns rather than panzers that halted the British advance. Rommel then attempted to drive eastwards again and Cunningham stopped his offensive. Auchinleck overruled then sacked him, replacing him with his own Chief of Staff in Cairo, Major-General Neil Ritchie. The battle would continue after all.

The panzers were now overstretched and being pummelled by the RAF's Desert Air Force, while the British had pushed forward and finally relieved Tobruk. Rommel tried to counter-attack but could make no headway against strong defence: it was now the turn of British artillery and anti-tank guns to halt the Axis armour. When the Italian Motorized Corps failed to join the attack on Tobruk on 5 December, Rommel accepted it was time to pull back. After one final assault on 7 December, he broke off and his battered forces sped back across the bulge of Cyrenaica. So the see-saw North Africa campaign continued.

Meanwhile, across the Mediterranean, Malta was soon to feel the wrath of the Luftwaffe once more. No one was more obsessed with the Mediterranean than Hitler, who constantly feared for his southern flank. With faith in his Italian ally completely gone, he now sent Field Marshal Albert Kesselring to command all Axis forces in the south.

Kesselring was known as 'Smiling Albert' because of his cheery manner, but this hid a grim ruthlessness and devout allegiance to the Führer. He correctly understood that the war in North Africa would be won or lost by whichever side won the battle of supplies, so with this in mind he determined to crush Malta as an offensive base.

Right: Fierce fighting at Sidi Rezegh during Operation CRUSADER.

Fliegerkorps II arrived on Sicily in December and in the New Year began pummelling the island. Over the next four months, its cities and harbours were smashed, airfields wrecked and air forces all but destroyed. Malta was an offensive base no more. It had become the most bombed place on earth.

Opposite: The Luftwaffe bombing Malta.

Both Kesselring and the Italian High Command had hoped to follow the Malta blitz with an invasion, but Rommel was keen to seize the initiative in North Africa and drive the British out of

Libya then Egypt, and there were not enough men or aircraft to do both at once. In the Soviet Union, the Germans were also planning a drive towards the Caucasus in the south-east. Rommel's flair and ambition appealed to Hitler, who now dreamed of linking up both forces through the Middle East. This was pure fantasy, but it meant an invasion of Malta would have to wait.

Rommel attacked on 26 May. Eighth Army was strung out over 40 miles of desert, from the Mediterranean to the Free French outpost of Bir Hacheim in what was called the Gazala Line. Infantry were placed in 'boxes' surrounded by wire entanglements and minefields and often separated from one another by a number of miles. Behind were the mobile units, such as those of Albert Martin and his fellows, and the British tank units. General Ritchie's dispositions made little sense, as behind was Tobruk, a garrison that had held out for nine months the previous year and already had defences in place. Rommel could have bypassed the town, but not for long, because the British in Tobruk would easily have been able to strangle his supply lines. This meant he would have had to turn and deal with Tobruk before charging off into Egypt and the Middle East.

Instead, he simply sent his mobile forces, including the Deutsches Afrikakorps, around the southern flank of the Gazala Line and came in around the back of the British positions.

Even then, Eighth Army had the chance to encircle Rommel's armour and crush him in turn, but chronic dithering at the top and a lack of firm and resolute generalship from Ritchie and his corps commanders ensured a golden opportunity to smash the German forces for good went begging. Instead, the Axis were able to dramatically regain the initiative and pick off Eighth Army units in detail, one by one. The 'Cauldron', a wide, shallow depression in the desert, became a scene of carnage as the British armour was largely destroyed by screens of anti-tank guns. Soon Eighth Army was in full retreat and then, on 21 June, Tobruk was surrounded and forced to surrender. It was a devastating and humiliating blow. British generalship at Gazala had been abject.

Eighth Army now streamed back into Egypt and to the Alamein position. This lay some 60 miles west of Alexandria and was almost the only place in the Western Desert that could not be outflanked because of the deep Qattara Depression some 40 miles to the south. What saved Eighth Army from annihilation was the Desert Air Force, who flew round-the-clock missions harrying the enemy at

Above left: 112 'Shark' Squadron P-40 Kittyhawks shooting up an Axis column.

Opposite: The Afrikakorps on the march

every turn and leap-frogging backwards from one desert landing ground to another. Since the fall of France in 1940, the RAF had been learning important lessons about how to provide close air support effectively to land forces. Men like Air Chief Marshal Arthur Tedder and the commander of the Desert Air Force, Air Vice-Marshal Arthur 'Mary' Coningham, were dynamic, charismatic and forward-thinking, and well served by tough, battle-hardened young squadron commanders. The contrast with Eighth Army's generals could not have been starker.

After the loss of Tobruk, Ritchie was fired and the Auk took over direct command of Eighth Army. Throughout July, his troops managed to hold off the newly promoted Field Marshal Rommel's Panzer Army Afrika. By August, both sides were exhausted. Churchill visited Egypt in early August and Auchinleck was now sacked too. General William 'Strafer' Gott took over Eighth Army but was then killed in a deliberate air attack as he flew to Cairo. The vastly experienced General Sir Harold Alexander took over as C-in-C Middle East, while Lieutenant-General Bernard Montgomery was given command of Eighth Army. Both announced an end to any more retreats. They would build up forces, retrain their men and, when ready, attack.

On Malta, meanwhile, the RAF had wrested back the air battle thanks to the arrival of good numbers of Spitfires, but the people were starving. A convoy in March had reached the island only to be sunk in harbour, while the next, in June, had been forced to turn back. In August, the most heavily protected convoy of the war set off from Gibraltar along the length of the Mediterranean: thirteen merchantmen and one tanker, protected by four aircraft carriers, two battleships, seven cruisers and thirty-two destroyers. Against them were 600 Axis aircraft, as well as submarines and fast torpedo boats. Operation PEDESTAL was an epic. Only four of the merchant ships made it, while the tanker, *Ohio*, was hit no fewer than ten times and even a Stuka dive-bomber crashed on her decks. She finally inched into Grand Harbour on 15 August, low in the water and towed by three destroyers. Malta had been saved.

Right:
The Ohio limping into Malta's Grand Harbour as Spitfires fly overhead.

Opposite : The SAS, operating deep in the Western Desert, under attack from Luftwaffe ME-109s.

It has often been claimed that British equipment was inferior to that of the Germans. That was not really the case. Nor was there much wrong with training methods. Eighth Army was now filled with men who had plenty of experience of fighting in the desert. The biggest problem was one of poor morale, as both Alexander and Montgomery recognized. This was their greatest challenge, but with no-nonsense pep-talks, new Sherman tanks from the US and plenty of hard training, they were soon able to turn things around.

Living and fighting in the desert was challenging for both sides. Water was in limited supply, food was monotonous and, in the case of the Germans and Italians, barely edible. Millions of flies swarmed around the men all the time, but especially when eating. There were sand flies, scorpions and other bugs to deal with. Desert sores were rife, and all the men were a long, long way from home. Sand storms, the *khamseen*, could suddenly sweep in and bury an entire truck. Daylight hours could be blisteringly hot, but nights freezing.

Those who embraced it could thrive, as British special forces, the Long Range Desert Group and SAS proved. Operating far behind enemy lines, the LRDG provided vital intelligence, while in the summer of 1942 the SAS proved increasingly effective, carrying out daring raids on Axis airfields and supply columns, then melting back into the desert once more. On 26 July, for example, in an attack on El Daba landing ground, the SAS destroyed thirty-seven German transport planes, all of which were vital for Rommel's efforts to rebuild strength.

With Malta resurgent as an offensive base, the British were able to attack Axis supply convoys from both sides of the Mediterranean and hit them hard. Many Axis ships went down that August, which was catastrophic for Rommel's new Panzer Army Afrika, especially since their lines of supply were so stretched. British supply lines were now both short and barely interrupted.

Rommel attacked on 30 August, but this time his attempted outflanking sweep was met by firm defence and by intense carpet-bombing by the RAF. 'Wave after wave of heavy bomber formations dropped their high explosive,' recalled Colonel Fritz Bayerlein, Chief of Staff of the Afrikakorps. There was no let-up, either day or night, and both Bayerlein and Rommel were lucky to survive.

The German commander began pulling back his forces on 2 September. The Battle of Alam Halfa had not achieved the breakthrough for which Rommel had hoped. 'Our last chance to win in the Nile Delta,' noted Bayerlein, 'had passed.'

With the Panzer Army now on the defensive, Montgomery began readying himself for his own attack. Intensive training and an increased build-up of forces meant he was not ready until the full moon in the third week of October.

Meanwhile, back in Britain, the build-up of American forces had been continuing since America's entry into the war the previous December. The plan had been to launch a joint Anglo-US invasion of Europe, but it quickly became clear that neither the British nor the Americans were ready. A large-scale Canadian raid on Dieppe in August had been a bloody failure. A successful invasion of north-west Africa, however, was more achievable. Operation TORCH was due to launch in November, after Eighth Army attacked in the desert.

Left: The Snipe action.

Opposite: General Montgomery.

The British offensive at Alamein began on the night of 23 October after incessant air attacks and a large-scale artillery barrage. The sound and sight of this barrage remained long in the memory, but it was largely a failure. Instead of focusing much of his artillery in the north, which was where the main attack was made, Montgomery chose to spread it down the length of the line. Furthermore, instead of firing in concentrations, each gun aimed directly ahead, where the impact of the landing shells was less.

This meant few of the mines, wire or Axis defences were destroyed, and it left the massed infantry and armour to fight a grinding, attritional and costly battle. Montgomery had said the fighting would last ten days and he was quite right. It did. With different tactics, however, it might have been over in a quarter of the time. Albert Martin found himself engaged in a desperate day-long battle as an anti-tank gunner at what became known as the Snipe action, but it helped stop the German armoured counter-attack on 27 October. By the end of the day, more than sixty Axis tanks littered the desert around them.

For Italian Lieutenant Giuseppe Santaniello, it was air power, more than anything, that broke the spirits of his men and himself. 'The RAF,' he noted in his diary, 'always wins.' In truth, it was

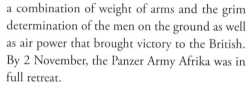

a combination of weight of arms and the grim determination of the men on the ground as well as air power that brought victory to the British. By 2 November, the Panzer Army Afrika was in full retreat.

Six days later, American troops landed in Vichy-controlled north-west Africa. The giant pincer movement to crush the Axis in Africa had begun.

Operation TORCH was, at the time, the largest amphibious operation the world had ever seen. Three separate invasion forces, one from the US and two from Britain, managed to land pretty much at the right place and on time. The Vichy French forces were quickly overrun and so the British First Army, containing the US II Corps, began its march on Tunis, while Montgomery's men snapped at the heels of the retreating Panzer Army Afrika.

Hitler's obsession with his southern flank continued, however, and he swiftly ordered large reinforcements. The distance from Sicily to north-east Tunisia was not far and, suddenly, Axis supply lines had shortened. Men, machines and aircraft were all hurried to form a bridgehead. It was also winter, and in the Mediterranean north of the country it soon began to

Left: American tanks: Stuart, top, and Grant, bottom.

Opposite: Battle of the Tebaga Gap.

rain and temperatures dropped. What had seemed like an easy victory slipped from the Allies' grasp.

By the third week of January 1943, Eighth Army had reached Tripoli then paused to regather strength. It was their turn to be a long way from their supply base – nearly 1,000 miles, in fact. Rommel, now greatly reinforced and with a second Axis army in northern Tunisia, chose this moment to strike back. On 14 February, he attacked the Americans advancing eastwards into southern Tunisia, pushing them back in disarray through the Kasserine Pass.

It was a great shock for the still inexperienced Americans, but the Axis counter-attack soon ran out of steam as Allied reinforcements were flung in to stop the rot. By 22 February Rommel's last-ditch attempt to affect the outcome in Africa had come to a halt.

Still Hitler sent more reinforcements to Tunisia. General Alexander had become 18th Army Group Commander, while the American General Dwight D. Eisenhower was promoted to Supreme Allied Commander. Alexander swiftly reorganized the front, sending green American units such as the 34th 'Red Bull' Division, who had suffered badly at Fondouk, off for battle-conditioning training. General George S. Patton took over command of II Corps after his predecessor, the hopeless General Lloyd Fredendall, was sacked.

Rommel made one last attempt to stem the advance of Eighth Army, but his counter-attack at Medenine on the south-east Tunisian border was swiftly defeated and on 6 March 1943 he left Africa for the last time, replaced by the Italian General Giovanni Messe.

Montgomery's next obstacle was the fixed defences between the coast and the Matmata Hills. While half his force headed towards the Mareth Line, the newly formed New Zealand Corps advanced wide into the desert in a 200-mile march around the back of the Matmata Hills and attacked through the Tebaga Gap. Despite a cumbersome armoured assault on the Mareth Line, this two-fisted punch, once again supported by the indefatigable Desert Air Force, was too much for the renamed Italian Panzer Army. By 27 March, Messe's troops were in retreat with Eighth Army following fast.

The Allies had now created the North African Tactical Air Force under 'Mary' Coningham, while both Eighth Army and a rejuvenated First Army were ready to close the net. Facing them was General Jürgen von Arnim's Fifth Panzer Army in the north and Messe's army now behind a new defensive line at Wadi Akarit north of Gabès. The endgame in North Africa was about to be played out.

Despite the brilliant work of the 4th Indian Division, who attacked through the mountains and outflanked the Wadi Akarit position, Eighth Army's X Corps was too slow to take advantage and so a golden opportunity to encircle and destroy the Italian Panzer Army was missed. With US II Corps attacking from the west, they finally linked up with Eighth Army, who now pursued Messe's forces northwards towards Enfidaville, where they were finally checked.

Throughout April 1943, the fighting continued as the two Axis forces were pushed back into an ever-narrowing bridgehead in the north-east of the country. Hitler continued to pour supplies into Tunisia, mostly now by air. It was a disastrous policy. On 16 April, the US 57th Fighter Group shot down seventy-four enemy aircraft, most of which were transports. 'What a day!' noted pilot Dale Deniston in his diary. 'What a day for making history!' It became known as the 'Palm Sunday Turkey Shoot'.

Opposite: USAAF P-38 Lightnings and RAF Spitfires wreak havoc during the Palm Sunday Turkey Shoot off Cap Bon.

Meanwhile, the 34th Red Bulls had returned from Battle School and managed to knock the Germans off the key Hill 609. The Americans were learning fast. US II Corps was now transferred to the north, Eighth Army held the line at Enfidaville, while several units, including the 4th Indian Division, were transferred to First Army for Operation VULCAN, the final assault in Tunisia.

The key attack was through the Medjerda Valley, which led directly to Tunis. The battle plan was the brainchild of the 4th Indians' commander, Major-General Francis Tuker, and was the perfect blend of massive firepower and infantry moving stealthily forward and surprising the enemy.

Today, the Battle of Medjerda is almost entirely forgotten, but it was fought against highly disciplined German troops and was one of the most perfectly executed battles the British carried out in the entire war. In the early hours of 6 May, massed night-bombers pummelled the German positions, followed by devastating artillery firing in concentrations on to one target after another – as should have been done at Alamein. Then 4th Indian Division attacked with stealth through long, reedy grass, achieving complete surprise. Many of the German units simply cut and ran, but as they fled they were hounded by yet more aircraft. A massive hole had been blown in the Axis defences and the road to Tunis was now open.

The city fell the next day, 7 May, while the Americans captured the second city, Bizerte. Axis resistance was crumbling fast. The Axis commander, General von Arnim, surrendered, rather fittingly, to General Tuker in the Cap Bon peninsula on 12 May, while General Messe signed the surrender document the following day. Some 250,000 Axis troops were taken prisoner, more than at Stalingrad in February of that year, along with a mass of aircraft, tanks, guns and ships. It was a major Allied victory.

At 1.16 p.m. on 13 May, General Alexander signalled to Winston Churchill: 'Sir, it is my duty to report that the Tunisian campaign is over. All enemy resistance has ceased. We are masters of the North African shores.'

Opposite: General von Arnim surrendering to General Tuker.

5: THE EASTERN FRONT
1941–1943

Operation BARBAROSSA was launched early on 22 June 1941, just a few weeks after the invasion of Crete, and was the largest clash of arms the world had ever seen. Germany had amassed more than 3 million men, a colossal number, yet in truth Adolf Hitler's forces were not really ready for a campaign on this scale. Hitler had originally intended to invade the Soviet Union once France and Britain had been defeated and Europe subjugated; as a veteran of the defeat of the First World War, he understood the danger of fighting on two fronts and overstretching Germany's meagre resources.

Yet Britain had not been defeated, and hovering in the background was the United States, with its huge economic potential and open hostility to Nazi Germany. Already Germany was running short of vital supplies, but especially food and oil, and plundering the Soviet Union now seemed the best chance of making up these shortfalls. Hitler was confident of success – after all, Germany had recently defeated mighty France in six weeks, while the Red Army had been given a bloody nose by lowly Finland during what was known as the 'Winter War' of 1939–40.

The trouble was, the Soviet Union was more than ten times the size of France and the Low Countries, and Germany had a force that was only slightly larger than that of the previous year when Hitler attacked in the west. What's more, he had only 30 per cent more panzer forces, the German elite units that had been the spearhead of victory in France. As in France, most German troops were to advance into Russia on foot and by horse. The difference was that the attack front for BARBAROSSA was some 1,200 miles long (see map on page 325).

Nothing less than complete annihilation of the Red Army would do, and really this had to be achieved within 500 miles – the effective range within which the Germans could operate with the kind of speed and weight of force needed before their supply lines became over-extended and their advance ground to a halt. This was a tall order even for an army full of confidence and flushed with victory. The invasion was also to be conducted with brutal violence. 'The upcoming campaign,' Hitler told his commanders, 'is more than a mere contest of arms. It will be a struggle between two world views.'

The General Staff of the Wehrmacht – the German armed services – had already put together a plan to take the farmlands of the Ukraine. This would mean starving some 20–30 million Soviet citizens, but Nazi Germany viewed it as a war of survival so this was considered regrettably acceptable. The Soviet leadership and intelligentsia were also to be exterminated. Hitler told his generals they had three months to win this victory, after which they would then turn back west and deal with Britain once and for all.

*Opposite:
German Heinkel
111 bombers
attack Moscow.*

To begin with, all seemed to go spectacularly well, helped by the Soviet leader Joseph Stalin's curious refusal to accept any warning sign of an imminent attack – and despite massive German build-up along the border in former Poland. In fact, BARBAROSSA had been the world's worst-kept secret.

Overwhelming force along what was initially a 500-mile front gouged out huge chunks of Soviet territory in the first fortnight of battle as the German armies swept forward, while above, the Luftwaffe hammered the Red Army's air forces. The Baltic States were swiftly overrun in the north, while in the centre much of former Poland was swept aside. Once again, the German armies seemed unstoppable.

Stalin appeared to have been briefly frozen with panic but quickly recovered. On 30 June he formed a war cabinet, the People's Commissariat of Defence (GKO), and the next day spoke to the people, appealing to their patriotism. At the same time, the security services were united under the People's Commissariat for Internal Affairs (NKVD) and ordered to clamp down even harder on defeatism and deserters, and to ensure there was no slackening of the struggle for survival.

Meanwhile, Hitler now began meddling in military matters despite having no qualifications for such high-level interference. On 19 July, he ordered that Leningrad in the north and the Ukraine in the south were the priorities and that his two precious panzer groups, currently pushing towards Moscow, should be sent to help with these drives once Smolensk, 360 miles south-west of the capital, had been crushed. The Soviet capital would be left to the Luftwaffe even though there were nothing like enough bombers to do the job.

Four days later, he changed his orders again, now demanding that the Luftwaffe support the southern drive and also the Finns, who were advancing against Leningrad in the north. He thought this would deter the British from intervening in the Arctic. At the time there was no possible way in which Britain could mount such an operation, something that was glaringly obvious to anyone with a basic knowledge of planning. Moscow was barely bombed at all.

Another directive was issued on 30 July and yet another on 12 August as Hitler obsessed over his flanks and the slowing up of their advance. By this time, the Red Army was starting to regain its balance, while the Germans were reaching the limits of their lines of supply.

Günther Sack was a young anti-aircraft gunner attached to the German 9th Division in Army Group South in the Ukraine. In the second week of July his team suffered a puncture on their gun carriage, which held them up, then on 15 July their truck broke down with a seized engine. Then the trailer broke again, so that it wasn't until the end of July that they finally caught up with the rest of the division. His and his crew's experience was a common one.

Meanwhile, a further 5 million men had been called up to the Red Army. The Soviets had been horrifically mauled in the opening stages of BARBAROSSA but they had not been completely defeated. Far from it. 'We very soon had to accustom ourselves,' wrote Hans von Luck, an officer in the 7th Panzer Division, 'to her almost inexhaustible masses of land forces, tanks, and artillery.'

The German advance was once again increasingly dependent on her railway network, but the Soviet Union operated on a different gauge. This meant changing the tracks as they moved east, because Stalin had also ordered a scorched earth policy as the Red Army fell back. All factories, bridges, farmland and infrastructure were to be destroyed so the Germans could not use it. On 24 June, Stalin had also ordered the establishment of a Soviet – or council – for Evacuation. The vast

Opposite: German troops advance into the Soviet Union on 22 June 1941.

bulk of the USSR's industry was to be moved lock, stock and barrel to the Urals, some 600 miles east of Moscow. By the beginning of August this was already well under way.

The Germans continued to win victories – and capture more prisoners than they could cope with. This meant many Soviet POWs soon starved to death, as there was already a shortage of food for the German troops without having to feed many more prisoners than they had expected. Word of the poor treatment of prisoners soon spread, and increasing numbers of Soviet soldiers now evaded capture and began to organize themselves to operate behind the lines as partisans. This further hindered the German supply lines to the front.

The Black Sea port of Kiev in the south was captured by the Germans on 19 August. It was another massive victory – but not massive enough. Hitler now agreed that the main effort should be focused on Moscow, but this involved an enormous redeployment of forces, which took time – too much time,

and a precious resource of which they were running short. Operation TYPHOON was launched on 30 September, three and a half months after the invasion had begun. And by this time, it had begun to rain.

Another 750,000 Soviet men were captured, but Moscow was still a long way off and the rain soon turned the rough roads to mud. Vehicles increasingly broke down or became stuck. Fuel could no longer be supplied in the quantities required. Casualties were mounting and manpower was running short. Replacements of men, machines and spare parts could not be found or delivered in the numbers needed. What made the Wehrmacht special was the speed with which it operated. But when it slowed down, it was not quite so special after all.

None the less, huge swathes of territory were now in German hands. In Moscow, the Soviet leadership was struggling to control the crisis. Although the German advance was slowing, by October they were just 120 miles from the capital. Civilians were ordered to help build an extra defence line, while General Georgi Zhukov was brought in to defend the city with massive reinforcements of troops. At the same time, more industry and even state archives were sent east to the Urals.

The Germans continued to close on the city, but rain had now given way to snow and a dramatic drop in temperatures for which they were simply not equipped. Only in the Luftwaffe had anyone thought ahead and ordered winter clothing. The army had none at all. Sixty miles from Moscow, Hans von Luck faced a Soviet counter-attack with Russian troops on skis and wearing white camouflage. 'We sensed catastrophe,' he wrote, 'and thought of Napoleon's fate.' Back in 1812, Napoleon's French army had been decimated by the freezing Russian winter.

Others feared the same. Colonel Hermann Balck visited the front in November and discovered panzer divisions operating at just a tenth of their strength in both men and machines. He was deeply shaken. Fritz Todt, the Armaments Minister, was horrified to learn that German tanks and vehicles were freezing up and unable to move while Soviet tanks could still operate in the extreme cold. With unusual frankness, he told Hitler at the end of November that the war against the Soviet Union could no longer be won.

Meanwhile, despite the vast losses suffered so far, General Zhukov was preparing to defend Moscow with no fewer than 1.25 million men, 7,600 guns and nearly 1,000 tanks. What's more, an incredible 2,593 industrial operations had been relocated in the Urals since June, along with 1.5 million railway wagons and much of the Soviet industrial workforce.

German troops advanced to within 30 miles of Moscow. Stalin and the GKO still feared the worst, but by this time most of the attackers were frozen, half starving and all but broken. On the night of 4/5 December, as temperatures plummeted further to minus 35, the Red Army counter-attacked, catching their enemy completely off guard. Suddenly it was the Germans who were on the back foot.

Six months earlier, Germany had had one enemy – Great Britain – but by the middle of December 1941 faced Britain, the Soviet Union and now the United States, following the Japanese attack on Pearl Harbor. Japan was an Axis partner and on 11 December Hitler declared war on America. By this time Nazi Germany was short of money, food, coal, oil and other vital resources necessary for war. In 1918, Germany had signed an armistice because it had run out of money and could no longer win. That moment had arrived again now, as men like Fritz Todt understood.

Hitler, however, refused to accept this and responded by sacking a number of highly experienced and brilliant commanders such as Field Marshal Heinz Guderian. He also fired the head of the army, Field Marshal Walther von Brauchitsch, and made himself Commander-in-Chief instead. This would mean more micromanaging and more rigid control. A key feature of the German Army's success had always been freedom of movement and the right of

Left: The German Army lacked adequate winter clothing.

Opposite: By contrast, ski-equipped Soviet troops wearing white camouflage were well prepared.

commanders to make swift, on-the-spot decisions. With Hitler directly in charge, there were now barriers to such rapid decision-making.

Moscow remained as out of reach as ever.

Meanwhile, to the north, Leningrad, Russia's second city, had been under siege since September. A major German objective, the city stood on a 30-mile-wide isthmus between the Baltic and Lake Ladoga. Finnish troops were pressing south from the north and had captured two thirds of the lake's shores, while the Germans were now within 10 miles of the city, having crossed the River Neva to the south, and had also reached the lake. The only lifeline to the city for the defenders was across the southern part of Lake Ladoga and via the railheads of the towns of Volkhov and Tikhvin on the far side.

The Germans planned to pound Leningrad into the dust with artillery and bombing. The starving civilian population would be deported east, the defending troops destroyed, and then the city would be levelled with demolition charges. There was to be no mercy.

German troops took Tikhvin on 9 November, but Leningrad was still grimly holding out. With the lake now frozen over, a passage was created across the ice from the far shore to the city; it was known as the 'Road of Life'. Even so, nothing like enough supplies were getting through. Hundreds of thousands of citizens were dying from a combination of starvation, water shortage and disease, their bodies often left where they died. The survivors were eating birds, then cats and dogs, then rats and even dead humans.

There were still large numbers of Red Army troops, however, and on 9 December, as the German attackers froze, they recaptured Tikhvin and then pushed the enemy back along a 90-mile stretch. The terrible siege, though, was still far from over.

'An interesting question is what are the Russians capable of doing in the spring?' noted Colonel Hermann Balck in his diary on 3 March 1942. 'One thing is clear,' he added, 'if we can grasp the initiative again, they will be finished.'

This was what worried the Soviet leadership, despite the catastrophic winter for the Germans and despite Red Army troops continuing to push German forces back along a wide front since December. Stalin and the GKO faced a tricky dilemma. Winter would soon be over and the traditional summer campaigning season would be upon them. The Germans would then, unquestionably, resume the offensive. Despite saving Moscow and holding on in Leningrad, and despite making some gains since then, the Red Army's situation remained perilous. Losses had been enormous, the relocation of war industry to the Urals had hampered the speed of

Right: Stalin and Marshal Timoshenko.

Opposite: The streets of Leningrad during the brutal siege.

production, and they were still learning lessons about how best to turn the tide against the enemy invaders. Manpower was not limitless, even in the Soviet Union. Nor could the will of the people to keep fighting be necessarily assured, despite totalitarian Communist rule. The conundrum facing the Soviet leadership was whether to go on the defensive and build up strength, or to strike first and try to upset the inevitable German offensive plans in the process.

At the urging of Marshal Semyon Timoshenko, Stalin decided to attack. A bulge in the line had been formed around the town of Izyum, south of the key city of Kharkov. By attacking north out of the salient and south from the north of Kharkov on 12 May 1942, they hoped to encircle the city and with it the German Sixth Army.

Unfortunately for the Soviets, the Izyum offensive was a disaster, as the Germans defeated the northern thrust and severed the salient, cutting off and encircling the main Red Army assault in turn. Another 240,000 Soviet prisoners were taken, along with 1,200 tanks and 2,600 guns. For Stalin and the GKO, the disaster could scarcely have been worse. Vyacheslav Molotov, the Foreign Minister, was sent to Britain then America to plead with the Allies to launch an offensive against Germany in the west as soon as possible. The possibility of the Soviet Union being completely defeated loomed heavily for Stalin and the GKO.

Meanwhile, in the skies, Luftwaffe fighter aces continued to rule. Men like Bubi Hartmann, Gerd Barkhorn and Günther Rall were amassing hundreds of aerial victories, using their superior skill, experience and machines to blow the Soviet air forces out of the sky.

Despite this dominance, however, the problems confronting the Germans had not gone away, as the newly promoted Major-General Balck discovered when he arrived at the front to take command of 11th Panzer Division. After BARBAROSSA, 11th Panzer had been reduced to a few battered remnants and even after rebuilding over the winter was still operating at only 60 per cent strength. They were far from alone, and the enormous scale of the Eastern Front, with ongoing shortages of food, oil and just about everything else, meant that Operation BLUE, the planned German drive south to the oilfields of the Caucasus, would be launched with less than they had had the previous summer and with longer lines of communication that would only get longer. What's more, the cream of German manpower had already gone, most of her finest young men obliterated by a year of fighting in this vast, unforgiving country.

Left: Bubi Hartmann (top), Günther Rall (middle) and Gerd Barkhorn (bottom).

Opposite: The Leningrad Philharmonic playing Shostakovich's new symphony in the ruins of the besieged city.

Nor was Operation BLUE the only German effort. Capturing Moscow had been abandoned for the time being, but Hitler had not given up hopes of taking Leningrad and General Erich von Manstein was planning to launch a renewed attack at the end of August.

The suffering of those in Leningrad is hard to comprehend. Over a million had perished since the siege had begun, but the onset of spring and then summer had seen the ice on Lake Ladoga melt. By July, over a million tons of supplies had been shipped across the lake to the city, while more than half a million civilians had been evacuated and some 310,000 troops brought in, along with large numbers of guns and ammunition.

In a striking act of defiance, it was these guns, along with those of the Soviet Baltic Fleet, that were able to silence German artillery early in August to allow the first performance in the city of Dmitri Shostakovich's newly composed Seventh Symphony, 'Leningrad'. To all those who braved going out to hear this incredible concert, the Leningrad Philharmonic played in perfect unison with the Russian guns. Miraculously, not a single German shell fell nearby. The event, broadcast around the world, was a stunning propaganda victory that struck a vital chord for Soviet patriotism.

On 19 August, the Red Army attacked from Volkhov, destroying the best part of two German divisions in the process. This time, their pre-emptive strike worked and von Manstein's offensive plans were scuppered. Leningrad also remained as tantalizingly out of reach as Moscow.

There was also a further operation by the Germans before Operation BLUE was launched. While most of the Crimean peninsula had been captured the previous November, the port and fortress of Sebastopol had remained besieged, stubbornly defended and supplied by the Soviet Navy, which had retained control of the Black Sea.

The Red Army had tried to relieve the city the previous Christmas by launching an amphibious assault on the Kerch peninsula further to the east, but this had been recaptured again by May 1942 and a renewed Axis assault on Sebastopol began. More units of the overstretched Luftwaffe were sent south to the Crimea, as were some 600 pieces of artillery, including two monstrous railway guns. The 'Dora' needed sixty steam engines just to move it and involved building new railway tracks, as well as tying up some 4,120 men. The shell it fired had a diameter of 80cm – almost one metre wide! Operating these two guns caused a logistical headache out of all proportion to its offensive benefits. As many as 500 men were needed just to fire it. 'An extraordinary piece of engineering,' noted General Franz Halder, Chief of Staff of the Army, 'but useless.'

Certainly the guns didn't secure a swift victory. By the end of June, Sebastopol still held out and the Germans then resorted to using poison smoke to clear the caverns below the city. Not until 9 July did the defenders finally surrender. The cost to both sides was huge, but was felt more keenly by the Germans, who had thrown an entire army into the final battle; 25,000 German soldiers died in that last offensive and 70,000 overall. Sebastopol also sucked up gargantuan amounts of resources at an average rate of 135 railway wagons a day. It was something of a Pyrrhic victory, while the grim defence did nothing but stiffen Red Army resolve.

When Operation BLUE was launched with a mighty artillery barrage at 2.15 a.m. on 28 June 1942, General Balck's 11th Panzer Division were at the front of the advance. By 9 a.m. they had crossed a vital river obstacle and, while under fire, Balck went forward to see his infantry, then accompanied his panzers as they sped forward. 'It was an intoxicating picture,' he wrote, 'the wide, treeless plains covered with 150 advancing tanks, above them a Stuka squadron.' The advance continued, but this time the enemy melted away, retreating before they could be captured. The Red Army was learning.

None the less, Operation BLUE appeared to be going well, although Hitler was beginning to

Opposite: Germany's massive 'Dora' railway gun fired shells that were almost a metre in diameter.

micro-manage once more. From the depths of his bunker, the Wolf's Lair in East Prussia, he insisted on sending two precious panzer divisions west to France then concentrating too many others against Rostov, leaving flanks dangerously exposed. When the folly of this became apparent, he flew into a fit of rage. Nothing was ever Hitler's fault. 'The situation is getting more and more intolerable,' noted General Halder. 'This so-called leadership is characterized by a pathological reaction to the impressions of the moment and a total lack of any understanding of the command machinery and its possibilities.'

Even so, Operation BLUE had smashed the Red Army's front and thereafter the German advance into the Caucasus was rapid. Maikop, a major objective, was captured, although its oil wells had been destroyed by the retreating Russians. Meanwhile, General Friedrich Paulus's Sixth Army was also advancing east towards Stalingrad on the River Volga.

The outskirts of Stalingrad were reached on 10 August, but by then the advance south into the Caucasus was beginning to slow as once again the supply lines began to stretch and Red Army resistance grew. The Germans were now more than 500 miles further on, the distance at which they could no longer operate with the speed and manoeuvrability that was the benchmark of their operational and tactical skill. They had exceeded what is known as the culmination point.

Hitler had dreamed of creating a mammoth Axis link between Rommel's forces advancing from Egypt into the Middle East and his armies in the Soviet Union, but this was pure fantasy. In fact, it was also absurd to believe they could capture the world's third-largest producing oilfields in Baku, even though that had been the prime strategic aim of Operation BLUE.

Such ambition was extremely flawed thinking for a number of reasons. First, the Red Army would destroy the wells in advance as they had at Maikop. Second, even if they didn't, the Germans had no means of either refining the oil or, more importantly, transporting it west. The only pipelines

were few and far between and all headed east to the Urals. Oil was transported around the world almost entirely by ship – as it still is today – yet Germany had neither shipping nor access to the world's oceans. The alternative was the railway, but the Reichsbahn was already operating at capacity and had nothing like enough oil wagons.

Incredibly, no one within the Reich appears to have considered any of this.

Instead, the Germans believed the Soviet Union was already on the point of collapse and that the capture of Baku would hasten its capitulation. However, because the Luftwaffe did not have the aircraft to bomb or spy on either Baku or the growing industrial relocation in the Urals, they had little idea that the Soviet Union was rapidly and very effectively increasing its

Left: Marshal Konstantin Rokossovsky.

Opposite: Hitler dreamed of capturing the vast Soviet oilfields in Baku on the shores of the Caspian Sea.

armaments production. Faulty intelligence, compounded by Hitler's desire always to listen to over-optimistic appreciations, meant Operation BLUE had been launched on an entirely false promise. For example, German intelligence reckoned the Soviet Union had 6,600 aircraft when in fact they had 22,000. They thought the Red Army had 6,000 tanks when the real number was 24,446. In artillery they were even further off the mark: 7,800 guns instead of the 33,000 that was the reality. These were very big errors.

As it happened, however, the Germans never reached Baku. Once again, their armies had run out of steam.

This marked the end for General Halder, who was fired in September. Ironically, as some of Germany's best commanders were finding themselves out of a job, the Red Army had learned much after more than a year of bitter warfare and a number of their very best commanders were now coming to the fore. One of those was General Konstantin Rokossovsky, of Polish descent and a man who had been on the receiving end of Stalin's purge of the Red Army in the 1930s. Most of the army's senior leadership had been executed – one reason for poor performance early in the war – and Rokossovsky had been lucky to lose only his teeth and a number of fingernails. Since his release from prison he had repeatedly proved himself to be one of Stalin's most capable and inspirational generals and had swiftly risen up the ranks as a result. By November 1942, he was commanding the Don Front, a group of armies facing the Germans at Stalingrad – and brilliantly so too.

As the winter of 1942 began to bite, it was clear that Paulus's Sixth Army was becoming horribly bogged down at Stalingrad, while the El Dorado of Baku was as out of reach as ever. Either side of Sixth Army were Axis allies: one Italian army to the north and a Romanian one on each side, and their forces were neither as well equipped nor of equal fighting quality as the Germans. Their fighting capacity had been further weakened by attrition and the advent of winter.

Realizing this, on 19 November the Red Army launched Operation URANUS to the north and south of the city. Through the winter mist, Russian troops attacked in thick snow like apocalyptic spectres, smashing their way through both Romanian armies to link up 35 miles west of Stalingrad. Trapped in the middle were more than a quarter of a million troops, including the remains of Sixth Army, once one of Germany's finest. By 24 November, a massive gap had opened up between the German forces to the north and those still in the Caucasus. How the tables had turned. Paulus asked permission to try to break out, but this was refused. Instead, the Luftwaffe were ordered to fly in supplies until Sixth Army could be relieved. They never managed a fraction of what was needed.

It was Rokossovsky's Don Front that was now ordered to destroy the Germans at Stalingrad. The offensive began on 10 January 1943. On the 16th, the main airfield was captured and with that the fate of Sixth Army was sealed for good. Against Hitler's wishes, Paulus surrendered on 31 January in what was the most crushing and devastating defeat so far suffered by the Germans in the war.

With the triumph of Stalingrad, Stalin now called for a renewed Red Army drive westwards using three fronts – that is, groups of armies. Soviet industry was producing increasing amounts of war materiel and more was coming from the USA and Britain, while the Red Army was showing signs of increasing competence. The plan was still overambitious, however.

Even so, by March the Germans had been thrown back between 200 and 420 miles. The Italian, Hungarian and two Romanian armies had all been utterly destroyed, and all the ground lost in the

Caucasus retaken. German forces west of Moscow had survived being encircled, but Kharkov had also been retaken – Hitler had forbidden any retreat from the city, but this time the SS Panzer Corps that held it ignored the order and pulled out on 15 February.

Despite these stunning reverses, suddenly it was the Red Army that was overstretched with lines of supply that were far too long. On 4 March, they halted their advances only for the Germans to counter-attack. Rather than allow themselves to be encircled, the Red Army sensibly fell back out of comparative danger, although it meant abandoning Kharkov yet again, as well as, some 250 miles to the north, Bryansk and Orel. The Russians did, however, hold on to the city of Kursk so that by the time the long, bloody and bitter winter fighting finally died down at the end of March there was a large bulge, or salient, sticking out some 60 miles to the west of the town and running some 150 miles north to south.

It was clear the lull was just that – a pause – and that the Germans would soon use the summer to go on the offensive once more. With the key cities of Orel and Kharkov to the north and south, it was also obvious that this large salient of rolling, well-cultivated farmland was where the next great battle would take place.

For Hitler and the Nazi leadership, the war in the Soviet Union had never been just about gaining food, oil and living space. There was also an ideological element: a battle of survival in which German 'Aryans' were fighting inferior 'Slavs' or Untermenschen – inferior beings. For the Nazis, it was a racial war. By making it so they were rather shooting themselves in the foot, however. During the 1930s, the Ukraine had suffered a famine in which millions had died. Many Ukrainians held Stalin directly responsible and even welcomed the Nazi invaders, but although some were absorbed into the Wehrmacht, many more faced barbarity. Villages were burned, people executed, and others rounded up and taken prisoner.

Soviet prisoners of war were also treated appallingly compared with western Allied POWs. Those who did not die of starvation and illness were forced into slave labour. So began a cycle of barely comprehensible violence and cruelty.

Large numbers of Soviet civilians and former soldiers who had fled the German advances or somehow escaped their clutches had, by the spring of 1943, become particularly vicious and increasingly effective bands of outlaws, or partisans, organized from within the Soviet Union by the NKVD, the Soviet intelligence service. These partisans were blowing up railway lines and roads, attacking convoys and ambushing any troops they could, while also passing back vital intelligence. In effect, the partisans had become a fourth armed service, and made the already difficult task of supply even harder for the Germans.

For the Germans, clearing the Kursk salient was an urgent priority. The bulge added around 150 miles to the front line, which was tying up some eighteen divisions. By straightening the line, they would free up those men and, more importantly, would destroy the main concentration of Red Army forces. These now included the Central Front, which had been formed back in February and which was commanded by Rokossovsky, as well as General Nikolai Vatutin's Voronezh Front in the southern part of the salient.

Hopes for the forthcoming battle were high. It would be a chance to restore prestige and confidence and show the world the Wehrmacht was far from beaten. From April and into June 1943, the

Opposite: (top) The German Army was guilty of terrible atrocities in Ukraine; (bottom) Partisan fighters, supported by Moscow, attacked German supply lines.

Germans began preparing for this next massive attack, code-named CITADEL.

It was Marshal Zhukov who persuaded Stalin and the GKO to stand firm, dig in, use the increasing amounts of war materiel coming from the Urals, and make the Germans fight for every yard. Only once the German attack had been blunted would the Soviets go on the offensive. For once, Stalin listened. In April, the Red Army began digging a massive series of defences. In all, there were five 'belts' around the salient and Kursk itself, and a further three behind. Each of these belts included several lines of bunkers, gun positions, minefields and wire. The entire population was evacuated from the outer zone and villages turned into small fortresses and strongpoints. Intelligence from partisans, from British code-breakers and from Soviet spies and signals intelligence made it clear the Germans would attack from two points, one in the north and one in the south. This, then, was where the defences were made strongest.

Soviet intelligence was so good that by the beginning of July they not only knew where the Germans would attack but with what and when. On the other hand, German intelligence was also good enough to know that Rokossovsky was staying in a small cottage halfway between Kursk and the north edge of the salient, and so on the night of 3 July, two days before CITADEL's launch, two planes came over and destroyed the house. By chance, however, Rokossovsky was not there. It was a lucky escape.

The Germans had amassed some 900,000 men, 10,000 guns, 2,700 tanks and 2,000 aircraft. General Kurt Student and the men of Ninth Army would attack from the north, while General Hermann Hoth's Fourth Panzer Army assaulted from the south. Inside the salient were some 1.3 million Red Army troops, double the number of German guns and 3,600 tanks. A military rule of thumb is never to attack without at least a three-to-one advantage, but not only did the Germans not have this, they were also confronting the most formidable defences they had yet come up against. Soviet air power was also on the rise with some 2,400 bombers, fighters and ground attack aircraft such as the Ilyushin Il-2 Sturmovik.

What's more, captured prisoners had revealed that the attack would begin in the early hours of 5 July 1943. In an effort to put the enemy off their stride, Rokossovsky had opened up 500 of his own guns first at around 2.20 a.m., along with a similar number of mortars and 100 Katyusha rocket-launchers. This certainly shook German confidence, but did not stop them launching an immense artillery barrage at around 4.30 a.m. Half an hour later, the Germans attacked from the south and at 5.50 a.m. they began their assault from the north.

The Fourth Panzer Army in the south was full of tanks, motorized infantry and artillery, and included new mighty Panther and Tiger tanks. It was the kind of armoured spearhead that had

Above left: The Red Army dug in around Kursk in anticipation of a renewed German offensive.

Opposite: The heavily armed Ilyushin Il-2 Sturmovik proved to be an effective ground-attack aircraft.

cut swathes through much of Europe, but now many of the new tanks broke down, while others found themselves being pummelled in turn by Russian anti-tank guns from their well-prepared positions. In the north, similarly prepared and well-sighted positions also intercepted the main German thrust. One after another, German tanks were hit and knocked out.

By 10 July, the Germans had managed to penetrate 20 miles in the south and about 7 miles in the north, and had reached only the third line of defence. The next day, 11 July, the panzers renewed their attack from the south. The fine summer weather was breaking and by the morning of the 12th, as the panzers neared the small town of Prokhorovka, thunderclouds were building. Joined by the II SS Panzer Corps with some 600 tanks, including 100 Tigers, they were now confronted by a counter-thrust from the Fifth Guards Tank Army.

The Battle of Prokhorovka, which followed that day, has often been called the 'greatest tank battle in history'. Although the numbers involved have often been wildly exaggerated, it did involve more than 800 on both sides. The Russians came off worst and left some 400 burnt-out hulks on the field of battle, but despite this, that same day Hitler called a halt to CITADEL. Two days earlier, the Allies had landed in Sicily, requiring a diversion of resources and especially Luftwaffe aircraft to meet this new threat – one that was far closer to home.

Now came the Red Army counter-attack. Rokossovsky's men, with a mass of tanks and artillery, ground down the best German efforts to hold on, gradually pushing forward. Orel was retaken on 4 August. At the same time, almost 100,000 coordinated partisans began what was known as the 'Railway War': blowing up railway lines in thousands of places, killing rail crew and paralysing the German lines of communication. On the night of 20/21 July, for example, they cut the main line from Bryansk in 430 places.

In the south, Vatutin's front was joined by another group of armies, the Steppe Front, and then Zhukov himself was sent forward to coordinate this massive combined counter-offensive there. The battered, exhausted and demoralized Germans had no answer. On 5 August, Belgorod was retaken. By midday on 23 August, Kharkov was once again in Soviet hands, and this time would remain so. In some fifty days of fighting, Red Army losses had been horrific but so had those of the Germans: some half a million dead, wounded and missing, and around thirty divisions destroyed. These were casualties they simply could not afford.

What's more, the Red Army was now a very

Right:
As German forces tired, the increasingly effective Red Army counter-attacked in strength, supported by air power.

Opposite:
The Battle of Prokhorovka.

different beast. The factories of the Urals, along with US and British convoys, were providing ever-greater firepower on the ground and in the air, while the Soviet commanders now understood the importance of the 'deep battle'. Five new tank armies were thrusting deep into the German line after any breakthrough, at great speed and with the support of large numbers of aircraft, before the enemy could pull back. It was proving very effective.

For the Soviet Union, this was the Great Patriotic War. Appealing to traditional Russian concepts of patriotism had been an effective ploy by Stalin, but the men – and women – of the Red Army were also made to keep fighting by extraordinary levels of brutality. Behind the advancing armies were NKVD troops who swept into newly retaken areas and arrested anyone suspected of collaborating with the Germans in any way whatsoever. These troops also dealt with deserters or those who made any other kind of infringement. One new lieutenant was executed at Stalingrad because several of his men had deserted before he'd even arrived at his post.

In July 1942, Stalin authorized the formation of *shtrafbats* – punishment battalions of former officers who had been demoted for perceived cowardice or lack of resolution. They were usually sent to the most difficult parts of the front. Clearing a minefield, for example, was the kind of task given to a *shtrafbat*: the men would simply be ordered to cross it until the mines had been detonated. There were also punishment companies – *shtrafroty* – made up of miscreant junior commanders. Life was very cheap in the Red Army, but especially so in these punishment units. Very few survived.

Women were also used widely from October 1941 onwards. The 'Night Witches' were an all-female night-bomber unit using old biplanes. Needless to say, casualties were high. There were also female fighter and dive-bomber units in the air force. Soviet women were used as snipers, and were often very effective too.

After Kursk, the Red Army continued to drive west into the Ukraine, using five army groups simultaneously. This autumn offensive became collectively known as the Battle of the Dnepr, the river that ran through this part of the Soviet Union. Rokossovsky's Central Front led the way, reaching the Dnepr north of Kiev in September and closely followed to the south by the Veronezh Front. Bitter fighting followed and Kiev was not retaken until 6 November, but it meant the old capital of the Ukraine was now back in Soviet hands and with it a huge bridgehead some 200 miles wide and 90 deep.

By the end of December, the entire front had shifted hundreds of miles westwards, the Crimea had been isolated, the Dnepr crossed and the Central Front had created a vast bridgehead that extended as far as the city of Karosten at the edge of the Pripyat Marshes.

The Red Army triumphed to the north as well. By January 1944, the Leningrad and Volkhov Fronts had amassed just under a million men and nearly 22,000 guns, while lying offshore was the Baltic Fleet. The Red Army attack began on 14 January and soon pushed the Germans back. The last German shell to land on Leningrad fell on 23 January and four days later, at 8 o'clock in the evening, the sky over the city lit up with a mass of colour as more than 300 guns fired a salute of triumph. After 880 days, the terrible siege of Leningrad was finally over.

There was plenty of hard fighting still to come, but no one, least of all the Germans, could now doubt the outcome.

Opposite: The 'Night Witches'.

The Soviet Union would have its revenge.

6: THE PACIFIC WAR
1941–1943

Early on Sunday morning, 7 December 1941, the inhabitants of the Hawaiian island of Oahu awoke to the sound of aircraft engines, guns and bombs exploding. Many thought it was another live firing exercise, but at 8.40 a.m. the local radio interrupted its programme. 'Please pay attention,' said the announcer. 'The island is under attack. I repeat, the island is under attack by hostile forces.'

In fact, the Japanese had first attacked fifty-two minutes earlier, when 353 aircraft swooped in low over the sea. Torpedo bombers had caught the United States Pacific Fleet at Pearl Harbor completely by surprise, and within minutes all eight battleships moored there had been hit. Meanwhile, dive-bombers screamed down over the island's air bases. A further 171 aircraft in the second wave roared in to attack a short while later, so that by the time the radio announcer told Hawaiians what was happening, the cream of the Pacific Fleet lay crippled: *California* had been half-sunk, *West Virginia* was ablaze and four other battleships were immobile and out of action. Worse, *Oklahoma* had capsized, while *Arizona*'s forward magazine had exploded, killing more than a thousand of her crew. Where once there had been 'Battleship Row' there was now a mass of twisted metal, angry flames and billowing thick smoke. And a lot of dead American servicemen. On the airfields, 188 aircraft had been destroyed and a further 159 damaged. Also hit were three cruisers, three destroyers and three other vessels.

Witnesses were stunned by how low the Japanese pilots flew. 'Hell, I could even see the gold in their teeth,' observed one American army officer. 'It was like being engulfed in a great flood, a tornado or earthquake,' said another. 'The thing hit so quickly and so powerfully it left you stunned and amazed.'

The devastating attack proved how badly the Americans had underestimated the Japanese. There had been, however, plenty of indications that Japan was heading towards war, although little that suggested the US Pacific Fleet at Pearl Harbor was the target.

Japan's growing aggression towards the West had been a long time in coming and at its core was the urgent need for resources. The origins for this change in Japanese ambition lay in the Meiji Revolution of 1868, in which the rule of the emperor was restored and the old feudal shogunate thrown aside. It was clear, though, that the country lagged industrially and commercially behind Britain, the United States, France and other global powers. In the decades that followed, Japan modernized very quickly, with a massive growth in industry and infrastructure. Shipyards were built, so too was a national railway, and the largely rural population began to migrate rapidly to the cities.

Opposite: The Japanese attack Pearl Harbor, Sunday, 7 December 1941.

The trouble was, Japan was fairly resource-poor and her burgeoning urban population and growing middle class needed the food and comforts of a modern, industrialized nation. Britain, similar in size to Japan, had a large global trading empire and overseas possessions. Now Japan began developing ambitions to have an empire of her own.

An obvious source of resources was China. Japan invaded Manchuria in north-east China in 1931, but while there were numerous engagements and sporadic fighting in the years that followed it was not until 1937 that Japan and China became embroiled in full-scale war.

Sweeping Japanese victories ensued, along with merciless brutality towards many hundreds of thousands of Chinese civilians. Yet the invaders were unable to complete their victory. The Chinese, under the military rule of General Chiang Kai-shek, offered more resistance than Japan had anticipated.

In fact, the continuing war meant Japan's situation was not improving but worsening, despite her gains. In the summer of 1939 there was a drought and a critical shortage of water, as well as of coal, which led to restrictions in electricity. The drought also led to a drastically reduced production of rice and to food shortages. By early 1940 the Japanese trade treaty with the USA had lapsed with no hope of renewal. Fear that imports, especially those from the US, would be cut off led to the urgent purchasing of overseas war materiel, which in turn meant foreign-exchange reserves were being allowed to run low.

By the autumn of 1941, Japan held most of the eastern coastal area of China and Indochina (Vietnam), but at great cost and with ongoing resistance and guerrilla fighting with which to contend. Militarily, Japan was reasonably well equipped with soldiers, aircraft and a large, powerful and modern navy, but was dependent on the United States, especially, for steel, oil and other essential raw materials. Once the American source was cut off, her ability to build on her gains would be limited unless she could successfully tap the resources of the Far East, the best of which lay in the hands of the British, the Americans and the Dutch.

The problem was, doing so would mean war with those powers. Throughout the 1930s, Britain and the United States had watched Japanese aggression with increasing concern. The Tripartite Pact between Japan, Germany and Italy in September 1940 set more alarm bells ringing. Fears grew further when Japan signed a non-aggression pact with her old enemy the USSR, then moved into Indochina, worryingly close to British-held Malaya and Singapore and the US Philippines.

Even so, the Allies felt Japan was unlikely to risk war any time soon, despite the latter sending increasing numbers of troops into Indochina. In an effort to deter the Japanese further, the US President, Franklin D. Roosevelt, imposed an embargo on all oil and fuel to Japan and stepped up supplies to China. Bombers were sent to the Philippines and the Pacific Fleet was posted to Pearl Harbor.

The Japanese Prime Minister, Fumimaro Konoe, offered to withdraw troops from much of China and Indochina and suggested talks, but his proposals were rejected by Roosevelt. Tragically, the Americans underestimated Japan's dilemma and in so doing overestimated the strength of their own hand.

Konoe resigned and was replaced by General Hideki Tojo, one of Japan's leading war hawks, and by early November 1941 both Emperor Hirohito and the new government had accepted that

Opposite: Japanese troops during the invasion of China.

war was now unavoidable. The plan was to strike rapidly and decisively, and in such a way as to give Japan breathing space to then grab vital British, Dutch and American possessions in the Far East. By the time America had recovered from the blow, they would hopefully come to some kind of settlement, but with Japan now holding a vastly widened and resource-rich Pacific empire.

After the First World War, the United States had largely withdrawn from the world stage. Her armed forces were dramatically reduced in size and Big Business vilified as 'merchants of death' for having profited from the war. Legislation introduced in the early 1930s imposed new restrictions and stifled the ability of American companies to make arms. There was also a prevalent belief that if a country had a large military, it would inevitably use it, and that the converse was also true. In short, the Americans had become firm isolationists.

By the outbreak of war in September 1939, the United States was languishing with the nineteenth largest army in the world, behind Portugal, and with just seventy-four fighter planes in the Army Air Corps, a cavalry still dependent on horses, very few tanks, no anti-tank guns at all and not one manufacturer of explosives in the country.

President Roosevelt was, however, becoming increasingly concerned that the Atlantic and Pacific Oceans were no longer the great defensive barriers they had once been. Technology was advancing fast. The trouble was, precious few agreed with him and another presidential election was due in November 1940. No one had ever before stood for three terms, but Roosevelt rightly believed he was the best person to steer the USA through the choppy waters ahead.

With the collapse of France in May 1940, he began the process of rearming, launching a major campaign to persuade Americans of its necessity. Restrictive legislation was repealed and key advisors from big business – the 'dollar-a-year' men – were brought in. In November 1940, he was re-elected for an historic third term, and with his authority and ability to shape US rearmament substantially increased.

Above right: At the outbreak of the Second World War, the US Army was small and old-fashioned.

Opposite: General Hideki Tojo (left) with Emperor Hirohito.

This meant that, while the United States had been in no way ready for war in September 1939, by December 1941 it was beginning to show its enormous industrial muscle. Tanks, aircraft and guns were starting to roll off the production lines in ever increasing numbers.

The US Navy was growing too. Of all the services, the navy had suffered the least in the inter-war years, and by December 1941 had 17 battleships, 7 aircraft carriers and 18 heavy cruisers, compared with the Japanese Imperial Navy's 10 battleships, 6 aircraft carriers and 18 heavy cruisers. Perhaps

more significant was the number of new US Navy warships under construction, including a further 15 battleships and 11 carriers. In contrast, the Japanese were building 3 new giant battleships and just 7 new carriers. Although the US Navy was only slightly largely than the Japanese Navy in December 1941, that gulf was set to widen.

Even so, the attack on Pearl Harbor stunned the Americans; Roosevelt said 7 December would 'live in infamy'. A few days later, Hitler declared war on the USA too, believing America would now focus all its efforts in taking on Japan. He was, however, very much mistaken, because the Americans and British had already agreed that Germany posed the greater immediate threat, not least because of its advances in science and technology, and this was reaffirmed at their first wartime conference in Washington that December.

A 'Germany first' strategy, however, did not mean the Americans – or British for that matter – would sit back in the Far East and Pacific. Far from it. Admiral Ernest King, the new commander-in-chief of the US Fleet, intended to strike back hard. And soon.

The attack on Pearl Harbor was, however, just the start of a series of superbly planned and dramatically fast strikes on British, Dutch and US possessions in the Far East. On 8 December, the US island of Guam fell within half an hour and Wake Island, 1,500 miles to its east, was also taken despite brave resistance from the small force of US Marines and construction workers there. Both islands were key stopping points and airfields in the Pacific. Borneo was invaded, while the British territory of Hong Kong was overwhelmed by 40,000 Japanese troops. Two of the Royal Navy's three battleships, *Prince of Wales* and *Repulse*, were sunk on the same day, 12 December. The Philippines were also attacked and vital airfields clinically knocked out. Manila, the capital, fell on 3 January.

Further defeats and humiliations followed. Malaya was invaded and, although the British forces were double the strength of General Tomoyuki Yamashita's in numbers, they lacked guns and any tanks, and had only 158 outdated aircraft compared with Japan's 617 modern planes. Yamashita's men were well trained and battle-hardened from the war in China; the British troops were neither. General Arthur Percival, the British commander, had allowed his forces to become too dispersed across the peninsula, which enabled the Japanese to defeat them in penny packets. Yamashita's naval strength was also vastly superior, which meant he could leapfrog his forces down the coast and so outmanoeuvre the British.

Kuala Lumpur, the capital of Malaya, fell on 12 January and the rest of the country by early February. This was followed swiftly by the fall of Singapore, where, on 15 February, Percival

Above left: Admiral Ernest King.

Opposite: The fall of Singapore.

surrendered 130,000 British, Australian and Indian troops. In terms of numbers, it was the worst defeat ever in British history.

Losses came at sea as well as on land. On 27 February a joint British, Dutch, American and Australian naval force was smashed at the Battle of the Java Sea, and the commander, the Dutch Rear-Admiral Karel Doorman, killed. These were catastrophic defeats. Quite simply, the British had been caught napping. With attention almost entirely on the war in the West, and under-estimating the imminence and strength of the Japanese threat, Britain had left her Far East colonies dangerously under-prepared. Malaya was Britain's richest territory, with crucial supplies of rubber, timber and quinine. Now Burma, which supplied British India and her interests in the Far East with oil, was also under threat.

Fierce battles continued in the Philippines and Borneo, while Australian New Guinea was also overrun, as were the Solomon Islands and Bougainville to the north of Australia. This threatened the crucial shipping channel between the US and Australia. The Dutch East Indies were also lost.

In the Philippines, the Americans retreated into the Bataan Peninsula, but throughout March were increasingly running short of supplies. Roosevelt ordered General Douglas MacArthur to fly to Australia rather than risk capture. 'I came out of Bataan,' he said on arriving there on 20 March, 'and I shall return.' The remaining US troops in the peninsula, malnourished and short of arms, finally surrendered on 10 April. Neighbouring Corregidor fell on 8 May. The loss of the Philippines was complete.

The many Allied troops who had suddenly become prisoners were now subjected to hell on earth. Their treatment in Japanese prisoner-of-war camps was appalling. Facing often random and extreme violence and deprivation, many simply did not survive their incarceration.

This excessive cruelty was a shock to the soldiers fighting the Japanese. Allied forces had a very different attitude to being taken prisoner than the Japanese, who had developed a code of discipline, sacrifice and military honour, borrowed in part from the old shogunate culture but given a new twist by the ultra-nationalist and militaristic elite that had emerged around the cult of the Emperor Hirohito. No one person exemplified this growing culture more than the new Prime Minister, Hideki Tojo.

Above left: Allied POWs forced to work as slave labourers on the Siam–Burma railway.

Opposite: Japanese soldiers on the attack in the Arakan.

'If two hundred Japs held a block, you had to kill all two hundred,' General Philip Christison would write some time later of his experiences of taking on the Japanese in Burma. 'None would surrender. None would retire.' Japanese soldiers regularly beheaded, crucified, eviscerated and beat those they captured. The Allies began to regard their enemy as inhuman, almost superhuman, such was their unshakeable discipline and preference for death over the dishonour of being captured.

Japan's soldiers, sailors and airmen were themselves subject to sadistic treatment and degradation in training. There can be little doubt that this brutalization and dehumanization affected how they treated Allied prisoners. But it meant that, on the ground, Japanese commanders could rely on soldiers to travel lightly with minimum comfort and maximum discipline and replenish supplies from those captured. Speed of manoeuvre was key.

Japanese naval fighter pilots were a case in point. The regular beatings they endured in training were seen as a form of education to harden them. Nothing, however, was greater than the fear of failure and the humiliation that came with it. Recruits spent a year training on the ground, including learning to improve their eyesight and the ancient principles of *kendo*, Japanese swordsmanship. Flying training was also intense and protracted. British and German pilots were sent to front-line squadrons after around 150 hours. For Japanese pilots, it was some 500.

They were flying superb aircraft too. The 'Zero', for example, based around an original aero-engine bought from the US, then copied and improved, was a machine that actually exceeded every one of its design specifications. It was light, fast, long-range, well armed and had fingertip agility. In early 1942 there was nothing in the Allied arsenal to touch it. Superb machines combined with exceptionally trained and highly disciplined pilots were proving a stunning combination and demonstrated how important Admiral Isoroku Yamamoto, commander of the Imperial Fleet, thought carrier-borne naval operations in the Pacific would be in the war that was rapidly unfolding.

For the first four decades of the twentieth century, it had been the battleship that had dominated the seas in times of war. That had now changed dramatically, which was why the prime target of the Japanese attack on Pearl Harbor had been the US Main Fleet's aircraft carriers. Yet stunning though that attack had been, not one American carrier had been at Pearl Harbor at the time. The US had been thrown a lifeline that Admiral King and the equally new Pacific Fleet commander, Admiral Chester Nimitz, were determined not to squander.

While the Royal Navy was playing a dominant role in the Atlantic and Mediterranean, it was agreed that the US Navy would take the lead in the Pacific. Admiral King's strategy was clear and based around two fundamental factors: first, Hawaii could not be allowed to fall; and second, nor could Australia (see map on page 324). He ordered Nimitz to make it his first priority to secure the seaways between Hawaii and the island of Midway, just to the east of the International Date Line, and the North American mainland. His second priority was to make safe the routes to Australia. Fiji and the Samoan and Tonga islands needed to be made secure as crucial strongpoints along the way, and from these bases a counter-offensive could be launched up through the Solomons, New Guinea, Borneo and then, in time, the Philippines. It was unquestionably the right strategy.

On 1 February, the US Navy's fightback began with a series of raids on shipping and airfields on the Japanese-held Marshall Islands. Although the material damage was less than was at first thought, the Americans learned vital lessons and their counter-offensive was under way.

Opposite: Japanese Zeros tussle with American Wildcats.

Further US carrier raids were mounted, but the first major naval clash came in May. The Japanese now plotted to disrupt Allied plans by invading and occupying Port Moresby in New Guinea and also the island of Tulagi in the Solomons. American cryptanalysts had broken Japanese codes, however, and, learning of their intentions, sent a joint US–Australian naval force of carriers and cruisers to intercept and stop the enemy.

Tulagi was invaded on 3–4 May, but the Japanese had been surprised to come under attack by American aircraft from the carrier *Yorktown*. They now advanced to meet the Allied naval forces, clashing in the Coral Sea on 7 May.

This was the first battle in which aircraft carriers engaged one another, and the Americans and Japanese lost one each and suffered damage to the others. On 8 May, US radar screens picked up enemy aircraft heading towards USS *Lexington* and Task Force 17, and her Wildcat fighters were scrambled to meet them. Then, at 11.13 a.m., lookouts spotted the black dots of enemy aircraft. As they approached, the attacking torpedo bombers split into two groups while enemy dive-bombers peeled over and down towards the *Lexington*, which was now taking evasive action by swerving frantically. The Japanese planes met a wall of anti-aircraft fire as well as the Wildcats. 'It seemed impossible we could survive our bombing and torpedo runs,' said Lieutenant Commander Shigekazu Shimazaki, the Japanese attack commander. 'Our Zeros and enemy Wildcats spun, dove, and climbed in the midst of our formations. Burning and shattered planes of both sides plunged from the skies.'

Despite the heroic defence, *Lexington* was hit by both bombs and torpedoes, but, amazingly, fire-damage parties managed to restore her to seagoing order before a series of explosions ensured the mighty carrier would have to be abandoned and scuttled.

With both sides suffering heavy losses of aircraft as well as ships, the battle ended as dusk fell on the second day. Crucially, the Battle of the Coral Sea ensured that the Japanese abandoned their plans to invade New Guinea.

Above right: The USS Lexington *under attack.*

Opposite: B-25s taking off on the Doolittle Raid.

Meanwhile, on land, Japanese forces were pushing the British out of Burma. Sent out to oversee the retreat and ensure vital oilfields were destroyed and denied to the Japanese was Lieutenant-General Harold Alexander. With his Burma Corps commander, Major-General Bill Slim, the British forces successfully escaped across the wide Irrawaddy River and back into India. Many Indian civilians living in Burma faced a more difficult flight and thousands perished. It was a tragedy for them and a further dent to British moral authority in India, where the Free India movement was growing stronger. India, the jewel in the British Empire's crown, now appeared under threat both from within and from the Japanese.

Despite their incredible successes, cracks were emerging between the Japanese Army and Navy over future strategy. While these disputes were going on, sixteen American B-25 bomber crews, led by Lieutenant-Colonel Jimmy Doolittle, had flown off the USS *Hornet* on 18 April and bombed Tokyo. Damage had been slight but it had shown the Japanese they were not invulnerable and helped Yamamoto's Pacific naval strategy. Instead of pushing into Ceylon (now Sri Lanka), which they had already attacked, and into India, as favoured by the army, Yamamoto instead won the internal battle with his defensive barrier strategy in the Pacific. His plan was to destroy the US Navy's carrier fleet then extend Japanese possessions with the swift capture of Samoa, Fiji and even Hawaii.

Yamamoto's aim was to lure the Americans into a trap around Midway, but hubris got the better of him. His plan was overly complex and based on faulty intelligence about US strength and morale. The consequence was a terrible error of judgement.

Yamamoto hoped to entice the US Pacific Fleet into battle by separating his forces, with his carriers and battleships several hundred miles apart. The plan was to attack the enemy carriers, then follow up with his battleships and cruisers, who would engage whatever American ships remained.

Once again, American code-breakers intercepted enemy signal traffic and learned of Yamamoto's plan. Because the Japanese forces were so far apart, they were no longer able to support one another. Furthermore, Nimitz's Pacific Fleet was stronger than Yamamoto had appreciated. In contrast, the Japanese still had two carriers out of action from the Battle of the Coral Sea.

The clash began on 4 June, with the two US Task Forces commanded by Admirals Raymond A. Spruance and Frank Jack Fletcher. Japanese reconnaissance flights were poorly mounted, and when their air forces approached they were picked up on radar, and US naval fighter planes scrambled to meet them. At the same time, American bombers were hurriedly sent to attack the Japanese carriers while the enemy aircraft were airborne and the ships were considerably more vulnerable. Japanese anti-aircraft defence was surprisingly poor and definitely an Achilles heel.

In the ensuing four-day sea and air battle, the Japanese lost four of the six carriers that had attacked Pearl Harbor six months earlier, one heavy cruiser and 248 carrier-based aircraft, while the Americans had just one carrier sunk – *Yorktown* – along with one destroyer and 150 aircraft. Losses of men were ten times higher for the Japanese.

Midway did not turn the tide against Japan, but it was a major victory for the United States and did decidedly shift the balance in the Pacific.

Guadalcanal in the Solomons, populated by 100,000 Melanesians, was a remote and underdeveloped British island of inhospitable jungle and hills, largely untouched by the modern world. From tiny Tulagi, which they had seized and occupied in May, the Japanese now landed troops on Guadalcanal and in early June started to build an airfield in the jungle.

A couple of weeks later, Admiral King ordered the US Navy to assault, capture and hold Guadalcanal – he was clear there could be no static defence. What's more, he insisted Operation WATCHTOWER, as it was to be called, was to take place in just five weeks' time, in early August. This was a massively ambitious undertaking. Overall command was given to Vice-Admiral Robert

Opposite: The Battle of Midway.

L. Ghormley, who had set up the headquarters of US South Pacific Forces in New Zealand just five weeks earlier. Troops were to come from the 1st Marine Division, who were mostly still at sea and had been promised six months' training in New Zealand before going into action.

A support air-and-supply base, from which the operation could be launched, was needed very quickly. The island of Espiritu Santo, more than 500 miles away, was chosen and, although far from ideal, would have to do. Naval construction battalions, known as 'Seabees', worked around the clock, under floodlights at night, for a month and, incredibly, by 28 July an airstrip had been built on Espiritu Santo.

Major-General Alexander Vandegrift, commander of the 1st Marine Division, had been speechless when he learned his orders. 'I could not believe it,' he recalled. His men had had no amphibious training and little was known about Guadalcanal. However, orders were orders. In the precious time available, he was determined to make his men as ready as they could be.

Despite intense training, the Marines felt barely prepared. However, luck was with them. Poor weather hid the advance of the vast US armada and amphibious force, while as the landing craft sped towards the northern Guadalcanal coast on the morning of 7 August, the seas had become as smooth as ice. The Marines landed on Guadalcanal unopposed and also quickly overran the Japanese on Tulagi following a naval artillery barrage that caught the enemy completely off guard. By the following day, the airfield, newly completed by Japanese labour, had been captured by the 11,000-strong force of Marines.

Under-defended Guadalcanal may have been, but the Japanese were quick to respond, hurriedly sending a force of cruisers and destroyers from Rabaul, some 650 miles away in New Britain, and scrambling naval aircraft to attack. Later that day, a furious air battle raged over western Guadalcanal and nearby Savo Island, while by the night of 8/9 August Japanese naval forces had reached the area and attacked the Allied screening force commanded by the British Rear-Admiral Victor Crutchley, VC. In the ensuing battle, the Allies suffered a heavy defeat, much of it watched by the Marines now digging in around the airfield. Dangerously crippled, it was decided the naval forces should withdraw, even though only half the supplies had been unloaded.

Understandably, the Marines felt rather abandoned. A patrol sent to clear the outpost of enemy troops at Matanikou, some miles to the west of the newly named Henderson Field, was butchered, but a heavier follow-up attack wiped out the enemy. Two squadrons of Wildcats and a further squadron of Dauntless dive-bombers also landed at the airfield. It seemed it was only a matter of time, though, before the Japanese reinforced the island.

As predicted, the enemy had every intention of retaking Guadalcanal and began gathering both troops and large naval forces. The first 917 men of Japan's 35th Infantry Brigade landed at midnight on 21 August well to the east of the Marines, then over 800 of them marched 9 miles to make a frontal attack on the Marines dug in on the western bank of the River Ilu, known to the Americans as Alligator Creek. It was a bloodbath. The Japanese were slaughtered, with just 30 survivors rejoining the 100-strong reserve who had remained behind where they had landed.

Meanwhile, more Japanese troops were on their way, as were considerable naval forces. The US naval task forces under Vice-Admiral Frank Fletcher also returned and on 24 August the two forces clashed, while the Japanese attacked from the air. A couple of months earlier, Guadalcanal had been

Opposite: 'Seabees' work on building an airstrip.

a remote and largely unknown island in the South Pacific. By the end of August 1942 it had become the scene of a bitter struggle on land, in the seas around it and in the air above.

The stage was now set for a truly decisive clash of arms.

While the Imperial Japanese Navy still had greater numerical strength, unless they delivered a knock-out and decisive blow against the Americans quickly, they would soon be ground down by the greater industrial strength of the United States. As it was, the remoteness of the Solomon Islands was already testing the logistical efforts of both sides to the utmost.

Both were now frantically trying to build up strength. More men, ships and aircraft were arriving from the US, while the Japanese were bringing up reinforcements via a system they dubbed the 'Rat Express': a fast destroyer would arrive at night from Rabaul, deposit men at Taivu Point in the Solomons, then scurry back. Between 29 August and 4 September, these ships landed almost 5,000 Japanese soldiers, now under command of General Kiyotake Kawaguchi.

His men attacked a long, 1,000-yard ridge that ran diagonally to the south of Henderson Field. This had already been picked out as a key feature and was defended by the Marines of Lieutenant-Colonel Merritt A. Edson's 1st Raider Battalion, who were well dug in and expecting an attack. It came at around 7.30 p.m. on 13 September, with wave after wave of Japanese charging with rifles, bayonets and swords into the lethal fire of American machine guns and Tommy guns. Once again, they were gunned down in their hundreds and their attack stopped dead. More than 1,200 were killed or later died of wounds. Fanatical 'banzai charges' were certainly terrifying to come up against but, as the Marines were discovering, disciplined defence could quickly turn them into suicide charges. This vital high ground became known as 'Bloody Ridge', but it was mostly Japanese blood that was spilled that night. By comparison, total American casualties – missing, dead and wounded – were 143.

Following this defeat, the Japanese Imperial General Staff began to fear that Guadalcanal would become the decisive battle of the war. They were not wrong. Troops were withdrawn from the ongoing battle in New Guinea to reinforce Guadalcanal, while the Americans brought in more men and also two more carrier task forces.

Right: Admiral Bill Halsey.

Opposite: US Marines storming the beaches of Guadalcanal.

But it was the Japanese who were winning the reinforcement battle. Over the first two weeks of October, a further 15,000 troops were landed by the Tokyo Express, while on the night of

13/14 October Henderson Field was pummelled by a barrage of 14-inch guns from the battleships *Kongo-* and *Haruna*, which churned up much of the airfield, destroyed key supplies of fuel and killed forty-one men. The Marines referred to it simply as 'the Night'.

By mid-October, General Vandegrift's men were beginning to despair, exhausted by the fighting and the conditions. They were short of food, stricken by malaria, dysentery and foot rot; the island was a brutal place in which to exist in the open, let alone fight. 'We all feared defeat and capture,' said one soldier. 'We were afraid they were going to leave us there.'

There was also a growing feeling among the Marines that the US Navy was not doing enough to support them – either aggressively at sea or in supplying them. The Japanese were willing to take risks, so why wasn't Admiral Ghormley?

On 15 October, Nimitz decided a change of command was needed. Ghormley was fired and Admiral Bill Halsey took over as C-in-C South Pacific. Aggressive, beloved of his men and a skilled tactician, his appointment came in the nick of time.

At the moment Bill Halsey took over, it was clear the Japanese were preparing a significant naval attack, but first came a major assault by land on Henderson Field on the evening of 24 October. Despite the exhaustion of the Marines, they once again cut down the attacking Japanese over the course of two nights. It was during these attacks that Sergeant John Basilone won the Congressional Medal of Honor, the highest US award for gallantry, for manning, moving and repairing several machine guns and holding his position until replacements arrived.

Out at sea, the biggest naval clash since Midway began on 25 October. Over two days, another bitter battle took place on sea and in the air. Eventually, the Americans withdrew after the loss of the carrier *Hornet*, and after *Enterprise* was badly damaged, but the levels of attrition were beginning to bite the Japanese hard. In what became known as the Battle of the Santa Cruz Islands, the Japanese lost far too many irreplaceable veteran aircrew – 148 compared with 26 American, and including 23 squadron leaders. The balance of power in the air war in the Pacific had begun gradually but decisively to shift in favour of the Americans.

Meanwhile, the Tokyo Express continued to land more troops – another 20,000 by mid-November – but more troops meant more mouths to feed and equipment to supply, which was beyond Japan's logistical capabilities. Their men now on Guadalcanal were living off little more than 500 calories a day. It was no way near enough.

General Vandegrift now ordered his Marines on to the offensive, pushing west towards Cruz Point. The Americans' grip on the island was starting to tighten.

In early November, Allied intelligence learned the Japanese were preparing to land yet more men and supplies, this time with the support of strong naval forces, and then to renew their attack on Henderson Field. Before they could do so, however, the Americans sent more Marines, as well as two army infantry battalions, food and ammunition, escorted by two naval task forces. The men and supplies were unloaded safely just a day before the arrival of the Japanese through the 'Slot' – the channel between Guadalcanal and Savo Island – on the night of 13 November. The American warships were badly outclassed by those of the Japanese, but they attacked anyway, in the hope of preventing enemy battleships from hammering the airfield once more. By dawn next day, wreckage littered the waters off Guadalcanal. The Americans had lost two cruisers and four destroyers, but

Opposite: Sergeant John Basilone won a Congressional Medal of Honor for his actions on Bloody Ridge.

a Japanese battleship, heavy cruiser and two destroyers had been sent to the bottom. More damaging for the Japanese was the loss of seven transport ships with most of the men aboard.

Admiral Halsey sent further reinforcements, including two battleships, and the next night the waters around Guadalcanal were once again alive with the thundering sound of battle. This time, the enemy naval forces were routed. The Japanese force had been the larger but had been defeated by superior gunnery and radar fire-control systems. In the morning, four more transport ships were run aground in a desperate effort to get troops ashore. Only around 2,000 Japanese soldiers were landed before each ship was hit and destroyed. Later, an enemy ammunition dump was spotted in the jungle, and hit with a massive explosion. The Japanese had just lost the battle for Guadalcanal.

Although there were over 30,000 Japanese troops on Guadalcanal, there was now no realistic way of supplying them. Morale deteriorated dramatically as the soldiers starved and became riddled with disease. By December, few more than 4,000 of them were fit enough to fight, as the Americans painstakingly cleared one bunker and tunnel after another.

By the start of February 1943, even the Japanese had had enough and began evacuating the survivors – a mere 10,000 of the 36,000 that had fought there. 'Hardly human beings,' wrote one Japanese soldier who saw them, 'they were just skin and bones dressed in military uniform, thin as bamboo sticks.' Most of the rest died. By comparison, the Americans lost 5,875 casualties, of whom 1,500 were killed.

The long and bitter struggle for Guadalcanal was finally over on 9 February 1943. It had been a humiliating and war-turning defeat for the Japanese. Technically, they were now standing still, running short of desperately needed resources, while growing numbers of factories in the USA produced ever more ships, tanks and aircraft.

In Arakan in north-west Burma, the British counter-attack was stopped in early 1943, but the Allies had now set up a highly effective air-supply line across the Himalayas from India to China. Suddenly and dramatically, Japan was on the back foot, her incredible early advances halted.

As if to underline this change of fortunes, American cryptanalysts learned that Admiral Yamamoto was flying from Rabaul to the southern end of Bougainville on 18 April. This was just within range

Left: Japanese transport ships run aground at Guadalcanal.

Opposite: American P-38 fighters attack and shoot down Admiral Yamamoto's plane.

of Henderson Field. On Nimitz's orders, at around 9.45 a.m. his plane was attacked by US P-38 Lightnings, shot down, and Yamamoto killed.

The Japanese news announcer broke down in tears as he announced Yamamoto's death. 'There is widespread sentiment,' wrote one Japanese diarist, 'of dark foreboding about the future course of the war.'

The end of the Guadalcanal campaign meant future action in the South Pacific moved into General Douglas MacArthur's agreed area of operations west of the 159th Parallel. Although commanding US Army troops rather than the Marine Corps, MacArthur was still dependent on the US Navy, but fortunately he and Admiral Bill Halsey gelled immediately. Together, they planned a series of leapfrogging operations, drawing on hard-won experience already gained in the Pacific and on the United States' burgeoning military might.

On 21 February, 10,000 soldiers and marines were landed on the Russell Islands, to the north-west of Guadalcanal. As soon as the islands were secure, Seabees arrived to hack out two more airfields. Nowhere was land, air and sea power more interconnected and mutually essential than here, in the South Pacific.

In the summer, New Georgia was captured; in the autumn, it was Bougainville's turn, the last of the Solomon Islands to return to Allied control. Earlier, a decision had been made by MacArthur and Halsey to bypass Rabaul entirely. Instead, the town would be pummelled and neutralized by air power, while finally, in December 1943, the 1st Marine Division, recovered after their ordeal on Guadalcanal, stormed the beaches of Cape Gloucester at the north-western end of New Britain. Weakly defended airfields were swiftly secured, while the large number of Japanese troops on the island retreated towards Rabaul and dug themselves in.

Japanese determination never to surrender worked entirely against them on New Britain and around Rabaul as MacArthur and Halsey's forces seized a ring of islands and bases, effectively cutting them off from the rest of the world. 'The Americans flowed into our weaker points and submerged us,' noted one Japanese intelligence officer, 'just as water seeks the weakest entry to sink a ship.'

Without doubt the Japanese combination of iron discipline and superb training had helped them win a string of stunning victories at the start of the Pacific War. They were, however, extremely inflexible. For Japan, there was only one way of fighting. Once committed to a plan, there could be no turning back; to do so was to admit failure. And failure was both dishonourable and totally unacceptable in the sadistic ultra-nationalistic culture that had evolved in Imperial Japan.

By the end of 1943, some 125,000 Japanese soldiers lay trapped around Rabaul. The pride of the Imperial Japanese Navy had been lost, its carriers pulled back, most of its experienced pre-war naval aviators killed, with more than 2,000 aircraft destroyed, while the next generation of warriors had neither the skills nor training of their predecessors.

In contrast, the United States was growing stronger by the day, and also increasingly battle-hardened. Green they may have been when the Japanese struck Pearl Harbor, but they were quick to absorb the lessons of war. Yet more and better ships, aircraft and weapons were arriving too. 'We've got so much equipment in the Pacific now,' wrote one officer, 'it's like shooting ducks out of your front living room.'

Many hard and terrible battles lay ahead but, in the Pacific, Allied victory was now assured.

7: THE BOMBER WAR

On the night of 14 November 1940, Coventry, an industrial cathedral city in the British Midlands, was hit by a large raid of German bombers – some 450, led by Kampfgeschwader (Bomber Group) 100 equipped with a navigation aid called *X-Gerät*. This used pulse radio technology to create beams that could be converged on a particular target. British intelligence had managed to crack an earlier German navigation aid, *Knickebein*, but not the new technology of *X-Gerät*, which meant the Luftwaffe's bombers reached their target accurately and without much interference.

The conditions for bombing were perfect: there was enough moonlight, not much cloud and a breeze in the air. Attacking in two waves and dropping a mixture of high-explosive heavy bombs and numerous much smaller incendiaries to set off fires, the gap between the waves was timed to perfection, with the second fanning the flames of the first. In all, 503 tons of bombs were dropped, including 139 1,000kg mines – the biggest the Germans had at the time – and 881 canisters of incendiary bombs.

The target had been Coventry's motor factories, but the centre was devastated. The beautiful cathedral and medieval heart of the city were destroyed as fires raged. It was the worst single attack so far in the Blitz – the bombing of Britain's cities that had begun two months earlier on Saturday, 7 September – and was a psychological and physical blow that deeply shocked both the wider public and Britain's war leaders. In all, 18,261 British civilians were killed by German bombing from the start of the Blitz on 7 September to the end of November 1940.

Coventry would not be forgotten – neither the method of the attack nor its effects.

When Germany invaded Poland on 1 September 1939, so starting what was to become the Second World War, they did so with the Luftwaffe flying above them and supporting the army's operations on the ground. Much had been written about the role of air power throughout the 1920s and 30s, but in truth no one was quite sure how it would manifest itself in the next war, despite its use in recent conflicts such as the civil war in Spain.

Air power and aeroplane technology were changing fast and, twenty years on from the last world war, machines were very different. However, it was a safe bet that air power would play a vital role and, clearly, whichever side controlled air space would have a crucial advantage.

In Britain, air power had been at the heart of rearmament from the mid-1930s. The Royal Air Force was reorganized into different commands: Training Command, Coastal, Bomber and Fighter. Each was to operate independently as what was known as a 'strategic' air force. Bomber Command would bomb enemy targets; Coastal would help protect Britain's waters; Fighter Command would

Opposite: The bombing of Coventry cathedral.

defend Britain's skies and was to be supported by the world's first – and at the time only – fully coordinated air defence system combining radar, observers, ground controllers and radio.

In Germany, the Luftwaffe had taken a different approach. Aircraft, whether bombers, fighters or reconnaissance, were grouped together into air corps and then air fleets. Their role was entirely to support the army on the ground, or as what is termed 'tactical' air power. Briefly, the Luftwaffe's Chief of Staff, General Walther Wever, planned to create an independent heavy bomber force, but when he was killed in a flying accident in 1936, his ideas died with him.

So it was that the Luftwaffe began the war with lots of fighter aircraft, Stuka dive-bombers and twin-engine 'medium' bombers, but no strategic bomber force. To begin with, this appeared to have been a good decision. As the army pressed forward, ahead of them Messerschmitt fighters shot down weak and out-of-date Polish aircraft, or bombers destroyed them on the ground. Screaming Stukas terrified soldiers and civilians alike, while the medium bombers pummelled the capital, Warsaw. No one doubted the role air power had played in Germany's rapid victory in Poland.

The Luftwaffe was again the German spearhead in subsequent attacks on Scandinavia, then France and the Low Countries in 1940. On 14 May, just four days after the Germans launched their attack on the West, the Luftwaffe's bombers struck Rotterdam in Holland, with devastating results.

Fifty-seven Heinkel 111s dropped bombs on the city centre, destroying 2.8 square miles of Rotterdam's heart and killing some 850 people. Chaos ensued. The frightfulness of war and the Armageddon brought by massed bomber formations, repeatedly forecast throughout the 1930s, suddenly appeared to be a reality. The attack on Rotterdam certainly hurried the Dutch decision to surrender.

The shortcomings of the Luftwaffe's structure were, however, laid bare during the Battle of Britain that followed. After the French armistice on 22 June 1940, Germany tried to bludgeon Britain into suing for peace through the use of air power alone. Attacks on Channel shipping in July were followed by more concentrated attacks on airfields, the British aircraft industry and other communications. For the first time, however, the Luftwaffe was operating on its own, strategically, and not in the supporting tactical role for which it had been designed.

Right: Heinkel He 111 bombers.

Opposite: The Ju 87 Stuka dive-bomber was a prime example of the Luftwaffe's focus on tactical air power.

The Luftwaffe's attempts to destroy the RAF did not go very well. They had never come up against a proper air defence system before and no longer had troops on the ground supporting them with follow-up actions. Their Stukas were being decimated now they were operating in skies where they no longer had complete control, while their medium bombers – mostly Dornier 17s and Heinkel 111s – could carry only about 2 tons of bombs. Nor were there enough of them. Only one airfield out of 138 used by the RAF was put out of action for longer than 48 hours. All the while, the strength of RAF Fighter Command was growing, not diminishing.

What's more, the bombers of Bomber Command were taking the attack to the enemy. The first raid on Germany had taken place on the night of 16/17 May 1940, while, whenever weather permitted, British bombers from Bomber and Coastal Commands were attacking German landing barges building up in the Channel ports as well as new Luftwaffe airfields near the French, Belgian and Dutch coast.

Then, on the night of 23/24 August, Bomber Command struck Berlin. The raid was not very successful in terms of damage, but was followed by three more attacks on the capital of the Third Reich. Incensed, and frustrated by the Luftwaffe's failure to subdue the RAF, Adolf Hitler, the German Führer, ordered reprisal strikes on London. The first deliberate attacks on the British capital arrived on Saturday, 7 September 1940, and would continue until the middle of May the following year.

The aim was no longer to destroy the RAF but to cause as much damage as possible and to break the morale of the British people. The 'Blitz', as it became known, had begun.

Although air-raid shelters had been built in readiness for such an assault and personal air-raid shelter kits issued, there were public shelters for only around half Britain's urban population. Civilian

casualties quickly mounted. There were 6,968 deaths and 9,488 serious casualties in September 1940, 6,313 and 7,949 in October and 5,004 and 6,247 in November, including the raid on Coventry.

Despite this carnage, Britain's factories continued to grow in number and productivity and there was no sign whatsoever of any collapse in morale. Britain's scientists were swiftly developing counter-measures against the Luftwaffe's night-time navigation aids in what became known as the Battle of the Beams. Soon after the counter-measure to *Knickebein*, one was also found for *X-Gerät*.

Nor was Bomber Command sitting still. The night after Coventry, over 100 RAF bombers attacked Hamburg and Dutch airfields used by the Luftwaffe. The Hamburg raid caused a number of fires and heavy damage to the Blohm & Voss shipyard, and was the most successful RAF bomber raid of the war to that date.

None the less, the Luftwaffe's largely night-time

Left: RAF Bomber Command Wellington and Hampden bombers on their way to Berlin.

Opposite: A Heinkel 111 bomber over Liverpool.

bomber assault of Britain continued. From airfields near the Channel, German aircrews did not always need *X-Gerät* to locate large cities such as London or ports like Southampton, Portsmouth and Liverpool. In February 1941, Hitler ordered his bombers to focus on Britain's ports. Between 19 February and the second week of May, there were sixty-one attacks of more than fifty bombers, of which forty-six were directed against ports. Liverpool was particularly badly hit. Some 316 bombers struck Merseyside on the night of 12 March, for example, and over 500 people were killed.

Despite the relentlessness and horrific damage caused by the Blitz, only 18,000 tons of bombs were dropped on London, a figure that would be dwarfed by what was to follow in the war. In mid-May 1941, with the Germans poised to launch their assault on the Soviet Union, the Blitz abruptly ended. It had fallen a long way short of achieving its aims and had cost the Luftwaffe dear. Britain was still in the war with its armaments production on the increase, while the Luftwaffe had more than 2,000 fewer aircraft with which to support the biggest military operation ever undertaken. Fears of aerial Armageddon had been largely unfounded after all.

The Luftwaffe would continue to use air power to try to subdue its enemies, but elsewhere it was just as unsuccessful. The tiny British island of Malta, for example, was not defeated despite in the spring of 1942 briefly becoming the most bombed place on earth. Depleted as it was by the middle of 1941, the Luftwaffe's bomber force also failed to play a significant role in the war against the Soviet Union. So much had been fruitlessly wasted on Britain.

The shortcomings of the Luftwaffe as a strategic air force had been matched, however, by those of Bomber Command, which had also discovered it had neither the numbers nor its bombers the capacity to deliver the kind of ordnance that would hurt Germany significantly. Nor did it have the navigational tools for the job. British bombers had far further to travel and navigate to reach German targets within the Reich than those of the Luftwaffe along the Channel coast had to reach Britain. At night, often with cloud cover and with only basic calculations – 'dead reckoning' – to help contend with variable wind speeds, Britain's bombers proved woefully inaccurate.

In August 1941, the Butt Report was published, an independent investigation into the accuracy of Bomber Command's bombing effort. Devastatingly, it revealed that only one in three bombers had been managing to drop its bombs within 5 miles of the target. It was a huge blow for Bomber Command and there were many who questioned the ongoing bombing strategy, which was, after all, using up a considerable amount of effort and resources, not to mention young men's lives. Although they were attacking at night because it was safer, bombing remained perilous.

There was to be no change of heart, however. Air Chief Marshal Sir Charles Portal, the Chief of the Air Staff, continued to believe strategic bombing would dramatically shorten the war and save the lives of many British servicemen. More importantly, the Prime Minister, Winston Churchill, was equally convinced air power was the key to ultimate victory. In any case, by mid-1941, British factories were producing more aircraft than any other country in the world. It was too late to change tack.

The answer was to improve the means of bombing. New, bigger aircraft were on their way. Some of the finest minds in Britain were dedicated to pushing the country's aviation industry to new levels of sophistication and technological advancement – incredible new navigation aids were in the pipeline and a superb new bombsight, the Mk XIV, known as the Blackett Sight, would start trialling in early 1942.

Opposite:
Another Heinkel
goes down to the
guns of a Fighter
Command
Spitfire.

It was bad news for German civilians, but collateral damage was not something that weighed too heavily on the minds of many of Britain's war chiefs at the time – not with parts of London and other cities in ruins and nearly 40,000 dead thanks to the Luftwaffe.

There was also new leadership. One man who had watched the Blitz with bitter interest was Air Marshal Arthur Harris. Standing on the roof of the Air Ministry in London, watching the fires raging over London, he had vowed, 'They will reap what they sow.' In February 1942, he became the new commander-in-chief of RAF Bomber Command. Like his boss, Sir Charles Portal, he was an avowed believer in the power of the bomber and in bringing Nazi Germany to its knees by pulverizing its cities and industrial infrastructure.

He also recognized that a major period of rebuilding was essential before Bomber Command could deliver the weight of force required to make strategic impact. Strategic bombing would have to be conducted on a far larger scale altogether. He needed lots more bombers, four-engine heavies, not twin-engine types, and especially the new Lancaster that was just coming into service. These would demand more airfields, and with concrete runways that could operate in all conditions. He needed much better navigation tools as well. None of this could happen overnight. Harris reckoned it would take a year at least until he was ready to launch his all-out strategic air campaign against Germany.

Even so, Bomber Command was not to stand idle. In April 1942, he launched a rare low-level daylight raid using twelve of his new Lancasters against the MAN diesel plant in Augsburg. In terms of damage caused it was highly successful, but the attacking force was decimated: only five returned safely. It underlined why night-time attacks had to continue.

Far greater success was achieved with the 'Thousand Bomber Raids'. Harris launched the first at the end of May 1942. On paper, Bomber Command only had some 400 bombers, but by scouring the Operational Training Units and other commands, and by using a number of largely obsolete aircraft, they managed to reach the magic number of 1,000 bombers. The first target was Cologne in west Germany, and the damage caused was considerable.

It also profoundly shocked Reichsmarschall Hermann Göring, the commander of the Luftwaffe, and the rest of the Nazi leadership. Two more such raids followed and, although it was too risky and stretched resources too tightly to repeat them regularly, they achieved their aim: Bomber Command was given a huge boost and their success did much to convince the sceptics that large-scale strategic bombing had a vital part to play in the ongoing war.

Above left: Bomber Harris.

Opposite: British bomb-aimer using the Blackett Sight.

Also arriving by the summer of 1942 were the commanders and first units of the United States Eighth Air Force, who were to operate alongside Bomber Command. The plan was to build up some sixteen heavy bombardment groups, each with 32 heavy bombers, and three pursuit – or fighter – groups of 75–80 fighters, as well as medium and light bomber groups.

They were commanded by Major-General Carl 'Tooey' Spaatz, another committed bomber man, although he was convinced that daylight 'precision' bombing was the way forward. A hugely experienced and intelligent commander, he had been an observer in England during the Battle of Britain and the Blitz. Nothing he had witnessed had dissuaded him from this firmly entrenched stance. 'The Germans can't bomb at night,' he observed. 'Hell, I don't think they're very good in daylight.'

Like Harris, Spaatz believed what was needed was ever-larger heavy bomber forces. The US had developed heavily armed B-17 Flying Fortresses and B-24 Liberators, but, because of the limitation of navigation aids, Spaatz was convinced accuracy could be achieved only in daylight. This would make the bomber force more vulnerable, but by flying his bombers in a tight defensive formation and equipping each one with thirteen .50-calibre machine guns, he believed heavy casualties could be avoided.

Spaatz had little chance to test his theories, as most of the Eighth's raids were short-range across the Channel, then most of his forces transferred to the Mediterranean after the joint Anglo-US invasion of north-west Africa in November 1942. Meanwhile, Harris continued sending his slowly growing bomber force to strike targets in Germany as well as the U-boat pens along the French Atlantic coast.

Not until the beginning of March 1943, however, and armed with a new directive from the Anglo-US Joint Chiefs of Staff to smash the German 'military, industrial and economic system', was Harris ready to launch his all-out attack. By then he had new navigation aids such as GEE, Oboe and now H2S, effectively the world's first ground-mapping radar. Marking targets was now in the hands of a special Pathfinder Force – or PFF – which flew ahead of the main bomber stream, armed with Oboe and H2S and using marker flares, helping ensure far greater accuracy when the bombs began dropping.

Above right: General 'Tooey' Spaatz.

Opposite: An RAF Mosquito of the Pathfinder Force drops flares over a target.

'I was at last able to undertake with real hope of success,' noted Harris, '. . . the task of destroying the main cities of the Ruhr.'

The Ruhr was the industrial heartland of the Third Reich and Harris's offensive began on the night of Friday, 5 March 1943, with an attack on Essen. He now had some 700 bombers, of which more

than 400 were four-engine heavies. What's more, it was a number that was, at last, significantly on the rise.

Some 442 bombers were used on Essen, dropping a mixture of incendiaries and 4,000 lbs – 2 tons – of high explosives. Despite cloud cover, Essen was devastated: 160 acres of destruction, with 53 separate buildings within the Krupp armaments factory hit, 3,018 houses flattened and a further 2,166 seriously damaged. At least 482 civilians were killed – more than on any single raid to date. A major new phase of the air war had begun.

While the Battle of the Ruhr was launched, Bomber Command was also preparing a one-off strike against Germany's mighty dams. The Möhne and Eder Dams were Germany's largest and were immense feats of engineering, providing water both for civilian use and for vital industrial processes. The Möhne and the Sorpe, another large dam, supplied the Ruhr, the Eder the city of Kassel. It was hoped that, if destroyed, their loss would be calamitous for Nazi Germany.

The dams were protected by vertical anti-torpedo nets, so the challenge was to get enough explosive over those nets and against the dam walls. This, however, had been considered impossible until Barnes Wallis, an engineer and assistant chief designer at Vickers Aviation, created a depth charge that could skip across water. The idea was that the bomb would 'bounce' over the nets, hit the dam wall, sink and then, at a certain depth, explode. The explosive power would be increased by the water pressure above – enough to smash the dams.

Harris had been against the plan, believing it a gross waste of resources on something that appeared too fantastical to have any chance of success. His bombers were used to flying at 18,000 feet or higher and not in formation. This would require a small force of Lancasters, specially adapted to carry the 4-ton bouncing bomb – code-named UPKEEP – to fly in formation at just 100 feet to stay below German radar detection, at night, over unfamiliar enemy territory and then drop the UPKEEP at a very precise spot dead centre of the dam and from an equally precise distance away. It seemed impossible. Even so, Portal, Harris's superior, gave Operation CHASTISE the green light.

A new squadron, 617, was formed, under the command of Wing Commander Guy Gibson, who was one of Harris's most determined young leaders. By March 1943, Gibson had flown seventy-two bomber missions, more than the fifty expected for two tours, and, notwithstanding his 'press on' reputation, was mentally and physically exhausted. None the less, he accepted the task and, despite less than ten weeks' training, on the night of 16 May 1943 he led nineteen Lancasters to attack the dams.

Gibson himself flew seven times up and down the defended Möhne Dam, drawing off enemy

*Above left:
Barnes Wallis.*

*Opposite:
A 617 Squadron
Lancaster drops
its bouncing
bomb during the
Dambusters raid.*

fire. The fourth bomb, dropped by Henry 'Dinghy' Young's crew, caused the fatal crack, so that by the time of the fifth run the dam had begun to crumble. Gibson then led the next assault on the Eder Dam, which, despite its location amongst steep hills, was also miraculously hit and destroyed. The Sorpe was badly damaged. Although eight crews were lost, the Dams Raid had been an incredible success.

Gibson's leadership during the Dams Raid was of the highest calibre and his Victoria Cross more than deserved. Huge tsunamis from the smashed dams caused apocalyptic damage, while the costs of repairing the dams and other infrastructure, at a time when the war was dramatically turning against Germany, were immense.

Bomber Command continued to hammer the Ruhr, but worse was to come for Germany. Operation GOMORRAH, an attack on Germany's second city and biggest port, Hamburg, was launched on the night of 27 July. Conditions were perfect and the British dropped millions of strips of tinfoil – known as 'Window' – to jam the German radar system.

Over three nights, some 3,500 aircraft smashed the city. The results were truly terrible. Some 42,600 German civilians were killed – more than had been killed in Britain during the entire Blitz. A further 37,000 were wounded and the old Hanseatic city was all but destroyed as a colossal firestorm developed – so big, so hellish, that the flames rose to nearly 1,500 feet. Around 6,200 acres out of 8,382 – around 80 per cent of the city – had been destroyed.

The Nazi leadership was shocked and appalled. 'A wave of terror radiated from the suffering city,' noted General Adolf Galland, the legendary Luftwaffe fighter commander, 'and spread through Germany.' The world had never before witnessed man-made destruction on such a catastrophic scale.

Harris's aim was to bring about the end of the war without the need for vast armies and the risk of losing a generation of young men, as had happened in 1914–18. He now planned ever heavier attacks, and next on his main target list was the capital of the Third Reich itself: Berlin.

By this time, the US Eighth Air Force was also building up its strength in Britain. General Spaatz was now commanding strategic air forces in the Mediterranean and Lieutenant-General Ira Eaker had taken over the Eighth. Eaker, like Spaatz, was a firm advocate of precision daylight bombing and had persuaded the Anglo-US Combined Chiefs of Staff that the Eighth should continue in this vein rather than join the RAF in night attacks as the British had been urging. He also argued convincingly that the priority bombing target should be the German aircraft industry. If the Luftwaffe could be destroyed, then strategic bombing would be easier as there was no question that enemy aircraft posed a far greater threat to Allied bombers than anti-aircraft guns.

Furthermore, the Allies planned to make a cross-Channel invasion of France in May 1944 and for that they needed air superiority over much of north-west Europe. Harris continued to believe massed night-time area bombing was the best way to win the war, but Eaker's plans were formally adopted as Operation POINTBLANK on 10 June 1943.

The trouble was, most of the Luftwaffe's assembly and components plants were inside the Reich, and beyond the range of Allied fighter escorts. Until mid-August 1943, the Eighth had not attempted any missions deep into Germany and casualties had been comparatively light.

That changed on 17 August, when 376 American bombers attacked the ball-bearing plant at Schweinfurt, some 100 miles east of Frankfurt, and the oil refinery and Messerschmitt plant at

Regensburg in south-east Germany. It was a terrible day for the Eighth: some 60 bombers, or 19 per cent of the attacking force, were shot down and destroyed, more than 550 aircrew lost, and a further 11 bombers had to be scrapped and 164 were damaged.

The bombing results against Schweinfurt and Regensburg had not justified the enormous effort and cost. Eaker realized he would have to send his boys back, but not until early October 1943 was the Eighth ready to have another crack at enemy targets beyond fighter range.

These new attempts were also very costly, culminating in a second attack on Schweinfurt on Thursday, 14 October. It became known as 'Black Thursday', as a further 60 bombers were shot down and 594 men lost. In fact, in seven days of missions into Germany, the Eighth had lost 148 heavy bombers. Despite the number of planes and men coming from across the Atlantic, that was not sustainable.

Nor was Harris's Battle of Berlin the success he had anticipated. If Hamburg had prompted any thought of a rapid end to the war through strategic bombing alone, this had quickly proved to be a false hope. This was because the Luftwaffe had been shocked into overhauling its air defence system. German night-bomber pilots were put into night-fighter planes – Me109s and Focke-Wulf 190s, known as the *Wilde Sau* (Wild Boars) – while increased numbers of two-engine night-fighters began attacking the British bomber stream en masse, equipped with improved radar and upward-tilting 30mm cannons called *Schrägemusik* to attack the unprotected belly of the Lancasters and Halifaxes. These were supported by superior early-warning systems and ground controllers. In ten raids on the capital of the Reich, Harris lost 239 aircraft – some 25 per cent of his force.

The Allied commanders were in crisis. The clock was ticking towards OVERLORD, the Allied invasion of France, air superiority was still a long way off, and the effects of bombing were falling some way short of expectation.

There was a crisis amongst the bomber crews too. Heavy losses were keenly felt on bomber bases in which crews were often housed together in hastily built Nissan huts. To return from a mission and find a row of empty beds where earlier there had been friends was hard to take. Everyone knew the odds of completing a 25-mission tour, in the case of the Americans, or a first 30-mission tour, in the case of Bomber Command, were not good. To many, it seemed impossible.

The weather didn't help. The winter of 1943 was particularly cold and bleak. Bill Byers, a Canadian pilot who had joined up with his

Left: Typically grim conditions on the ground at an RAF bomber station.

Opposite: Focke Wulfs of the Wilde Sau *night-fighters in action.*

identical twin brother, George, used to take his crew up on a test flight during the day just to get above the cloud and see some sunshine. George had been lost on his third mission; they had been inseparable all their lives until that night of 3 November.

Bomber crews rarely flew two days – or nights – in a row, and in between could visit pubs, local cinemas and generally do what they liked, although options were limited. RAF bomber crews would be told in the morning they would be flying that night. The target would be revealed during the briefing a couple of hours before take-off. They would be given supper, then they would collect their flying gear and head to their aircraft. Just taking off in quick succession, in the dark or thick cloud, was dangerous enough. American bombers flew in formation but RAF crews flew in a 'stream' – that is, out of formation. At heights of 18,000 feet or more the temperature fell below minus 40 degrees. Danger was constant: from collision, from anti-aircraft fire – 'flak' – or, most deadly of all, from night-fighters. Flying bombers was brutal.

Life was much better for the Allied fighter pilots. US and RAF pilots were reaching their squadrons far better trained than their German equivalents. All had at least 350 hours in their logbooks; German pilots were lucky if they had 100. Allied airmen were then rapidly able to improve further thanks to excess numbers of pilots per squadron, plentiful supplies of fuel and a core of combat-experienced men to teach the new boys the ropes. Their aircraft and tactics were also superior to those of the Luftwaffe.

The ingredient missing was a long-range fighter that could escort US heavy bombers deep into Germany, but by the late summer of 1943 the solution had been found. Back in May 1940, the British had commissioned North American Aviation, a small company in California, to produce a new fighter. The result was the P-51 Mustang. Despite a sleek, streamlined design and incredible manoeuvrability, the Allison engine was underpowered and the new fighter was a disappointment.

Then, in October 1942, the Rolls-Royce test pilot Ron Harker suggested putting in a new Merlin 60 engine and the Mustang was totally transformed. At 20,000 feet it could fly at 430 m.p.h., and at 35,000 feet a staggering 455 m.p.h. – 70 m.p.h. more than the Luftwaffe's fighters.

The position of the radiator also helped produce jet thrust and incredible fuel efficiency. The Merlin engine, which could be built under licence in the US by Packard, had transformed the Mustang into a superb fighter. Then, in the summer of 1943, an extra fuel tank was placed behind the cockpit. With two further auxiliary drop tanks added to each wing, it was discovered it could fly a stunning 1,474 miles. That took it to beyond Berlin and back. And that was a game-changer.

The challenge was urgently to get enough of these new P-51Bs to England in time to make a difference. The first Mustang fighter group of three squadrons was operational by December 1943, with more on their way. Eighth Air Force also received a change at the top. Spaatz returned to England to take overall command of all US strategic air forces in England and Italy, while Major-General Jimmy Doolittle took over the Eighth. Doolittle was a young, dynamic and pioneering aviator who immediately gave orders for his fighters no longer to close-escort the bombers but instead actively to seek out all enemy fighters and attack them. On the way home they were ordered to shoot up any enemy airfields they saw too.

Allied air commanders had been planning an all-out round-the-clock assault on the German aircraft industry for some months, but not until the third week of February 1944 were the conditions right: a big enough gap in the weather and enough long-range fighters.

Opposite: A P-51 Mustang in flight.

Operation ARGUMENT began on the night of 19 February with Bomber Command hitting assembly plants at Leipzig. The following day it was the turn of the Eighth. Later in the week, the Fifteenth Air Force in Italy also joined the fray as the biggest air battle of the war to date was played out over the skies of Germany.

'Big Week', as it became known, destroyed 70 per cent of the factories targeted, but where it really hurt the Luftwaffe was in the loss of pilots. In February 1944, Germany lost 2,605 aircraft – a devastating number. The battle for air superiority was not over, but the tide had been turned in favour of the Allies.

Allied bomber losses during Big Week were 6.6 per cent for Bomber Command and 6 per cent for the Americans, far more manageable figures than had been suffered by the Eighth earlier when flying far into the Reich. It also suggested that flying by night was no less dangerous than flying by day. What's more, the dramatic increase in the sophistication of navigation aids, bombsights and target-marking techniques meant Bomber Command no longer needed to settle purely for massed

area bombing. Those days were over, yet Harris remained wedded to the same strategy he had championed on taking over the command back in February 1942.

In early March 1944, the Eighth joined Bomber Command in attacking Berlin, and with some success now the bombers were escorted by ever-greater numbers of long-range fighters. Harris finally ended the so-called Battle of Berlin on the night of 30 March when he sent his bombers to Nuremberg, site of the infamous Nazi rallies of the 1930s. It was a disaster for the Allies. 'Wholesale slaughter,' wrote Flight Lieutenant 'Rusty' Waughman, a Lancaster pilot in 101 Squadron. He reckoned he had seen at least sixteen bombers go down as the RAF planes were mauled by German night-fighters. 'All of us were pretty tired and shaken!' Waughman added in his diary. Bill Byers had also been on the raid, although he had perhaps been saved by engine trouble that forced him to turn for home early.

Nuremberg would prove the costliest mission of the entire war and confirmed what was already crystal clear to all but Harris: that his vision of massed bombing was not going to bring about the sudden wholesale collapse of the Third Reich. Throughout March and April of 1944, the Allies – and the Americans especially – continued the

Left: Upwards-firing cannons known as Schrägemusik allowed German night-fighters to attack undetected.

Opposite: P-51B Mustangs escorting B-24 Liberator heavy bombers.

strategy of POINTBLANK: to grind down the Luftwaffe and win air superiority over much of western Europe. By now the famed 4th Fighter Group was also equipped with Mustangs. Led by Lieutenant-Colonel Don Blakeslee, before America's entry into the war they had originally formed three volunteer squadrons in the RAF. By early 1944, they were one of the most experienced and highly skilled fighter units in the West and, under Blakeslee's tough, confident and aggressive leadership, the 4th soon had a number of rising aces amongst their number. Men such as Don Gentile, John Godfrey and Jimmy Goodson were becoming household names and able to pass on their knowledge to the new pilots arriving fresh from the States.

By contrast, the old guard of Luftwaffe aces was slowly but surely being whittled down in number as desperate German air commanders made them fly on relentlessly. Fighter pilot losses were utterly unsustainable as new pilots were arriving at front-line squadrons with ever-fewer hours in their logbooks, little chance to train further because of fuel shortages and expected to fly inadequate models of Messerschmitt 109s, not an easy aircraft for the inexperienced to master. Losses through accidents now exceeded 50 per cent. Those who did get airborne were facing American pilots with greater skill and experience, flying superior aircraft. The Germans were being slaughtered.

By mid-April, the Allies had finally won control of the skies over western Europe – and in the nick of time for D-Day. General Dwight D. Eisenhower, the Supreme Allied Commander for the invasion, now took formal control of the strategic air forces as D-Day, set for 5 June 1944, drew closer.

Left to right: John Godfrey, Don Gentile and Jimmy Goodson.

Many high-level discussions had taken place over how best to use the strategic air forces to support the forthcoming invasion. Spaatz argued strongly for attacking all German fuel supplies, from Ploesti in Romania – the only oilfield available to Nazi Germany – to various depots and synthetic-fuel plants throughout the Reich. Air Chief Marshal Sir Arthur Tedder, the Deputy Supreme Commander, favoured attacking larger railway centres, marshalling yards and depots in support of the work of the Allied tactical air forces now striking bridges, railways and the German communications network.

In the end, both plans were adopted, although Tedder's Transportation Plan had the priority up to the invasion. Harris, meanwhile, was deeply opposed to playing second fiddle to someone else's

Opposite: RAF Tempest pilot Roland Beamont tips the wing of a V-1 flying bomb to send it spinning out of control.

plan and would have preferred to keep on hitting German cities. There were also concerns that the Transportation Plan, much of which would be targeted at France, would lead to terrible loss of civilian life amongst those they were about to liberate. However, Bomber Command, especially, proved more than up to the task, attacking their targets with success and comparatively little loss of life – and, interestingly, frequently with greater accuracy than their American allies operating by night.

At the same time, Spaatz's Oil Plan was also under way. By the end of May 1944, this was really hurting the Luftwaffe and Germany as a whole, so much so that the Luftwaffe moved a number of flak units from cities to protect synthetic-fuel plants.

Meanwhile, the Germans had started directing V-1 flying bombs to southern England and V-2 rockets were on their way. Their launch sites, despite being very difficult to hit accurately, were now relentlessly targeted too.

On most days, the Allies could now call on around 2,500 heavy bombers to pummel Germany, but the demands on these resources were considerable. D-Day was finally launched, successfully, on 6 June 1944, but throughout the Battle for Normandy, strategic air forces were repeatedly called upon to support operations on the ground with attacks on Caen, Saint-Lô and numerous other targets, including port cities like Le Havre. After Normandy, there were further ground operations to support, such as MARKET GARDEN, the failed Allied airborne attempt to cross the Rhine at Arnhem.

By the end of September, however, Eisenhower had handed back direct control of the Allied strategic air forces, their successful support of the invasion of Europe completed. The question now was how best to use the mass of heavy bombers to quicken the end of the war. So much had changed. The Luftwaffe, though not beaten, was a shadow of its former self. The Allies had thousands of heavy bombers not hundreds. Accuracy, though still not 'precision', was considerably improved.

Spaatz urged a continuation of the Oil Plan, while, predictably, Harris had not wavered from his preference of continuing to hammer German cities. Unquestionably, both strategies were dramatically reducing Germany's ability effectively to continue the war, but although the outcome of the conflict was in no doubt, Hitler and the Nazi regime made it clear they intended to continue fighting to the bitter end.

Although by this stage of the war it was questionable whether daylight bombing was any more precise than that conducted by night, the Americans were certainly more concerned with the morality of deliberately targeting cities, with their large civilian populations, than were the British.

So the bombing continued. Officially, Allied bombing policy was for oil targets to be the priority and transportation the next most important. In reality, Harris was able to pay lip-service to this directive while still targeting city centres, and especially those cities around the Ruhr industrial area. Cologne, Essen, Dortmund, Koblenz – all were wrecked by the weight of bombs. In all, in 1944, British bombers dropped more than 440,000 tons of bombs on Germany. In the entire Blitz back in 1940–41, the Luftwaffe dropped only 18,000 tons on London.

In February, the Russians asked the Allies to bomb Dresden in eastern Germany. A beautiful medieval city, it was none the less an important rail hub for German troops heading to the southern Eastern Front as well as to Italy. There were also some 127 different factories in Dresden involved in war work. These two factors made it an entirely justifiable target.

However, when Bomber Command attacked in two waves with 805 aircraft on the night of 13/14 February 1945, they targeted the medieval centre, not the military barracks to the north or the marshalling yards. The conditions were ideal, with clear skies and a light wind. Very quickly, a firestorm developed and, tragically for the civilian population, Dresden had far from enough air-raid defences. Latest figures suggest more than 19,000 were killed that night, but Josef Goebbels, the Nazi propaganda chief, cynically claimed 120,000 had perished and hailed it as a British atrocity.

The following night, Chemnitz was attacked, and ten days later, so too was Pforzheim, where one in four civilians was killed. Würzburg was 90 per cent destroyed by the RAF in February 1945, to no obvious military advantage.

The strategic bombing of Germany continued to the very end of the war, and Bomber Command continued to prove it could bomb with skilful precision when asked to do so. In April 1945, 617 Squadron, the Dam Busters, hit the newly built Valentine U-boat assembly plant near Bremen. RAF photo reconnaissance had been watching its construction carefully and realized that, while some of the roof was 15 metres thick with concrete, other parts were just 5 feet. The Dam Busters flew over before a single U-boat had been completed, targeting the weaker part of the roof with 10-ton Grand Slam high-explosive bombs. The attack was entirely successful.

Berlin was attacked for the last time on the night of 20 April 1945 and Hitler's home in the Bavarian Alps at Berchtesgaden was smashed a few days later. The Third Reich lay in ruins and, although by the end of April the Red Army was swarming over Berlin, it was mostly bombs dropped

by the RAF, and to a lesser extent the Americans, that had reduced it to a broken, post-apocalyptic shell. That so many other German cities lay in shattered ruins was also largely down to Harris's bombing policy. Almost a million tons of bombs had been dropped on Germany during five long years of Bomber Command's air offensive and cost hundreds of thousands of lives. Almost one in two Bomber Command aircrew was killed during the war.

The morality of the Bomber War has been debated ever since, but there is no doubt that the hammering of Germany caused immense material and economic damage and shortened the war. Air power also allowed the Allies to put fewer men into the front line on the ground. Despite the cost, it did unquestionably save Allied lives.

And the moment the Nazis surrendered, the bombing stopped.

Left: Loss rates were appalling. Only one in two Bomber Command aircrew could expect to survive the war.

Opposite: The bombing of Dresden.

8: THE WAR IN ITALY

At dusk on 9 July 1943, the Allied invasion force was approaching Sicily. Those on board the fleet could see Mount Etna rising into the sky in the distance. Operation HUSKY was the largest amphibious invasion ever mounted: some 160,000 British, American and Canadian troops and more than 14,000 vehicles in over 2,590 vessels of varying sizes and supported by a staggering 3,600 aircraft. This mammoth undertaking had set sail from Alexandria in Egypt, from northern Tunisia and tiny Malta, brutally besieged in the first years of the war but now the launch pad for the Allied invasion of Axis-dominated Europe.

Above the invasion fleet was an impressive armada of gliders and aircraft carrying paratroopers. It was the first time the Allies had mounted a large-scale airborne operation, although this part of the invasion was soon to turn into a fiasco. The Allied airborne troops were all highly trained and motivated, but were being delivered by woefully ill-prepared aircrew who had been given little chance to train with the troops they were due to deliver, and especially not at night. To make matters worse, strong winds had started to whip up over the Mediterranean.

American paratroopers from the 82nd Airborne Division were to capture key features that would then make the tasks of the landing US infantry that followed easier, while British glider troops were to secure intact a key bridge, Ponte Grande, to the south of the city of Syracuse. In the event, both paratroopers and glider troops were tragically scattered to the four winds. Only 425 out of 3,500 paratroopers even got close to their objectives, while only four out of 144 gliders landed on their drop zone. It was a shambles and a poor start to the invasion.

It had been agreed at the Casablanca Conference back in January 1943 that, after winning the war in North Africa, the Allies would invade Sicily. The aim was to get a foothold in Europe, knock Italy out of the war and threaten Nazi Germany from southern Europe. The trouble was, victory in Tunisia was not completed until 13 May 1943 and planning for HUSKY, as the invasion was code-named, had to begin long before that and without any real knowledge of what the strength of enemy defence might be.

It was a mind-bogglingly complex operation that involved coalition air, land and naval forces. General Sir Harold Alexander, the Allied land commander, wanted to concentrate his forces as much as possible. On the other hand, Air Chief Marshal Sir Arthur Tedder, commander of Allied air forces, knew that having control of the skies was essential and that Sicily was awash with airfields in the east, west, centre and south. He hoped for multiple landings and for the ground troops to capture all the island's airfields swiftly.

*Opposite:
The Allied
invasion force
approaching
Sicily at dusk on
9 July 1943.*

There was also the need to keep the enemy guessing as to where they might strike. Complex deception plans were put in place to suggest the Allies would be landing in Sardinia or Greece but not Sicily. In the end, the plan for HUSKY went through eight evolutions, but it was finally agreed that British Eighth Army, under General Bernard Montgomery, should land in the south-east and the American Seventh Army, commanded by General George S. Patton, in the central-southern part of the island. Allied air forces would roam far and wide, destroying as many Axis aircraft as possible on the ground and in the air prior to the invasion.

Allied air forces did superbly well. The tiny island of Pantelleria to the south-west of Sicily was bombed into submission by 11 June, while Sicilian airfields and communication centres were hammered so hard in the days leading up to the invasion that only just over 100 Axis fighters remained on the island by the time the invasion got under way. Other targets were hit across the Mediterranean.

The Italian dictator, Benito Mussolini, and Field Marshal Albert Kesselring, the German commander-in-chief in the Mediterranean, were both convinced the Allies would land in Sicily despite their deception measures and even though Hitler believed it would be in southern Greece. There were, however, sufficient doubts and differences of opinion in Axis minds that preparation was needed for every eventuality. By the end of the first week of July, Kesselring had two German divisions in Sicily, although the Hermann Göring Division had only just arrived. He placed it in the centre of the island and moved the 15th Panzer-Grenadier Division, which had been based centrally, to the west instead. This move was completed by 6 July but meant neither division knew the terrain in which it now found itself. This was to prove a critical mistake.

Overall command on the ground was left to the Italian General Alfredo Guzzoni, who had a number of infantry divisions as well as large numbers of coastal naval forces. What neither the Germans nor the Allies knew, however, was how well these more than 200,000 Italian troops would fight. Although the Italians were generally poorly trained, there were bunkers, large numbers of coastal gun batteries and other artillery and they would be fighting for Italian soil.

On paper, at any rate, Sicily looked a very tough nut for the Allies to crack, despite the success of the air forces.

Although the Americans faced fierce fighting at Gela, especially, broadly speaking the invasion went far better than the Allies could have hoped, and that was despite the chaos of the airborne assault. Although fewer than seventy British glider troops attacked Ponte Grande rather than 2,000, they not only secured the bridge but managed to hold on to it too. The Special Raiding Squadron – the SAS as they had been in North Africa – arriving by landing craft and led by Major Paddy Mayne, successfully scaled cliffs and destroyed three vital coastal batteries for the loss of just one dead and two wounded. It was a brilliantly carried out attack.

Meanwhile, British troops came ashore to very limited and sporadic opposition and swiftly moved inland. By nightfall, they were entering Syracuse, one of the key invasion objectives.

The next day, the Italian Livorno Division and the men of the Hermann Göring, some in massive Tiger tanks, counter-attacked at Gela and several German panzers almost reached the sea. Personally commanding the defence on the beach was General Patton and, thanks to his leadership, determined fighting from the Americans and the brilliant work of a group of anti-tank gunners, the Axis counter-attack was successfully repulsed.

Opposite: SRS attacking Capo Murro di Porco.

By 12 July, General Dwight D. Eisenhower, the Supreme Allied Commander, was aboard a ship off the southern coast and, seeing thousands of vehicles and men already ashore, realized the Allies would now win on Sicily. Curiously, watching the same thing from a piece of high ground inland, was the German General Fridolin von Senger und Etterlin. He drew exactly the same conclusion as Eisenhower.

It would not be plain sailing for the Allies, however.

Montgomery's plan had been for Eighth Army to sweep up to Catania, a sizeable port on the east coast, then swiftly on to Messina in the north-eastern part of the island, where Sicily lay only a mile or so from the boot of mainland Italy. Patton's Seventh Army was to support Eighth Army's flanks. The key was to get on to the plain of Catania – one of the few flat parts of the island – quickly, before the enemy regained their balance.

First, though, it was essential to ensure the invasion did not fail. That trumped all other considerations. This was why Alexander had supported the decision to front-load the invasion with troops rather than vehicles. As it turned out, Italian resistance was less than had been feared and so the British infantry were left to move up towards Catania largely on foot. Sicily in July was scorching hot, diseases such as dysentery and malaria were rife, water was in short supply and the Germans very swiftly reorganized themselves.

German troops, under Colonel Wilhelm Schmalz – one of the highly experienced and capable combat commanders who made German troops such a tough proposition – formed blocking forces along the main axes of the British advance. Delaying the British allowed Kesselring, largely cutting General Guzzoni out of the loop, to move the bulk of his forces back to a rough defensive line overlooking the Catania Plain and with their guns set up in the foothills of Mount Etna.

At the same time, leading units of the 1st Fallschirmjäger – Parachute – Division were flown in to secure Ponte Primosole, the one key bridge on the Catania Plain that led north. Ironically, British paratroopers were also dropped to seize the very same bridge. British and German airborne troops landed on the same drop zones just hours apart.

A bitter and bloody battle followed around Primosole Bridge. In the extreme heat, the dead soon began to putrefy. Lieutenant David Fenner, whose 6th Durham Light Infantry were thrown into the battle on the night of 15 July, was shocked by the scenes of carnage and sight of flies feasting on twisted carcasses.

Above left: Aerial battle over Sicily. Allied fighters shoot down Me109s and Macchi 202s.

Opposite: German Fallschirmjäger landing on drop zones near the Primosole Bridge.

The British finally took the bridge on 17 July, but precious time had been lost. Not only was the bridge repeatedly put out of action in the days that followed, but the Germans had regained their balance and were now firmly dug in overlooking the Catania Plain. Repeated attempts to break through were stopped in their tracks.

This prompted a rethink by Montgomery, who now pushed forward the Canadians and the 51st Highland Division to try to break through further west of the plain. Here, though, the terrain was much hillier and greatly favoured the defender. The Canadian Hastings and Prince Edward's Regiment – known as the 'Hasty Ps' – were given the task of attacking one such hilltop strongpoint, the town of Assoro. Led by Major Lord Tweedsmuir, son of the adventure writer John Buchan, they scaled an almost vertical side of the mountain by night, took the observation post on the summit and then held out until Allied artillery finally forced the Germans to pull back. It was an extraordinary action, but Assoro was followed by another hilltop to be captured, then another and another.

Monty's left hook had forced the Americans into a supporting role, which did not please General Patton. On 17 July he visited Alexander and asked to be allowed to head westwards to capture Palermo.

Patton was given his wish, and with most German troops now behind a defensive position, the San Stefano Line, which cut off the entire north-east of Sicily, the Americans swiftly overwhelmed the remaining Italian forces in the west of the island. Palermo was taken in triumph on 22 July. Helping the Americans had been the tactical support given by the Mafia, brought to heel under Mussolini but now given a new lease of life by the Allies. Don Calò Vizzini, the senior Mafia figure on Sicily, encouraged Sicilian troops to lay down their arms. Most did.

The main battle, however, continued along the San Stefano Line. In the sweltering heat and dust the fighting was brutal. Thin soil and rocky ground meant stone splinters from mortars and artillery were lethal for both sides. On the Catania Plain, meanwhile, the British were losing more casualties to malaria than to battle. The Allies might have had superiority in numbers, fire-power and air support, but the landscape favoured the defenders. Sicily was a tough, demoralizing place in which to fight.

Hitler had now ordered one of his best commanders, General Valentin Hube, to take command of XIV Panzer Corps on Sicily with two more divisions. His brief was to hold Sicily for as long as

Above left: Canadians assaulting Assoro.

possible. Known by his men as 'Der Mann', Hube now swiftly bypassed Guzzoni, absorbed Italian artillery units into his own, and prepared further defensive lines in the north-east of the island.

For the Italians, meanwhile, Sicily was proving the straw that broke the camel's back. They wanted out of a war for which most had never had much enthusiasm and from an alliance with partners they mostly despised.

On 24 July, the Fascist Grand Council voted to overthrow Mussolini. Initially refusing to resign, he was forced to stand down the following day by the Italian king, Victor Emmanuel. Although the new government, under Marshal Pietro Badoglio, told their ally they would continue to fight alongside them, these were empty words, as the Germans were well aware. Almost immediately, the Italians began armistice negotiations with the Allies, while at the same time the Germans prepared Operation AXIS, the occupation of Italy and Greece, for the moment the Italians pulled out of the war.

While these high-level events were going on, the battle continued to rage on Sicily. Agira, Regalbuto, Troina and Centuripe became bywords for the bloody, bitter and attritional fighting as the British, Canadians and Americans wrested one hilltop town after another. Catania was finally captured on 5 August.

The German defence was being ground down, however. Fortunately for them, the north-east of Sicily narrowed to a tip, which meant that, as they fell back to the next defensive line, fewer men were needed to defend it. Remaining Italian troops began evacuating across the narrow Strait of Messina in the first week of August, and the Germans on the 11th. With some 333 anti-aircraft guns massed on each side of the Strait, it was impossible for Allied bombers to fly in and attack at low-level or for naval warships to get close.

In all, 62,000 Italians and 39,569 German troops were safely evacuated, along with 9,605 vehicles. Although the Allies were disappointed that so many enemy troops escaped, thirty-six days in which to capture a heavily defended island such as Sicily had been a considerable victory.

That same day of victory, 17 August, Italian surrender negotiations were agreed. Although willing to switch sides, they were to be 'co-belligerents' rather than formal allies. That same day, the Allied Joint Chiefs of Staff also agreed to invade southern Italy.

Right: American troops enter Palermo.

The Americans had been reluctant to do this, as they were worried it was a further distraction from the main strategy, which was a cross-Channel invasion of Nazi-occupied France from southern England. However, General George Marshall, the US Chief of Staff and most senior general, came round to the idea for three main reasons. First, decrypts of German coded traffic revealed that, if the Allies invaded, Hitler planned to pull his forces back to a line some 200 miles north of Rome between Pisa and Rimini. This suggested the Allies could easily capture the Italian capital, a major psychological victory.

The second was the chance to capture a group of airfields in central-southern Italy at Foggia. Heavy strategic bombers could then be based there, allowing the noose to be further tightened around Nazi Germany. In particular, Germany's one oilfield, at Ploesti in Romania, could be bombed from Foggia. Finally, it was also hoped fighting in Italy would draw German troops away from north-west Europe before the invasion of France, planned for the following May.

Without telling the Italians the exact details or timings of their plans, the Allies intended to land Montgomery's Eighth Army in southern Italy first, followed by an armistice announcement a few days later and then, the following day, Lieutenant-General Mark Clark's US Fifth Army would make an amphibious invasion of Italy at Salerno, just to the south of Naples. It was confidently expected that General Alexander's 15th Army Group would be in Rome by Christmas.

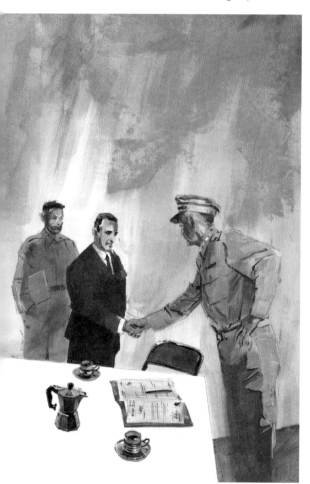

The invasion of Italy was still fraught with risk, however. There were some seventeen German divisions in Italy by this time – in Sicily there had never been more than four. The Germans knew Italy was likely to quit the war, which was why they had prepared Operation AXIS to flood both Italy and Greece with German troops and disarm the Italian armed forces the moment they did so. And actually, the strategy was initially to resist an Allied invasion but then carry out a methodical withdrawal to the Pisa–Rimini Line. This was based on the assumption that the Allies would never try to fight their way up the peninsula but instead would move north in a series of outflanking manoeuvres by sea. In reality, the Allies had nothing like the shipping and landing craft the Germans thought they had – much of that used for Sicily had already been sent to the Pacific or back to Britain. The cross-Channel invasion planned for May 1944 remained the strategic priority for the Allies.

Eighth Army landed on the toe of Italy to almost no opposition on 3 September, while

Left: The Italians sign the armistice.

Opposite: German anti-aircraft gunners furiously defend the Strait of Messina.

British paratroopers captured the port of Taranto, complete with much of the Italian fleet. The armistice was announced on 8 September, much to the surprise of the Italians, who for some reason had become convinced it would be on 12 September. Caught completely off guard, the king and Marshal Badoglio fled Rome, while German troops swept in and successfully disarmed much of the Italian Army. They would now be no help to the Allies.

The landings at Salerno took place the following day, but because of the shortage of shipping, Mark Clark's Fifth Army came ashore with just three divisions in the first assault, of which two were British. It was very nearly a catastrophic failure.

Meanwhile, German commando troops had sprung Mussolini from his prison in the Gran Sasso in the southern Apennines and installed him as a puppet dictator of the new fascist Socialist Republic of Italy – the RSI. It meant the north was subject to even stricter Nazi-dominated control.

To the south, the Allies landed successfully at Salerno, but their situation quickly became precarious. Eighth Army was advancing from the toe, but was still some way to the south, while the lack of any support from the Italians meant Field Marshal Kesselring decided to throw the weight of the newly formed German Tenth Army against Salerno.

Although the beaches were good for landing, they lay in a semicircular amphitheatre surrounded by hills from which every move could be seen. British and American troops also landed too far apart to mutually support one another, and by 11 September the Germans were furiously counter-attacking with five divisions. At one point, the situation became so critical that General Clark came ashore and personally took command of some anti-tank guns. Eighth Army was urged to hurry from the south and massive extra air and naval support was brought in. Allied fire-power from the air and sea made all the difference. By 16 September, General Heinrich von Vietinghoff, the German Tenth Army commander, decided it was time to pull back. One last counter-attack was made on 17 September to mask their withdrawal, but the Battle of Salerno was over. It was not, though, the start to the Italian campaign that the Allies had hoped for. Nor was it about to get any easier for them.

Hitler, stirred by the determined defence at Salerno, now changed his orders and told Kesselring he wanted him to fight for every yard. There was no longer to be a swift retreat to the Pisa–Rimini Line.

The trouble was, the Allies had set their strategy in stone: the overall priority was still to be the capture of Foggia and the build-up of the new Fifteenth Air Force. That meant giving them, rather than Alexander's armies, the lion's share of shipping capacity and fuel. To make matters worse for the Allies, the Mediterranean sunshine in which the Italian campaign had been planned rapidly disappeared, replaced instead by weeks of endless rain and, with it, mud. Although the Foggia airfields were in their hands by 1 October, the narrow, mountainous nature of Italy meant it was not an easy place in which to advance. From the mountains, rivers ran down to the sea, across the path of the Allies.

Highly mechanized and using a large number of vehicles, the Allies needed roads. There were, however, only four main routes leading to Rome. One passed through the centre, which was too mountainous. Another ran along the eastern Adriatic coast and a third beside the western Ionian coast; the latter was narrow and the mountains too close for manoeuvre. Only one other main road was available: Highway 1, the old Roman Via Casilina, which ran north–south from Rome inland from the west coast. All were fairly easy for the Germans to block.

In the rain and mud, Eighth Army began pushing up the Adriatic Coast, while Fifth Army headed up the Via Casilina. All the way, bridges were blown and the roads lined with mines and booby traps. The confidence and hopes with which Italy had been invaded were quickly dampening. By Christmas, Fifth Army was still some 70 miles south of Rome. The River Volturno had been crossed but now they faced a major new defensive position: the Gustav Line.

While the Allies had been slogging their way northwards, the Germans had been creating a formidable defensive position that ran the width of Italy. A network of bunkers, mines, wire, mortar pits and gun positions, it was strongest around the town of Cassino. Here the Via Casilina emerged through narrow passes into the Liri Valley, an expanse around 5 miles wide that ran much of the way to Rome. Highway 1 hugged its eastern side, passing through Cassino. Towering above was the Monte Cassino massif, the end of the mountain spur on which stood a famous Benedictine monastery.

As the Allies were all too aware, the Germans had observers and guns aimed on any attempt by Fifth Army to break through into the Liri Valley. General Clark first tried to burst through by forcing a crossing over the River Rapido at the southern end of the valley. The 36th Texas Division was given this dubious honour and were cut to pieces in the process. After the disaster of the 'Bloody Rapido', an outflanking manoeuvre was attempted further up the coast at Anzio on 21 January 1944. This involved collecting precious shipping needed for the planned Normandy invasion, but although a bridgehead was secured, the attacking force was not strong enough to force the Germans to abandon the Gustav Line.

Next, at the end of January, Clark sent the 34th 'Red Bull' Division up on to the Monte Cassino massif, while the French Expeditionary Corps, largely made up of colonial North African troops, attacked further east in the mountains around Monte Abate. In the rain, cold and brutal conditions, the fighting was bitter and costly. Both the French and the Red Bulls made important gains but were unable to dislodge the Germans from the heights.

The Anzio landings had been meant to relieve the pressure at Cassino, but in February a further attack was made on the massif in an effort to take the strain off the beleaguered troops in the bridgehead. By this time, the Gustav Line at Monte Cassino had been reinforced with paratroopers of the 1st Fallschirmjäger Division, and Major-General Francis Tuker, the 4th Indian Division commander,

Above left: A column of troops moving over a Bailey bridge through the rain, mud and mountains.

Opposite: The Salerno landings.

suggested instead attacking further east where the enemy was less strong, cutting the massif and then isolating it. His immediate superior, Lieutenant-General Bernard Freyberg, commander of the New Zealand Corps, was unfamiliar with mountain warfare and so disregarded Tuker's idea. Instead, he ordered a direct attack on Monte Cassino – just as had been attempted before. This time, though, the strategic air forces, now based at Foggia, were called upon to plaster the position.

Tragically, the request to hit the entire massif did not reach the air forces and instead they focused on the beautiful monastery, which was pulverized. The Germans, who had not been using it, promptly created enviably strong positions amidst the rubble. Not only had an architectural and religious gem been destroyed, the enemy position on Monte Cassino had become stronger, not weaker. When the 4th Indian Division attacked, they predictably failed, just as previous attacks had done.

In March, Freyberg launched a further attack, this time hoping his troops would bludgeon their way through the town. The attack was also preceded by heavy bombing, which destroyed Cassino entirely. Once again, the rubble and ruins aided rather than hindered the Germans. A lot of men were being killed and wounded and an entire town smashed for very little gain. These were not the Allies' finest few weeks of battle.

Among the difficulties facing the Allies at Monte Cassino had been the weather as well as the terrain. Alexander's forces were highly mechanized and dependent on both fire and, increasingly, close air support provided by the tactical air forces. However, with the poor weather, air power had been less able to help. Nor had the troops on the ground been able to bring their huge advantage in mechanization to bear. Rather, pack mules had been the best means of transport.

But summer was on its way, and Alexander brought the bulk of Eighth Army, now commanded by General Oliver Leese, across the mountains alongside Fifth Army and began preparing a large-scale attack to smash the Gustav Line once and for all and capture Rome. Operation DIADEM was launched with a huge barrage of artillery fire on 11 May 1944.

The expectation was that Eighth Army would break through in the Liri Valley and speed down the Via Casilina. At the right moment, US V Corps at Anzio would then break out and, it was hoped, trap the bulk of the German Tenth Army in an encirclement.

The recently arrived II Polish Corps attacked on Monte Cassino. Theirs had been an extraordinary journey. Most had been captured by the Red Army back in September 1939 and sent to Gulags. After the German invasion of the USSR in June 1941, they had been released and told to muster in Kazakhstan, 2,000 miles to the south. There, many had suffered from an outbreak of typhus and malaria, but the survivors had made their way to Iraq, where the British had equipped and begun training them. After completing training in Palestine, they had been sent to Italy. Their first action was on Monte Cassino, which, after brutal fighting, they finally captured on 18 May.

DIADEM did not develop as Alexander had imagined. Eighth Army struggled in the Liri Valley as they came up against the next line of defences, the so-called Senger Line, while the mass of streams and waterways all needed bridging, which took time. Lieutenant Ted Wyke-Smith was one engineer who helped build 26 Bailey bridges in 28 nights, an astonishing achievement; but despite this, the congestion of men and Eighth Army vehicles in the Liri Valley meant progress was slow.

Rather, it was the Free French, on their left and fighting through the mountains, and US II Corps,

Opposite:
The bombing of
Monte Cassino.

pushing along the west coast, who had the greatest success, pressing far ahead of the British and Canadians. It meant that by the time V Corps was ordered to burst out of the Anzio bridgehead, the remnants of the battered German Tenth Army were streaming down mountain roads further east. Not one German soldier retreated down the Via Casilina.

Instead of going all-out to cut Highway 1, as had been the original plan, General Clark now found his Fifth Army ahead of Eighth and facing a second German Army, the Fourteenth, dug in behind the next defensive position – the Caesar Line to the south of Rome. With this in mind, Clark now turned his forces to face them square on. To begin with, it seemed as though his men were banging against a brick wall, but then the Texans, recovered from their ordeal on the Rapido, found a gap in the German defences in the Alban Hills. Exploiting this weakness, the German line was swiftly blown wide open. Fourteenth Army fell back in disarray, and on 4 June Fifth Army entered Rome.

DIADEM was a huge victory – not only had German Tenth Army been badly mauled, but Fourteenth Army had been routed, making it a greater triumph than had originally been hoped. The cost to the Italians, however, was a terrible one. Cassino was entirely destroyed – barely a single building still stood – while the bomb craters were filled with stagnant water infested with malaria. Most of the surrounding villages and towns suffered similarly. The 60-mile stretch between Rome and Cassino was devastated. Many civilians had been killed and maimed and many more forced to flee to the mountains or find shelter in caves. 'To live in little caverns dug by us,' said Leonardo Bocale, 'without any facilities for hygiene, without a life, without knowing what our future could be, tossed like animals . . . we were abandoned: culturally, materially, spiritually.'

A stain on the Allied victory was the treatment of Italian civilians by men of the French Expeditionary Corps, who went on the rampage – raping, stealing and murdering untold numbers. These troops had fought superbly, yet in the flush of victory they ran amok. They were not the first troops in history to do so, nor would they be the last, but their actions added to the torment of the Italians, most of whom the previous September had thought the war was over. The fallacy of that belief had been brutally exposed.

Elsewhere in the south, now largely under Allied Military Government, inflation was out of control, food scarce and much of the infrastructure destroyed. Gangsters ran the black market. With

Above left: The Poles fighting on Monte Cassino.

Opposite: Fifth Army troops pass the Colosseum in Rome.

many men either prisoners-of-war or transported to Germany as forced labour, it was left to the women to try to keep their families alive. They were paying a terrible price for Mussolini's entry into the war back in 1940.

Meanwhile, the Allied armies in Italy were slogging their way north from Rome and initially making great strides as the Germans fell back in disarray. In this narrow, mountainous country, however, it did not take long, nor many troops, for the shattered remnants of their two armies to set up blocking lines.

More German soldiers and supplies were hurriedly sent south through the Alps, while labourers continued to build the twin defensive lines of the Gothic Line, a truly formidable position that ran the width of the country and had always been seen as Germany's main line of defence in Italy.

First, though, came the Trasimeno Line in southern Tuscany and Umbria. A ten-day battle from 20 to 30 June saw the Allies bludgeon their way through at a mile a day before encountering numerous blocking lines as they headed to Florence. All the way, climbing blue in the distance, were the peaks of the Apennines, a constant reminder of what faced them to the north.

Florence, declared an 'open city' by Kesselring, was still contested by the Germans. All the bridges across the River Arno were blown except the beautiful Ponte Vecchio, too narrow, in any case, for military traffic. Italian partisans also tussled with fascist militia. Not until 4 August was the city finally captured by the Allies.

By this time, Alexander had lost a quarter of his forces to Operation DRAGOON, the Allied invasion of southern France. He had argued in vain that it was better to exploit the success of DIADEM and use the morale of victory and momentum to push through the Gothic Line that summer and then on through the Alps, either into France or the Balkans.

The same day that Florence fell, Field Marshal Alexander met with General Oliver Leese, the British Eighth Army commander, at Orvieto airfield. It was a scorching hot day, so they talked under the wing of a Dakota aircraft, which offered some shade. The plan had been for Eighth and Fifth Army to continue fighting side by side to assault the Gothic Line in the centre.

Leese, though, now suggested moving Eighth Army to the Adriatic coast, where the mountains were less pronounced and where the Via Adriatica, the main coast road, could be the prime axis of advance. Alexander wanted his army commander to fight on ground of his choosing and was also aware of tensions between Leese and Clark, so agreed. But it meant a two-week delay in attacking while Eighth Army moved across Italy.

Leese had intended to use his V Corps along the coast – it was his strongest, with five divisions – with the Canadians in the hills on their left flank. However, it was pointed out to him that the Germans were now experts at blowing bridges and mining roads, so, at the last moment, he switched them around. The Canadians, however, had only two divisions and the Via Adriatica was still the main axis of advance for Eighth Army and, because it did not run through mountains, had been the main reason for switching the line of attack to the coast. Now, V Corps, with its strength, scale, heavy armour and vehicles, was to advance inland, across narrow winding dirt roads. It was not a good decision, because the Canadians did not have the strength in depth to push through along the Via Adriatica, whereas V Corps had.

Eighth Army began its assault of the Gothic Line on 25 August.

Opposite: German Fallschirmjäger defending the north bank of the River Arno in Florence.

Eighth Army managed to get through the first defences of the Gothic Line, Green I, by 2 September, but then, as Kesselring reinforced this part of the front, German resistance stiffened. Eighth Army reached Green II and was held up at the Coriano Ridge. V Corps was struggling in the foothills of the Apennines, and the Canadians were running out of steam. And it had begun to rain.

Meanwhile, Fifth Army had captured Pisa and pushed the Germans back to the Gothic Line in the centre and west. There were two main inland passes through the mountains: the Futa Pass was the easier route, but Clark decided to surprise the enemy by attacking through the narrower Giogo Pass. This was protected on either side by Monticelli to the west and Monte Altuzzo to the east. Although not held in any strength by the 4th Fallschirmjäger Division, it was none the less a daunting objective for the Americans of the 91st and 85th Divisions. Despite the attackers having formidable artillery and close air support, these peaks could be taken only by infantrymen slogging their way up narrow ridges and prising out each machine-gun nest and mortar position one by one.

Clark's men attacked on 12 September and, after a bloody and brutal battle in which both Germans and Americans fought heroically and with terrible casualties, the Giogo Pass was captured on 18 September. The bodies of many hundreds who fought there have never been recovered.

In the rain, the Allied armies continued to batter their way against the second line of German defences. During its assault on Monte Grande, the US 88th Division lost nearly 10,000 casualties in two weeks' fighting. Each peak fought for was an epic of grit, determination and sacrifice.

Civil war had now effectively broken out in the north of Italy. Young men who did not want to be called up into SS police battalions or Mussolini's new divisions were increasingly fleeing to the mountains to become partisans. Although ill-trained, they rapidly became a major thorn in the side of the Germans, who, suffering from relentless Allied shelling and fighter-bomber attacks, now faced no let-up away from the front line either. Both German troops and fascist militias became embroiled in *rastrellamenti* – round-up operations to try to crush these insurgents. Kesselring reckoned partisans killed at least 30,000 German troops – over two divisions. He instigated a brutal rule of terror in which ten civilians were summarily executed for every one German killed. The beautiful towns of northern Italy were lined with hanged corpses, while mountain villages such as Sant'Anna di Stazzema and San Terenzo became scenes of appalling civilian massacres.

Above left:
The Americans assaulting Monte Altuzzo.

Opposite: A group of Stella Rossa partisans.

Many partisans were highly politicized, and often communist, but the Stella Rossa, operating in and around the Monte Sole massif to the south of Bologna, were a rare exception. Led by the charismatic 'Lupo', over the summer of 1944 they captured vital plans and made life very difficult for the Germans.

By the end of September 1944, and with the front just 10 miles to the south, the Stella Rossa had become an increasing problem. On the 29th, through the mist and rain, a large *rastrellamento* was launched, led by men of the 16th Waffen-SS Division. Partisans, the elderly, women and children were all rounded up and shot, and their homes destroyed. In all, 762 were murdered. It was the largest single civilian massacre in all of western Europe during the war.

Despite the loss of so many troops back in July, by the end of October Alexander's Allied armies had come within a stone's throw of breaking through the Gothic Line defences completely and bursting out into the Po Valley. Yet it was not to be. With the onset of winter and another bout of appalling weather, it proved tantalizingly beyond them. Casualties were simply too high and, as the secondary theatre since the Allied invasion of Normandy two days after the fall of Rome, Italy had not been the priority for reinforcements. As it was, Alexander had a staggering twenty-four different nationalities fighting in his armies, even including an infantry division from Brazil.

On 29 October, he briefed his commanders about his winter plan, which was to place his forces on to the defensive. This also meant ordering the partisans temporarily to lay down their arms and wait until the following spring. For these resistance fighters, this was a catastrophic blow. They now faced a long, bitterly cold winter as outlaws, with diminishing supplies, hunted by Nazi police and fascist militias.

Meanwhile, Field Marshal Alexander also now had to deal with the Allied liberation of Greece and the Aegean, and on 23 November he was promoted to Supreme Allied Commander, Mediterranean. He had no hesitation in recommending that Mark Clark replace him as Army Group commander in Italy.

Heavy snow fell on northern Italy that winter of 1944–5, but as spring slowly dawned, so Clark began preparing his forces for what would be the final offensive in Italy.

The winter was once again bitter. In the mountains, snow lay thick on the ground, making life miserable for all. Mussolini, still puppet dictator in the north, had become subdued and withdrawn, sensing the end was near, while General Karl Wolff, the senior SS commander in Italy, was even actively pursuing secret peace talks with the Allies. This was something Kesselring was not willing to countenance, however, which meant there would still be one last major battle.

By the beginning of March, Clark had crystallized his plans, once more favouring a two-fisted approach, with a big push by Fifth Army in the centre and with Eighth Army attacking at two places. One of these would involve crossing Lake Comacchio to the north of Ravenna, using 'fantail' amphibious tanks. The key, Clark realized, was to build up as much strength as possible while at the same time denying supplies to the enemy, then to hit them swiftly and very hard.

Since resources in northern Italy were, by this time, extremely scarce, most German supplies had to come from the Reich and south through the Alpine Brenner Pass. Allied air forces hammered this route, despite facing nearly 1,000 anti-aircraft guns in the narrow valley. Their efforts paid off. The

Opposite: American fighter-bombers shoot up German supplies heading south.

previous autumn an average of thirty-eight trains had passed through each day, but by March 1945 the figure was just eight. Fuel supplies had dwindled to almost nothing.

At the same time, the Allies had been rearming the partisans and also sending increasing numbers of liaison officers, both American and British, to help train and coordinate their efforts. These irregulars were now instrumental in playing havoc with German supply lines.

By dawn on 9 April 1945, the Allies were ready. The final battle was about to begin.

German resistance was initially stiff, with fierce battles all along the front, but the Allies kept bludgeoning their way through. Eighth Army successfully crossed Lake Comacchio, outflanking German positions, while on 20 April Bologna finally fell. Despite orders to the contrary, von Vietinghoff now gave the signal for his armies to fall back across the River Po.

At this moment, the glue that had kept the German forces defending Italy so doggedly for over a year and a half finally gave way. Cohesion crumbled as the Germans fled in disarray, ruthlessly pursued by Allied fighter aircraft. Terrible scenes were played out at the Po. Vehicles were destroyed, equipment abandoned and horses shot, while many of those unable to cross on the few ferries available drowned trying to swim.

General Wolff was urging Kesselring and von Vietinghoff to surrender, but neither would do so without the authority of Hitler. Meanwhile, on 25 April Mussolini fled north, only to be captured by partisans and executed along with his mistress, Clara Petacci. Their bodies were brought to Milan and, with three other leading fascists, hung upside down from butcher's hooks. Partisans now exacted their revenge on thousands of fascists as brutal blood-letting took hold.

The German surrender was finally agreed on 29 April, without Hitler's authority and with Wolff presenting it to von Vietinghoff as a *fait accompli*. It took effect at 2 p.m. on 2 May. The long, bitter war in Italy was part of the wider and ultimately effective Allied strategy of tightening a noose around Nazi Germany. For all its brutality, the conflict there saw not only the end of fascism but tied down large numbers of German troops, materiel and resources right to the very end. The enormity of that sacrifice and achievement should not be forgotten.

9: THE BATTLE FOR NORMANDY

At just sixteen minutes past midnight on Tuesday, 6 June 1944, the first Allied troops touched down on French soil when the first of three gliders landed beside a swing bridge on the Caen Canal, code-named 'Pegasus'. On board were twenty-eight men of D Company, the Oxfordshire and Buckinghamshire Light Infantry, part of the British 6th Airborne Division. Incredibly, the pilot, Jim Wallwork, had landed on precisely the right spot, despite it being night-time and despite strong westerly winds. In fact, as the glider slid to a halt, the nose gently nudged the perimeter wire protecting a German gun position at the eastern end of the bridge.

Jumping clear of the wreckage, they charged the enemy positions, firing their automatic weapons and hurling grenades. The lead officer, Lieutenant Den Brotheridge, was fatally shot in the neck as he ran to the far side of the bridge, but apart from this tragic blow the airborne men quickly secured the bridge as planned, supported by two further loads of troops whose gliders similarly landed exactly where they were supposed to.

A few hundred yards to the east was a second bridge, code-named 'Horsa', spanning the River Orne, which ran parallel to the canal. Although only two of the three gliders allocated successfully landed there, the men swiftly and efficiently secured that bridge too. The initial D-Day objectives had been captured intact, as planned, and on schedule.

These troops were the first of some 20,000 airborne soldiers dropped in the early hours of D-Day. It was the task of the 6th Airborne Division to secure the eastern flanks of the invasion front and the job of two US airborne divisions, the 82nd and 101st, to hold key ground along the western flank, at the base of the Cotentin Peninsula.

The airborne landings might have signalled the start of the Allied invasion of Normandy, but the battle for France had, in many ways, begun a lot earlier. Britain and her allies in the United States and Canada, especially, had been able to amass vast numbers of men and quantities of war materiel in the United Kingdom – more than enough to win the day in Normandy – but the challenge was how to bring them swiftly and successfully across the English Channel into Nazi-occupied France. The Allies, despite gathering an enormous invasion fleet, still had only enough shipping to transport a fraction in one go.

The moment they landed, therefore, the race would be on to see who could bring decisive numbers of troops and supplies into the bridgehead – or battle zone – more quickly. Would it be the Allies, at the nearest point more than 80 miles away across the sea, or the Germans, travelling across land? This was where air power came in. Allied air forces could slow up the Germans' ability to supply

Normandy by destroying railway marshalling yards, locomotives and wagons, key bridges and roads and also the German radar and communications network. This often meant bombing and attacking at low level, which in turn meant ensuring there were no Messerschmitt or Focke-Wulf fighters hovering above as they did so.

Fortunately for the Allies, winning control of the skies was achieved after a long, bitter air battle over the winter of 1943/44, and by mid-April their air forces had secured air superiority over most of north-west Europe. This allowed the full weight of Allied bomber forces to hammer the enemy transportation network in the nine weeks before D-Day. And very successfully too.

An early plan for Operation OVERLORD, the code-name for the invasion, had been developed back in 1943, but it was not until British General Sir Bernard Montgomery was made overall Allied Land Commander that this was significantly enlarged.

Although the main architect of the plan, Montgomery was answerable to his chief, US General Dwight D. Eisenhower, the Supreme Allied Commander, and was also working hand in hand with his navy and air force counterparts, Admiral Sir Bertram Ramsay and Air Marshal Sir Trafford Leigh-Mallory. Under him was a large tri-service and multinational planning team.

Rough plans were approved in February 1944 and presented on 7 April. The flanks would be secured with the help of airborne troops: the Americans in the west at the foot of the Cotentin Peninsula, and the British and Canadians in the east, between the River Orne and the Caen Canal and, 5 miles further to the east, the River Dives. There would then be five major landing beaches, code-named Utah, Omaha, Gold, Juno and Sword. Monty would have liked more troops in the initial waves, but shipping was the constraint. Although the invasion fleet would be almost 7,000 vessels, which included 4,127 landing craft of various shapes and sizes, that was enough to carry only 135,000 men plus accompanying equipment and materiel on D-Day itself. It sounded a lot but, as all the Allied commanders were keenly aware, it was not enough to guarantee victory by any stretch.

On 15 May, Eisenhower called a final commanders' conference and asked them all to express any misgivings they might have. No one voiced any. Everyone accepted it was the best possible plan for the resources they had available. The challenge would be to secure a foothold and then build up strength as quickly as possible before a major German counter-attack.

Right: Monty briefs Allied commanders.

Opposite: Rocket-armed Typhoons wreaked havoc on German supply lines.

By the summer of 1944, Nazi Germany was emphatically losing the war. Hitler's armies were being pushed back along the Eastern

Front and in Italy too, and her cities were being systematically destroyed by Allied strategic bombing. Despite this, the Führer insisted on fighting on. His scientists were developing so-called 'wonder' weapons, which he hoped might still turn the tide, while he knew that crossing the Channel would not be easy for the Allies. His black-and-white world view had always seen the Third Reich as either lasting a thousand years or descending into Armageddon, but he was certainly not about to countenance defeat, no matter the shortening odds. Germany would fight on.

Protecting the European coast from the Arctic Circle in Norway to the border with Spain was the Atlantic Wall – not a solid continuous structure, but a series of 9,671 concrete bunkers and emplacements housing a mixture of guns, machine guns, mortars and men. Linking them were wire entanglements and minefields. Inevitably, some parts were stronger than others – the Pas de Calais was the best protected – but while Normandy was less well defended, the Germans still had around 75,000 men in the area and, by June 1944, 913 concrete structures and some 6 million mines.

Most of the divisions guarding the coast were poorly trained and equipped, and un-mechanized – dependent on their feet and horses – but in France and north-west Europe there were some ten mobile divisions, all of which were well trained and motivated, oversized and bristling with weaponry and vehicles. The challenge for the Germans was where to position these. Should they guess where the Allies might land and place them all close to the front? Or hedge their bets and keep them spread widely to cover any eventuality?

In the nine weeks before D-Day, Allied air forces dropped a staggering 197,000 tons of bombs on France alone; the Luftwaffe had managed just 18,000 tons on London during the entire nine-month Blitz. There had been huge concerns about civilian loss of life, but casualties, although still some 15,000 before D-Day, were a fraction of what had been feared. All bridges across the River Seine had been destroyed, hundreds of locomotives had been shot up and marshalling yards pummelled. By the beginning of June, 76 out of 92 radar stations along the Atlantic coast had been knocked out of action too. On 28 May, 78 Luftwaffe fighters were shot down – and the closest was about 500 miles from Normandy, demonstrating that most of the German air force had been pushed back deep into the Reich. Control of the skies of northern France, a prerequisite for any amphibious invasion, had been emphatically achieved.

By the beginning of June 1944, the invasion armada had been assembled and the troops involved consigned to camps all along the southern coast of England, with the British and Canadians in

Above left: A concrete bunker on the Atlantic Wall.

Opposite: Lancaster bombers pound occupied France before D-Day.

the east and Americans in the west. An immense deception operation, Operation FORTITUDE, had long been in action, with double agents and imaginary agents feeding bogus information and creating fake forces and even a completely fake army group spread across Britain. The aim was to keep the Germans guessing where and when the invasion would take place.

Meanwhile, final details of OVERLORD had been agreed and were being put into practice, with every man allocated the right aircraft, ship and landing craft, and follow-up forces and supplies ready and waiting too. The logistics were mind-bogglingly complex.

After the beautiful sunshine of late May, the weather in early June turned against the Allies. A delay of twenty-four hours was advised by the meteorological teams, but even on the night of 5/6 June as the invasion was launched it was not certain the predicted good-weather window would hold.

A massive further challenge was how to clear enough of the minefields laid by the Germans in the Channel. A particularly dense mine barrier lay 7–10 miles off the Normandy coast. Tides and currents, combined with the need for enough clear routes through for the shipping to support five invasion beaches, posed a massive headache for the naval planners. The solution was the biggest single mine-clearing operation of the entire war, as a staggering 255 minesweepers working in teams cleared and marked two channels running out from each landing beach. That it was achieved in rough seas at night ahead of the main invasion force is testament to the extraordinary skill of those involved. It remains a largely forgotten episode that deserves far greater recognition.

Meanwhile, airborne troops were dropped at the western and eastern ends of the invasion front. In the east, the key bridges across the River Orne and the Caen Canal were captured intact in a brilliantly executed operation by British glider troops, while, despite chaos, confusion and scattered troops, all five bridges over the River Dives were destroyed. German counter-attacks from the east would be blocked by the lack of bridges, while Allied reinforcements could use the intact bridges to support airborne troops and secure the all-important high ground in between.

In the west, American paratroopers were also scattered, but secured all their objectives successfully, even managing to kill the German general of the 91st Luftlande Division, which was holding the southern Cotentin Peninsula.

With airborne troops successfully securing the flanks, the main invasion forces neared the Normandy coast. Heavy bombers preceded them but, in their anxiety not to hit the landing craft, many of their bombs fell too far inland. Offshore naval bombardments were, however, very successful. The weight of Allied naval fire was immense. One shell fired from 6 miles out at sea by HMS *Ajax*, for example, hit the shield and breech of a large German coastal gun. Supporting the Americans at Omaha Beach were 183 heavy-calibre guns of over 90mm diameter and many more cannons. In contrast, the Germans had just 32 guns of 50–88mm diameter directly defending Omaha and nothing larger.

At certain points on Omaha, the Americans landing in the initial waves were slaughtered, but others got across the beach with comparative ease. German defences, hammered by offshore naval guns and running short of ammunition, were knocked out one by one. Fighting continued all day, but the outcome there had been secured by mid-morning. Proportionally, the Canadians at Juno were worst hit, but also managed to push the furthest inland. Utah Beach was captured with very few casualties, while the British suffered at Gold and Sword, but still managed to secure a clear toehold.

The German response was illogical and poorly executed. General Erich Marcks, the local corps commander, sent his mobile reserve – serviced by French trucks and bicycles – after the American airborne troops and then changed his mind. By the time they entered the battle on the afternoon of 6 June, it was too late: they were exhausted and were largely destroyed. Field Marshal Erwin Rommel, the overall German commander in Normandy, was away, his chief of staff was still drunk in the early hours after a particularly heavy dinner, while the precious panzer divisions were not allowed to move until Hitler gave the order.

Hitler was never an early riser and, even once up, prevaricated from his home in the Bavarian Alps. Not until after 4 p.m. on D-Day did he finally authorize the panzer divisions to move. The nearest, the superb Panzer-Lehr and 12th Waffen-SS Panzer Division 'Hitlerjugend', thus lost precious hours.

None the less, the Allies had still fallen some way short of their D-Day objectives, including the key city of Caen. The British advance from Sword had been held up by the best sited and equipped strongpoint along the entire invasion front, code-named Hillman. This had been captured late on 6 June and by the morning of the 7th the British and Canadians were advancing towards Caen once more. By the afternoon, one battalion of Canadian troops – around 800 men – and a handful of Sherman tanks were nearing Carpiquet, the airfield to the west of the city, when they were counter-attacked by the newly arrived vanguard of the 12th SS. Strong in both weaponry

and highly motivated young troops, the 12th SS were a formidable force and had orders to throw the Allies back into the sea. Despite this, they managed to push the Canadians back only a couple of miles before Allied artillery and dogged Canadian defence stopped them in their tracks. In their frustration, they executed thirty-seven Canadian prisoners and some of the wounded were deliberately crushed by panzer tracks.

It was a highly significant battle that proved that, in the wide open farmland around Caen, going on the offensive would not be easy, whichever side was attacking. After all, the 12th SS had been unable to smash Canadian infantry and armour that had initially been badly undersupported. It also set the tone for the brutal and extremely violent fighting that would follow.

Right: Troops of the 12th SS 'Hitlerjugend' Division on the move to Normandy.

Opposite: Normandy before the landings.

The Germans now began sending reinforcements as quickly as possible. There were numerous low-quality infantry divisions in Brittany and elsewhere, but it was on the ten available elite mobile divisions that German chances in Normandy depended. Fortunately for the Allies, because of Hitler's illogical decision to split up control of the panzer divisions and spread them far and wide, getting them to Normandy swiftly was not going to be an easy task.

Their difficulties were also greatly exacerbated by the work of Allied air power before the invasion, which had strangled rail movement across France. The 12th SS-Panzer Division had been the first to reach Normandy, followed by the Panzer-Lehr, arguably the best-trained panzer division in the German armed forces. They had been due to reach the front on 7 June and with 12th SS and 21st Panzer, already in Normandy, were to make a coordinated counter-attack that day. Instead, during the 60-mile journey from Le Mans, the Panzer-Lehr were harried all the way; now the cat was out of the bag, and the Allied air forces could concentrate on supporting the invasion directly.

The long summer days also helped the Allies and hindered the Germans: the moment the Germans ventured on to roads in daylight, fighter-bombers swept down upon them. 'Sitting along the road were burnt-out trucks and bombed field kitchens and gun tractors,' wrote Captain Alexander Hartdegen, 'some still smouldering, the dead lying beside them. This horrible scene was the backdrop to our journey.'

Not until the evening of 8 June did the Panzer-Lehr enter the line, but they were unable to attack until the following day. By then the chance of a swift coordinated counter-attack was slipping away.

The broken arrival of panzer divisions meant a gap soon developed between the Panzer-Lehr and the 12th SS, so the newly arrived British 7th Armoured Division, the Desert Rats of North Africa fame, were hastily ordered forward to try to burst through and then swing round south of Caen. Early on 13 June, the vanguard reached the small town of Villers-Bocage, 12 miles south-west of the city. Unfortunately for them, leading elements of a heavy German Tiger tank battalion had also arrived near the town overnight and caught the British by surprise. Although over two days of fighting the Germans suffered heavily too, it had been the last chance for the British swiftly to out-manoeuvre the enemy around Caen.

On the other hand, though the Germans were only able to move freely during the hours of darkness, Allied mastery of the skies allowed the Americans, British and Canadians to bring across a constant stream of supplies. While this meant ever more men, tanks, guns, ammunition and other materiel, another priority was building airfields. Incredibly, the first was open for business behind Omaha Beach on the evening of 7 June. By the 15th, five had been built, using bulldozers, graders and rolls of pierced-steel plating, or 'PSP'. By 20 June, a staggering twelve airfields had been built. As a result, fighter-bombers no longer had to fly back to England to refuel and re-arm, and ensured they spent more time when airborne over the battlefield and, in turn, more time shooting up

Left: Pierced-steel plating allowed the beaches to be used as airfields.

Opposite: Tiger tanks at Villers-Bocage.

anything German that moved. General Marcks was killed by Allied fighter planes, while General Leo Geyr von Schweppenburg's Panzer Group West headquarters was also badly hit and so too were the panzer divisions heading to the front. The Allies were winning the battle of the build-up.

Then a huge storm swept in. A key part of the Allied build-up was the creation of two Mulberry harbours, each the size of Dover. These astonishing feats of engineering involved constructing huge, 200-feet-long concrete blocks to create a harbour wall, plus a floating jetty. Each harbour was towed, in parts, across the Channel then sunk in place, but between 19 and 21 June the ferocious storm knocked Allied plans awry. The American Mulberry was largely destroyed and, although the British harbour at Arromanches survived, some 800 landing ships were also lost.

This meant that by the third week in June Montgomery was missing an entire corps of three divisions that he had counted on having in place by then. Aware from decoded German radio messages that more panzer divisions were en route to the Caen sector and that the enemy was planning a concentrated counter-attack, Monty and his Second Army commander, General Miles Dempsey, knew they needed to launch a major attack themselves in an effort to chew up new panzer units as they arrived and before they could organize themselves into a coordinated assault.

Before the invasion, Monty had predicted being 50 miles inland by the end of June, yet the advance had been nothing like as far as that, and with German V-1 flying bombs now falling on the British capital, impatience over the perceived lack of Allied progress was quickly growing in London and Washington.

On 25 June General Dempsey launched an attack towards the Rauray Ridge, key high ground some 12 miles west of Caen. British armour and infantry clashed with the Panzer-Lehr and 12th SS. In one action, a single Sherman tank of the Sherwood Rangers Yeomanry knocked out one Tiger, two formidable Panthers and two Panzer IVs.

The attack on the Rauray Ridge was to draw the enemy away from the main assault, Operation EPSOM, just to the west of Caen, which was launched the next day, 26 June. Bad weather ensured there was not the usual air support, while the rapidly increasing number of panzer units reaching the area, combined with a shortfall of Allied troops as a result of the storm and continued poor weather, made a decisive British breakthrough unlikely.

Attacking meant infantry and tanks advancing over open fields behind a barrage of artillery, which invariably never gave quite the protection hoped for by those advancing.

Right: A Cromwell tank leads the advance during Operation EPSOM.

Opposite: A Sherman tank of the Sherwood Rangers Yeomanry.

Waiting for them were well-dug-in German troops with artillery, tanks, anti-tank guns, mortars and machine guns. Aware that Germans, without fail, always counter-attacked, British commanders were, in effect, using the infantry and armour as bait: the moment the Germans emerged from their foxholes and cover, down came the full force of Allied fire-power, from the immense weight of artillery but also from offshore naval guns and, when skies were clear, their air forces.

At the start of EPSOM, the British troops of VIII Corps pressed forward, making ground but 2 miles short of their first-day objective, the River Odon, which ran west–east across the axis of advance. German resistance was fierce and not until late on 27 June did British troops get across and start pushing up the far slopes towards a commanding rise known as Hill 112. The following day the high point was captured, but by then more and more panzer units were reaching the battle and being flung into the counter-attack. By 30 June, elements of no fewer than seven panzer divisions were desperately attacking the British salient, now dubbed the Scottish Corridor after the spearhead, the 15th Scottish Division.

The full weight of Allied fire-power now poured down on the German counter-attack, smashing these newly arrived units before they had had a chance to familiarize themselves with the ground or organize properly. Even so, fearing the British troops on Hill 112 were becoming isolated and in danger of being cut off, on 30 June General Dempsey ordered them to pull back to shorten the salient and ensure the front remained secure. EPSOM was halted and, while there had been no decisive British breakthrough, because the Germans had flung newly arriving panzer units straight into the fighting, their casualties had been so heavy that they had now lost their last chance of a fully coordinated large-scale counter-attack.

Meanwhile, in the western half of the battlefront, the Americans were simultaneously pushing south towards St-Lô and also north-west up the Cotentin Peninsula towards the port of Cherbourg. Here the ground was dominated by the *bocage*, a network of small fields fenced by dense hedgerows grown on raised banks. The bocage was every bit as difficult an area through which to fight as the wide-open farmland around Caen, but for different reasons. Here, it was hard to see what lay ahead, while tanks simply could not get over the raised banks and hedgerows. This left the infantry horribly exposed. Casualties among front-line units were appalling. The 4th Infantry Division, which had lost just a handful of men on D-Day, suffered 100 per cent front-line casualties within a fortnight as they battled up the Cotentin.

Rommel had urged Hitler to allow him to evacuate the Cotentin, but the Führer had refused. Instead, three entire German divisions were lost as Cherbourg finally fell on 27 June. Three days later, the last German troops in the peninsula were forced to surrender too.

For those back in London and Washington, looking at their maps, it still seemed as though the Allies were barely moving. On one level, this was true, but in this highly attritional phase of the battle the Allies were slowly but surely grinding down the Germans, chewing them up bit by bit and all the while growing in strength, while German troops and reinforcements continued to struggle to reach the front. In the same time that a million Allied troops reached Normandy, the increasingly battered German divisions received just over 10,000 replacements. Despite casualties, the US 4th Division was soon back at full strength, while equivalent German units continued to be flung into the fighting with ever-decreasing numbers of men.

Opposite: American troops endured heavy fighting in the bocage.

Much has been made of the Germans' tactical flair and their ability to organize themselves swiftly into *Kampfgruppen* – battle groups. Discipline was certainly good, especially in the panzer divisions, but they also had less to organize than the Allies. With no Luftwaffe to speak of, fewer guns, vehicles and no naval support, they could coordinate actions more quickly. There was a freedom of manoeuvre because of their materiel poverty.

In contrast, the Allies had to organize and coordinate infantry, tanks, engineers and artillery, along with offshore naval guns and air forces. It was logistically tricky to plan operations across three services while ensuring there was also the strength in depth to support a major offensive. These were the constraints of Allied materiel wealth, and a lack of tactical chutzpah was the result. None the less, this materiel-heavy, steady grinding down of the enemy was incredibly effective. The lines on the map might have been moving slowly, but this mattered less than those in London and Washington feared.

One of the issues was Montgomery's prediction before D-Day that the Allies would be 50 miles inland seventeen days after the landings. That had proved false, but was based on previous experiences against the Germans in North Africa, Sicily and southern Italy, when they had retreated in stages. Quite reasonably, the Allies had expected the Germans to do the same now, not least because it made little military sense for them to remain within firing distance of Allied naval guns.

Rommel had pleaded with Hitler to be allowed to retreat from Normandy, but Hitler insisted they hold firm and fight for every yard, and sacked General von Schweppenburg and Field Marshal Gerd von Rundstedt, the most senior German commander in the West.

The German commanders were exasperated by the Führer's interference – even those in the Waffen-SS. 'The constant use of piecemeal tactics enraged me,' wrote Kurt 'Panzer' Meyer, the commander of the 12th Waffen-SS Division. 'What had happened to the days of the big armoured offensives?' All they could do was fight ferociously and try to hold on for as long as possible. The brutal battle would continue.

None the less, they still held Caen and, after the British withdrawal, once more had Hill 112. This decision of General Dempsey's has often been criticized, but his salient was being attacked on both sides by elements of the 9th SS, 2nd SS, 10th SS, 1st SS and 2nd Panzer Divisions, and the risk of those troops at the front of the British thrust becoming isolated and surrounded had been too great. Now,

Left:
Fierce fighting on Hill 112.

Opposite:
American troops battling to secure Hill 192 near St-Lô.

though, with the front line secure and the enemy blunted, it was time for the British to swing back the battering ram and attack again.

With Cherbourg and the Cotentin Peninsula now in Allied hands, the Americans began pushing south on a broad front towards the town of St-Lô, but found it every bit as hard to make ground as the British and Canadians did around Caen. The Germans had flooded the low ground, making large areas impassable, while they tenaciously held on to the ridge line to the north of Caen. The dense network of small hedgerow-lined fields and winding sunken lanes was ideal for defence. The Americans had to prise each field from the enemy one by one. This would have been easier had Sherman tanks been able to burst through the bocage and blast enemy positions with their main gun and machine guns, and with the infantry operating first behind them and then mopping up. However, the tanks simply could not climb over the high mounds at the base of the hedgerows, which meant the infantry had to operate alone and were being decimated as a result.

On the ridge to the north-east of St-Lô repeated attacks by the Americans could not find a way through. An important and particularly troublesome feature was Hill 192, near the village of St-Georges-d'Elle, which had commanding views all the way back to the coast and which was covered by a patchwork of dense hedges and lanes. It had first been attacked on 11 June, but the Americans had failed to capture it. They had tried again, but by the beginning of July it was still in German hands and the men on both sides had dug in as artillery and mortar shells rained down and snipers picked off anyone who showed their head above the parapet.

A major assault on Caen, Operation CHARNWOOD, was launched on the night of 7 July when 467 heavy bombers flew over and pummelled the northern edge of the city in an effort to hammer German lanes and pave the way for the armour and infantry attack that would follow. Many bombs struck the city, which had already been badly hit, and made Allied progress through the town more difficult because of the rubble. Bitter fighting between the Canadians and the 12th SS also took place around the airfield. None the less, by 9 July British and Canadian troops had finally taken the city.

By this time, the 12th SS were so badly mauled after a month of fighting that they had been all but destroyed. 'They had gone to war weeks before with fresh, blooming faces,' noted their commander, Kurt Meyer, as he watched them pull out of Caen. 'At this point, camouflaged, muddy steel helmets cast shade on emaciated faces whose eyes had, all too often, looked into another world. The men presented a picture of deep human misery.'

Near St-Lô, the Panzer-Lehr had been moved to face the Americans and immediately launched an attack on 9 July on instructions from higher up the chain of command. Already under strength, and without any time to prepare, they hit a wall of American fire and suffered further terrible casualties. In one panzer battalion not a single junior officer remained. After this, the Panzer-Lehr went on to the defensive, its tanks being used as anti-tank guns and crews not daring to move by day. 'In general,' wrote Major Helmut Ritgen, 'we lived in the ground like foxes.' Still, though, the lines on the map seemed to be barely moving for the Allies. Impatience at the top was mounting.

While British troops were flung at Hill 112 once more, General Dempsey began planning a new major attack to clear the Bourgébus Ridge to the south-east of Caen and, he hoped, to shatter

German resistance and finally break out of Normandy. At the same time, General Omar Bradley, the US First Army commander, was also making plans for a major attack from the north-west of St-Lô. Both Eisenhower and his deputy, Air Chief Marshal Sir Arthur Tedder, had high hopes for Operation GOODWOOD, as Dempsey's new assault was to be called, but Montgomery had more realistic expectations. He did not, however, share his doubts for a breakthrough with Eisenhower or Tedder because he wanted the full support of the heavy bombers before the attack was launched and suspected this might not be granted for a lesser operation.

Because infantry casualties in British Second Army had been high so far, Dempsey chose to attack with his three armoured divisions, a deviation from the prescribed tactics. GOODWOOD was launched on 18 July. The bombers caused huge damage, upturning not only Tiger and Panther tanks but even the newly arrived 76-ton King Tigers, and the British armour, following on, initially made headway. By the afternoon, however, progress was slowing. In the end, GOODWOOD achieved exactly what Montgomery had predicted: the British had advanced 7 miles and captured the Bourgébus Ridge, but there had been no decisive breakthrough. Some 493 tanks had suffered battle damage, but because of the incredible system of battlefield maintenance and the huge standardization of parts for Allied equipment, within twenty-four hours a staggering 218 were back in action and in forty-eight hours a further 62.

What's more, GOODWOOD had ensured seven of the ten German mobile divisions had remained rooted in the British and Canadian sector.

This was good news for the second major Allied offensive, Operation COBRA, soon to be launched by the Americans. That troublesome high point, Hill 192, was finally captured on 12 July and thereafter the Americans slowly but surely pushed the Germans back. St-Lô was taken at long last on 19 July.

Like Montgomery, Bradley also wanted to use heavy bombers to soften up the enemy before his attack, but together with the American air commanders chose a different approach. His bomber force would drop a massive 72,000 smaller 100-pound bombs over a clearly defined area 3.5 miles wide and 1.5 miles deep. These would pulverize any German troops without churning up the ground so badly that it would be impassable to the attackers who followed. A device for uprooting hedgerows – a giant fork that protruded low on the front of a Sherman tank – had also been trialled and some 60 per cent of First Army's tanks had been swiftly equipped with these 'rhinos'. A huge force of more than 2,000 tanks and tank destroyers was amassed, along with 1,000 artillery pieces. It was an immense concentration of force – more than for any other single operation in Normandy so far.

Bad weather scuppered the planned launch of COBRA on 24 July, but the next day the weather was better and, on cue, the bombers arrived and began blitzing the German positions. Smoke drifting back caused some to drop their bombs wide and on to the waiting American troops. More than 100 men were killed and nearly 500 wounded.

For the Germans, the bombing was horrific. Two-thirds of what was left of the Panzer-Lehr were destroyed and a German paratrooper regiment effectively annihilated.

Despite this, initially the American infantry struggled to make much headway. The armour was then thrown in with orders to carry the infantry and just keep driving forward. On 26 July, the dam

Opposite: American armoured troops during the breakout after COBRA.

finally burst as the Germans could hold out no longer. Suddenly the enemy was in full retreat, and in daylight too. New VHF radios had been put in the lead tank of each armoured column and in the fighter planes above so that those in the air and on the ground could communicate. This Armoured Column Cover quickly proved a great success, as aircraft were able to warn troops on the ground of German troop movements up ahead, as well as hitting targets and paving the way for an increasingly rapid advance.

Meanwhile, in the centre of the Allied line, Dempsey was launching his latest attack after the capture of Hill 112. With his units brought back up to strength after GOODWOOD, on 30 July he attacked southwards from Caumont with two thrusts, VIII Corps on the right and XXX Corps on the left. BLUECOAT, as the operation was named, was a great success, with VIII Corps, especially, showing a new level of tactical verve and flexibility and pushing the Germans back a further 15 miles. Once again, the enemy had desperately tried to stem the flow and so had sent yet more panzer and infantry divisions to meet the British assault.

At the same time, Allied fighter-bombers were attacking the retreating Germans following COBRA. Vast columns were smashed and left burning, while American armoured columns, hot on their tails, harried them. Near the village of St-Denis-le-Gast, a German column was trapped nose-to-tail for 3 miles. Some 100 tanks, 250 vehicles and horse-drawn wagons were left in flames.

It was now time for General George S. Patton's Third Army to enter the battle. His men had been building up in Normandy and were activated as Bradley took command of the new US 12th Army Group. With a key bridge that crossed into Brittany captured intact on 30 July, Patton ordered his men to press on south and west with all speed, while the American First Army, still flush with the success of COBRA, turned eastwards. These were frenetic days, the Allied breakout from the battle of attrition in full flow.

By 1 August, it was blindingly obvious to all the senior German commanders in Normandy that the battle was lost. Rommel had been badly wounded in an air attack back on 17 July, throwing the German command into further disarray. Field Marshal Günther von Kluge, now in overall command in the West, accepted he needed to pull his forces back and across the River Seine with all speed or face losing both Seventh Army and what remained of his panzer forces, now renamed the Fifth Panzer Army.

Hitler, however, refused to countenance such a move. On 20 July the Führer had narrowly avoided an assassination attempt and since then his paranoia had grown. He now mistrusted his generals even more and his insistence on micro-managing had worsened. Then came the bombshell. On 2 August, a directive arrived from Hitler ordering von Kluge to counter-attack towards Avranches on the south-western Normandy coast. An armoured force of nine panzer divisions was to be hastily assembled and, supported by a thousand fighter planes, was to strike west and split the Americans in two. It was to be called Operation LÜTTICH.

Meanwhile, Patton's forces were sweeping through Brittany, capturing much of the peninsula and effectively besieging the ports. Other units were pushing on south and eastwards in a wide thrust. With First Army still pressing east to the north and the British and Canadians preparing to make a further strike south from Caen, the Germans were suddenly in danger of being completely encircled.

Despite this rapidly worsening situation, Hitler still insisted on launching LÜTTICH. Von Kluge had assembled only four panzer divisions, not nine, and only one of them, the newly arrived 116th Panzer Division, was in good shape. However, its commander thought the plan was so bad he deliberately ensured they were not ready in time. Even worse, British cryptanalysts had decoded enemy radio traffic and so Bradley learned the day before that a German attack towards Avranches was being planned.

Throughout the Normandy battle, the moment German troops assaulted they tended to be absolutely hammered as the full weight of Allied fire-power rained down on them, and this was the case with LÜTTICH when it was finally launched in the early hours of 7 August. Although the town of Mortain was quickly overrun by the Germans, a key hill was not. Here a battalion of the US 30th Division clung on and could not be budged.

The German attack was soon running out of steam. The thousand Luftwaffe fighter planes were nowhere to be seen – a few hundred had attempted to take off from airfields near Paris but had been swiftly pounced upon by Allied fighters. Everywhere, the German advance was faltering under the weight of aggressive counter-attacks by the Americans and continued pummelling from the air.

One of the reasons LÜTTICH ended up being so half-hearted was that one German division after another had been turned north to face the advancing British and Canadians. The Canadians launched TOTALIZE on the night of 7 August, heading south from Caen directly towards the

key town of Falaise. The plan was to strike south by night, wait for the heavy bombers to pound German positions, then advance again and wait for the bombers to come over a second time the following day.

As it happened, the advance south was so successful it might have been better to have cancelled the second wave of bombers but, such were the logistical complications of coordinating these operations, this was not possible. Instead, the Canadian and British ground troops were left twiddling their thumbs while they waited, allowing the beleaguered 12th SS time to organize some kind of defence. That afternoon Kurt Meyer threw his last tanks into the battle and they were, inevitably, hit hard. Michael Wittmann, one of the most celebrated and decorated panzer 'aces' in the Waffen-SS, was among those killed.

Meanwhile, the Allies were now preparing to launch a second amphibious invasion of France, this time in the south across the Mediterranean. There had been much debate over another such operation, not least because many of the forces involved had to be withdrawn from Italy at a

Left: During Operation LÜTTICH the German armour faced destruction from the air.

Opposite: The last throw of the dice in Normandy.

moment when there had been an opportunity to exploit the success of the fall of Rome back on 4 June. The debate had continued, but the landings were eventually given the go-ahead in July, as it was felt the additional ports of southern France would help with the swift conquest of the whole country. In addition, General de Gaulle of the Free French was very keen to see French forces take part in the liberation.

Operation DRAGOON, the Allied invasion of southern France, took place on 15 August, with a mixed US and French force commanded by General Alexander Patch. Resistance was limited and the landings were a success, costing the Allies fewer than 500 casualties and opening up vital port facilities. German attempts at counter-attacking also floundered thanks to the sabotage efforts of the French Resistance crippling enemy lines of communication.

Back in Normandy, the net was closing in around the Germans as American forces from the south and west, and the British and Canadians from the north and centre – now bolstered by a Polish armoured division – pressed towards them. On 16 August, Falaise was captured and the remaining German troops were forced to flee down narrow country lanes before the neck of the so-called Falaise Pocket closed for good. In the valley of the River Dives, the crossing points became jammed with tanks, half-tracks, lorries and horse-drawn wagons desperately trying to escape the fighter-bombers and Allied artillery. Few succeeded. The scenes of carnage were appalling. One of the most beautiful parts of northern France had been turned into the Corridor of Death.

American, Canadian and Polish troops met on 19 August. In all, the Normandy battle had lasted seventy-seven days, so although the pre-invasion estimates had not been realized, overall the campaign was over thirteen days earlier than Montgomery had predicted. At its end, two entire German armies had been destroyed – only some 50,000 escaped, along with barely two dozen armoured fighting vehicles out of the 2,500 that had been sent to Normandy. It had been a brutal battle in which daily casualty rates had been, on average, worse than for the Somme, Verdun and Passchendaele in the First World War. Normandy was, though, by any reckoning, a stunning Allied victory.

Opposite: For German forces trapped in the Falaise Pocket there was no escape from the Allied fighter-bombers that attacked round the clock.

10: THE WAR IN BURMA

Early on Sunday morning, 6 February 1944, Brigadier Geoffrey Evans had just reached his new post: 9th Brigade headquarters in the Arakan in north-west Burma. He was to be serving under Major-General Frank Messervy, the fearless commander of 7th Indian Division, which was in turn part of Fourteenth Army. Part of a three-division front, strung out between dense jungle and hills, they were separated from the neighbouring 5th Division by a long ridge of peaks known as the Mayu Range. A single narrow track, the Ngakyedauk Pass, had only just been completed, roughly hacked out across this mountain chain via a number of treacherous hairpin bends. This was the only link to the western coastal part of the Arakan.

No sooner had Evans reached his new command, however, than he received a horrifying signal. 'Early this morning,' he was told, 'the Japs overran Frank Messervy's headquarters at Laung Chaung. Nobody knows whether he or anybody else got away.' Laung Chaung was to the north; the Japanese were supposed to be to the south. It was vital, Evans was told, that the division's administrative area – a clearing in the jungle a mile or so to the north of 9th Brigade HQ, and the division's supply dump – be saved.

Evans neither knew where the administrative area was, nor had a clear picture of how his new brigade was disposed, but with map in hand and the rain pouring down, he set off. The situation could hardly have been worse. They were clearly surrounded, cut off, and in one of the most inhospitable places to fight in the world. And he had only a handful of men to defeat thousands of fanatical Japanese – an enemy they had yet to beat in battle. The prospects did not look good.

So far, the Burma campaign had been one humiliation after another for the British. Ignominiously pushed out in the first half of 1942, they had vowed to retake the country, and so the much-strengthened Eastern Army had thrust southwards into the Arakan at the end of that year. Barely had they crossed the border, however, than they came up against strong enemy defences, already dug into the hills. Despite throwing ever more infantry into the line, Lieutenant-General Noel Irwin's men had got nowhere, unable to master the challenges of the jungle or work out ways of breaking down the networks of Japanese tunnels, trenches and foxholes.

An attempt had been made to fight the Japanese on their own terms by sending a column of some 3,000 men under Major-General Orde Wingate into north-east Burma to attack Japanese supply lines. The Chindit Expedition, as it was known, had achieved little, suffered a lot of casualties and sucked up a lot of much-needed resources. In the Arakan, despite repeated attempts, General Irwin's men had made no progress at all, while in the skies the increasingly battered and obsolescent

Opposite:
Burma was one of
the most remote
and inhospitable
places in the
world in which
to fight.

Hurricane fighter planes had also been unable to win mastery from the Oscars of the Imperial Japanese Army Air Force.

The monsoon had arrived in May and the fighting had stopped. The Japanese in Burma had been content to go on the defensive, as had the British. General Irwin had been sacked, along with a number of other senior British commanders. The last man standing was Lieutenant-General Bill Slim, who by the beginning of October 1944 was Acting Eastern Army Commander – an army as low on morale as it was on ideas about how to beat a fanatical and highly disciplined enemy in this terrible jungle terrain.

Slim was holed up at the former viceroy's lodge at Barrackpore. A large and ornate villa lying on the banks of the Hooghly River, it was hot, stultifying, and surrounded by the dense, creeping suburbs of northern Calcutta.

Despite these conditions, Slim used the time to try to work out a plan for transforming British fortunes in Burma and swiftly isolated four major challenges. The first was one of logistics in this inhospitable part of the world: the heat, the phenomenal amount of rain, the almost total lack of modern infrastructure along the Burma front, the distances involved and the terrain all conspired against the modern, mechanized army.

The second was to train this army to a level where they could effectively take on the Japanese – no easy task for a force made up mostly of conscripts and volunteers drawn from a hugely religious and ethnic diversity. The third was to substantially improve the health of the army, which was struggling in an area rife with malaria, dysentery and a host of other horrible diseases. And the fourth was dramatically to improve the army's disastrously low morale and rebuild a sense of belief and confidence.

Which was the toughest challenge was hard to say. Each was big enough, but collectively the task facing Slim and British fortunes in the area was Herculean.

The diversity of Eastern Army was enormous. There were Brits, Punjabis, Kashmiris, Pathans, Gurkhas from Nepal, as well as Sikhs, Hindus and Muslims. These required as many as thirty different ration scales each day – a huge amount of food to find, and especially so along an 800-mile front with only a handful of roads, two railway gauges and a number of rivers to cross.

The British and American war chiefs also recognized that South-East Asia urgently required both greater supplies and a change at the top with the introduction of a Supreme Allied Commander South East Asia in line with other Allied commands. The man they chose was a 43-year-old cousin of King George VI, Admiral Lord Louis Mountbatten.

Mountbatten's appointment raised eyebrows to say the very least, but he was dashing, glamorous, well connected, and the polar opposite of the archetypal moustachioed, silver-haired British Indian Army general. Just the man, in fact, to reassure the Americans and to bring a dose of much-needed energy.

Slim and Mountbatten first met on 22 October 1943, soon after the new Supreme Commander's arrival in South-East Asia. Mountbatten immediately liked the sound of what Slim was telling him and, against all protocol, there and then appointed him as permanent army commander with a mandate to transform his new command and the promise of full backing. In a signal of new intent, Slim also asked whether the name of his army might be changed. Mountbatten agreed. Eastern Army became Fourteenth Army. A new era had dawned and with it, they hoped, a change in Allied fortunes.

Slim immediately set to work on the solutions. Because of the lack of stone, kilns were set up and a brick road built from southern Bengal into the Arakan. Chinese were brought in to establish duck farms near the Burma front south of Imphal in the north-east, while goats, sheep and chickens were also reared locally where possible. Vast areas were turned over to the production of vegetables, while more dehydrated food was supplied from India. Further roads, like the Ngakyedauk Pass, were hastily constructed by army engineers.

Slim also quickly set about resolving the dire number of casualties lost to sickness. So far in 1943, 120 men had been pulled out of the line through illness for every one suffering combat wounds. Malaria had struck 84 per cent of those in Eastern Army per year. Dysentery also ravaged most men at some point. The answer was no longer to send them back to hospitals far from the front but to establish new Malaria Forward Treatment Units – tented hospitals just behind the front line. Those suffering

would reach these within 24 hours rather than disappearing to Calcutta and elsewhere. Once better, they would be sent straight back to the front. What had before meant months out of the line could now be resolved in a couple of weeks. Taking malaria tablets also became compulsory, as did wearing long trousers and shirts with the sleeves rolled down.

Training was also much improved. Everyone was to be instructed in jungle-warfare techniques – whether infantry or service corps, such as cooks and drivers. They were taught to use the jungle to their advantage and not to fear it.

Slim's biggest anxiety, however, was that of low morale. Fear of the Japanese soldier was high. He had become a superman – vicious, almost inhuman, maliciously cruel and savage. Tales of captured British soldiers being used for bayonet practice or beheaded were rampant. Compounding the problem was a feeling of not being appreciated back home. They had become the 'Forgotten Army'.

Slim knew he had to reverse this corrosive malaise. The improvements in training, supplies

Left: The Eastern Army was trained to use the jungle to its advantage.

Opposite: Bill Slim with Admiral Lord Louis Mountbatten, Supreme Allied Commander South-East Asia.

and food played a big part, but so too did regular visits by both him and Mountbatten. A message of growing confidence and self-belief was delivered by them to each and every man in person.

Air power was also critical. Back in 1942, Lieutenant-General Harold Alexander, who had safely led the British out of Burma, had identified a way to defeat the Japanese. The enemy moved so fast by travelling light and resupplying using captured materiel. The answer was to stand firm, come what may, and deny the Japanese this bounty. With supplies dropped from the air, stubbornly holding ground ought to be possible, but to do that, control of the skies was needed. The Japanese Army Air Force had to be neutralized first.

The trouble was, British Hurricanes were evenly matched against Japanese Oscars and not fast enough to catch enemy reconnaissance planes known as Dinahs. The answer was to send over precious Spitfires, far superior in speed and rate of climb. To do so from Britain was a further enormous logistical challenge, but in September 1943 the first of these precious aircraft arrived and more soon followed.

Each newly equipped squadron was pulled out of the line and given intensive further fighter training at Amarda Road, south of Calcutta, while new Wireless Observer Units were established on the ground at 20-mile intervals all along the Arakan border and into the Chin Hills, with radio links to fighter control. Enemy aircraft could now be intercepted, and by superior aircraft too.

The rewards were not long in coming. Three Dinahs were shot down in November, as well as a growing number of Oscars. Then, on New Year's Eve 1943, the fighter pilots of 136 'Woodpecker' Squadron, in their Spitfires, attacked twelve enemy bombers and nine fighters, destroying or badly damaging every one for the loss of no pilots of their own. In the air, at any rate, the British had at long last got the better of the Japanese.

While the British were reorganizing their command structures, building up strength and training, the Japanese were also making ready for offensive operations of their own. And ever since the end of the last Arakan battle and the arrival of the monsoon, the man beating the loudest drum for action had been the commander of Japanese Fifteenth Army, General Renya Mutaguchi.

A tough, highly experienced but arrogant general, Mutaguchi aimed to strike deep into north-east India through the Plain of Imphal, then, having captured the large stockpiles of British supplies, press on to Dimapur. He was convinced that if they could successfully take Imphal and then Dimapur, the gates to India would be open; Dimapur was not only a major British railhead, it was also the key to unlocking the mighty Brahmaputra Valley, which was wide and open and very hard to defend.

Elsewhere in the Pacific, the Japanese were losing ground, but Mutaguchi hoped that such a drive into British India would prompt an uprising and the end of the British Raj: the jewel in the British Empire's crown would become the jewel of Imperial Japan instead. At the same time, a strike into Assam would capture airfields from where supplies were being flown over the Himalayas and into China to support General Chiang Kai-shek's Chinese Nationalists. Without those supplies, the Chinese would be finished and Japan could then turn the tide of the war.

Further up the chain of command, however, there was concern that Mutaguchi's vision was far too ambitious. Instead, Imperial General Headquarters in Tokyo sanctioned an offensive into

Opposite: The arrival of Spitfires in 1943 changed the balance of power in the air.

India to capture the key British town of Imphal, but the operation was to be limited. Its aim was to prevent the British from ever re-entering Burma rather than to conquer India.

Operation U-GO, an attack into India towards Imphal, was given the go-ahead on New Year's Eve, but for Mutaguchi's attack to succeed General Masakazu Kawabe, commander of Japan's Burma Area Army, recognized that an attack in the Arakan was needed as well in order to draw British troops away from the central part of the front around Imphal.

With Operation HA-GO, General Kawabe intended to mount a lightning strike using 55 Infantry Group, part of Twenty-Eighth Army, and commanded by Lieutenant-General Shozo Sakurai. Like Mutaguchi, Sakurai had little respect for the British. 'It's child's play,' he said, 'to smash the enemy in the Mayu Peninsula.'

First, the British 7th Division, in the middle of the line, would be surrounded, isolated and annihilated. Then they would do the same to the 5th Indian Division on the western coast of the peninsula, leaving the third British division, the 81st West African, cut off and easy prey. The British would need reinforcements and these would have to come from the centre of the front. That, in turn, would fatally weaken the British position at Imphal.

The first signs that the Japanese were on the move in the Arakan came on the night of Friday, 4 February 1944, when patrols heard and spotted Japanese columns moving forward along the Kalapanzin River to the east of the 7th Indian Division. By the afternoon of the 5th, General Frank Messervy was told by Captain Anthony Irwin, commander of an organization of local Muslim irregulars called 'V Force', that the Japanese had already reached Taung Bazaar, far to the rear.

'Don't talk such bloody nonsense, Anthony,' Messervy replied. But it was true. For all Slim's preparations, the British had been caught completely by surprise. Disaster beckoned.

On reaching the administrative region of 7th Division on the morning of 6 February, Brigadier Geoffrey Evans ordered the area to be hastily turned into a defensive stronghold, swiftly renamed the Admin Box. It was too late to bring in any reinforcements. The other two brigades of the 7th Division, to the east and to the south, were told to stay put and not give a yard. Within the Box, two squadrons of Lee tanks of the 25th Dragoons had joined the division in the previous days, having successfully made the lethal crossing over the Ngakyedauk Pass at night and without discovery by the enemy. These 30-ton beasts were equipped with a main 75mm gun, as well as a smaller 37mm and a machine gun, and that they were there at all was entirely down to General Messervy, who had successfully argued that such tanks could operate in this terrain, though many others had scoffed at the notion. Having headed north to try to save division HQ, they arrived back that afternoon, as did General Messervy himself and a number of his staff. Attacked and caught up in hand-to-hand fighting, they had managed to kill several of the enemy and then give them the slip.

Also arriving was 2nd Battalion, West Yorkshire Regiment, while already there were the brigade signals and a number of service troops, muleteer, drivers, cooks, administrative and medical staff. It was not a lot, and the entire position, featuring two lonely tree-covered hills amidst an open expanse some three-quarters of a mile square and surrounded by dense jungle-clad hills, was vulnerable to say the least.

'Your job,' Brigadier Evans told his men in the Box, 'is to stay put and keep the Japanese out.'

Opposite: The Japanese 55 Infantry Group advance through the Arakan.

The Japanese first attacked the Admin Box that night, Sunday, 6 February, with tracer, screams and firing suddenly ripping apart the inky dark. They made no progress at all, but the following day cut off the Ngakyedauk Pass and then, once night fell, attacked again. This time, they caught the Medical Dressing Station, killing doctors and staff and dragging the wounded into the jungle, the screams of their victims heard by the rest of the defenders. Evans's orders – supported by Messervy – were for no man to leave his position at night under any circumstances. They were all to hold their ground.

Shocked though the defenders were, the attack on the MDS only stiffened their resolve. The following night, when the Japanese attacked yet again, the enemy were cut to pieces. In fact, night after night, the Japanese attacks failed. Several times, they advanced down the same *chaung* – dried river bed – and were slaughtered. One of the hills – Ammunition Hill – was attacked, but the tanks of the 25th Dragoons blasted the trees with their main guns and sprayed the area with machine-gun fire.

Because of the growing success of the RAF in the air, Dakotas were able to drop supplies on the beleaguered division on 8 February and into the Admin Box three days later, on the 11th. Another night, the Japanese charged across the open dried paddy fields from the north, only to be met by the machine guns of the 25th Dragoons and stopped in their tracks. The following morning, the plans for HA-GO were taken from the body of a dead officer.

The Admin Box had become a terrible place. Lying where they had fallen were hundreds of Japanese dead, and in the heat they soon began to rot. Vultures circled, while the stench became unbearable.

The defenders were suffering too – casualties were mounting with the relentless shelling by day and enemy infantry attacks by night. By 14 February there were some 400 defenders in the new 'Hospital Nullah' established after the destruction of the MDS. Yet despite these losses and despite mounting exhaustion, they were still holding on, as were the isolated battalions to the east and south, helped by the arrival of more supplies by air.

With every passing day, however, the enemy attacks were lessening as they increasingly ran short of men, ammunition and food. Sakurai's men were starving. What's more, British reinforcements were fighting their way south. On 16 February, Major Charles Ferguson Hoey, a Canadian-born company commander in the 1st Lincolns, won a posthumous VC while leading the charge against a Japanese strongpoint on Hill 315, overlooking the Box. The attack failed to take the position but the enemy were further weakened there.

By day, meanwhile, the defenders of the Box were aggressively patrolling further and further, supported by the tanks of the 25th Dragoons. On 22 February, the Ngakyedauk Pass was reopened and the wounded evacuated, while two nights later the Japanese finally pulled back, although not until 25 February was Hill 315 retaken. The Battle of the Admin Box was finally over.

Counter-attacking, the British pushed the Japanese back further. It was the first time the British had inflicted a defeat on the Japanese and, although there had been 3,506 casualties in the fighting, only a smaller number had been actually killed. The Japanese, by contrast, left 5,000 dead in and around the Admin Box and lost a further 2,000 in the fighting that followed.

Opposite: RAF success meant troops could be resupplied from the air.

The Japanese Operation HA-GO had been the first punch of a two-fisted attack designed to draw British troops to the Arakan, but despite its failure, U-GO, the invasion of India towards Imphal, was still to go ahead, as Slim's intelligence was well aware. And despite orders for a limited operation, Mutaguchi still planned to strike not only towards Imphal but further north towards Dimapur too. A fanatic, he hated the British and believed fate had handed him the chance to lead the Japanese to victory in India. Assam would be conquered, Bengal would revolt against the British Raj, then so too would the rest of the country. Britain would be forced to withdraw, humbled and humiliated. America might then make terms and Japan would win its war. He fervently believed this was his destiny: to deliver victory to the Emperor and his country.

General Slim knew the Japanese attack was coming, but not the scale or ambition of Mutaguchi's plans. That Imphal was the prime objective, though, was clear and, now familiar with his enemy, Slim knew they were expecting the British to act the way they always had – and retreat. He realized that if he did exactly that, the Japanese would think the British were the ineffective, flighty, morale-crushed force they had always been. So he planned not a withdrawal but a fighting retreat, in which the Japanese divisions would be increasingly ground down and degraded. It was certainly a bold plan, but the Admin Box had shown that his men were of a different calibre than they had been a year before. He believed they were now equal to the challenge.

They were far better led too. Slim had personally chosen all his senior commanders. Men like Generals Stopford, Messervy, Gracey, Cowan, Briggs and Roberts were tough, tactically astute, beloved by their men and by now very experienced. Slim hoped that by the time his divisions had fallen back to Imphal, the Japanese would already have suffered badly. The enemy's lines of supply would be woefully stretched, while Fourteenth Army's would be shortened. After two years' fighting the Japanese, Slim also knew they were unlikely to retreat in a hurry, so he intended to hold them at Imphal, grind them down further, then counter-attack. And annihilate them.

The challenges of operating in this inhospitable part of the world were such that only by an emphatic victory would Fourteenth Army have enough of a free hand to re-invade Burma successfully from the north. It was, though, unquestionably a high-risk strategy. If it failed, the whole of India, and possibly even the course of the entire war against Japan, could be at risk.

In fact, Slim's plan went awry almost from the outset, with the first of several near-disasters. Protecting Imphal was IV Corps under Lieutenant-General Geoffrey Scoones. His three divisions were all far apart: one to the south-east protecting the road from Burma across the Shenam Saddle Hills, another to the south covering the other route into Burma, the Tiddim Road, while a third was in reserve around Imphal itself.

Scoones and Slim had anticipated Mutaguchi's attack beginning on 15 March, but the southern thrust up the Tiddim Road began a whole week earlier. Men from the Japanese 33rd Division had already crossed the Manipur River and were moving north and to the west of the Tiddim Road to block the British retreat.

Left: Slim's strategy relied on shortening his own supply lines at the same time as stretching the enemy's.

Opposite: Major Charles Ferguson Hoey leads the attack against Hill 315.

Major-General David 'Punch' Cowan, the British 17th Division commander, swiftly realized what was happening, but Scoones discounted the intelligence of the Japanese outflanking moves. He knew it was essential they didn't withdraw too soon and so ordered Cowan to keep his men where they were. Fortunately for the fate of Imphal, Cowan ignored Scoones and ordered his men to start falling back. It was the right decision. He was the man on the spot, he trusted his own judgement and, by pulling his men back when he did, unquestionably not only saved his division, but averted disaster.

The Tiddim Road saw some extraordinary fighting – Japanese and British troops were interspersed along the road like a Neapolitan sandwich but, supported by the RAF, Cowan's men successfully fought their way back to Imphal, reaching the southern edge on 4 April and so badly mauling the Japanese 33rd Division that the enemy no longer had the strength to push on through to the city. It had been a close-run thing, but to the south, at any rate, Slim's strategy was working.

Elsewhere, however, other disasters loomed. To the south-east of Imphal ran the road from Burma over which the beaten British had retreated in May 1942. Now it was the axis of advance for the Japanese 15th Division under Major-General Tsunoru Yamamoto. Major-General Douglas Gracey's 20th Division had already prepared a series of defensive positions along the Shenam Saddle and here they made their stand.

Once again, though, the decision to withdraw was given very late and to only roughly prepared positions. The defence 20th Division put up was out of all proportion to what the Japanese had come to expect from British and Indian forces. Bitter fighting took place here – scenes of devastation likened to the battlefields of the Somme were the result.

However, while Gracey's men were successfully holding the Japanese onslaught along the Shenam Saddle, more enemy columns were bypassing them to the north, including Lieutenant-General Kotoku Sato's entire 31st Division.

Mutaguchi's men were now attacking from all around. Slim described the battle as being like the spokes of a wheel with Imphal the hub. By the beginning of April, Japanese forces were attacking down a number of these spokes – including, most worryingly, from the north. It was to the north of Imphal that the British had most of their supply bases as well as airfields – located there precisely because they were thought to be safest. Slim had intended to lure the Japanese towards Imphal, but had not meant them to get as close as they now were. To make matters worse, Sato's men were also heading towards Kohima, way to the north of Imphal (see map on page 324). If they managed to take this shallow saddle successfully and cut the road to Dimapur, catastrophe would loom.

The 50th Indian Parachute Division arrived at Sangshak to the south-east of Kohima in mid-March. They were commanded by Brigadier Maxwell Hope-Thompson, who, at just 31 years old, was the youngest brigadier in the Indian Army. He posted his Gurkha and Indian battalions around the area, intending to acclimatize and train his men further before they were posted to the front line. Little did he realize the front line was coming to him.

Opposite: 20th Division defensive positions along the Shenam Saddle.

The leading elements of the Japanese 58th Regiment, Sato's spearhead, clashed with C Company, 502nd Battalion, on 17 March. Surrounded, the Indians fought ferociously but were slaughtered almost to a man. During C Company's final charge, one of the officers even put a pistol to his head rather than be taken prisoner.

Hope-Thompson now knew he was facing a sizeable Japanese formation. Cut off, and with barely enough supplies and neither mines nor wire, both essential for strong defence, he decided to bring his men together to face the full fury of the Japanese attack. He chose the village of Sangshak to make his stand.

The first major assault on the position came on the evening of 22 March. The Japanese attack was launched as the sun was setting and straight at the dug-in Gurkhas. It was a massacre. One observer said it was like an optical illusion, with the Japanese tumbling as they all fell. Ninety men out of 120 in the company were killed within minutes.

From then on, the Japanese shelled and mortared the defenders by day and made increasing numbers of attacks by night. Both sides were soon suffering debilitating casualties, but yet again, on the body of one Japanese officer, the complete enemy plans were found. And they showed that the main target for Sato's 31st Division was Kohima.

Incredibly, the brigade's intelligence officer managed to slip through the Japanese positions and walk all the way back to Imphal, where he handed over this golden piece of information. Meanwhile, for four days and four nights, the defenders grimly hung on.

Finally, on 26 March, after being sent a clear signal over the radio to withdraw, Hope-Thompson ordered those still standing to try to break out. At around 11 p.m., having fired the last of their mortar and artillery shells, they made a dash for it – and were entirely successful. The fighting had cost them dearly, but for all their sacrifice Sangshak had had far-reaching and decisive consequences.

Meanwhile, Slim landed at Imphal on 29 March to confer with Scoones and his senior commanders. Neither had expected the Japanese to move so quickly or on such a broad front and, since the plans captured at Sangshak had not yet reached them – although they were aware there was a major enemy force to the north – they were unsure whether the enemy was heading for the tiny hill village of Kohima or the main railhead and supply base of Dimapur.

A further urgent threat also had to be faced, as forces from the Japanese 15th Division were fast approaching Imphal from the north-east and were now just a few miles from the airfield at Kangla. Yet it was in this moment of crisis that the Allies' superior air power was about to become a decisive factor. Fleets of transport planes could, in theory, move entire brigades, and even divisions, up to the Imphal front. The trouble was, these were mostly American and were being used to fly 'the Hump' – the route over the Himalayas into China to supply Chiang Kai-shek's forces.

Fortunately, the very strong working relationship between Mountbatten and Slim had led to mutual trust. Consequently, when Slim asked

Right: Bill Slim confers with IV Corps Commander Lieutenant-General Geoffrey Scoones.

Opposite: The 50th Indian Parachute Division's last stand at Sangshak.

for an urgent diversion of US transport aircraft to support Fourteenth Army, Mountbatten didn't hesitate, even though he should have asked permission from the US Chiefs of Staff. But he didn't. He knew he had to make a decision right now, and had the courage of his convictions to do so. Flight after flight landed at Imphal Main, bringing in the battle-hardened 5th Indian Division from the Arakan. It was the first time ever a division had been brought into battle by air alone – and they arrived in the nick of time.

Japanese troops were already on the Nungshigum Ridge to the north of Imphal when the newly arrived 5th Division first clashed with them. From Nungshigum, Imphal was in sight, and from this dominating position the enemy could launch an assault on the town. Somehow, some way, the new arrivals in 5th Division had to clear the enemy from this vitally important ridge.

On 13 April, dive-bombers and Hurri-bombers were sent to bombard the Japanese, then Indian infantry supported by Lee tanks attacked. Every one of the infantry and tank officers was killed or wounded, so it was left to the NCOs, the sergeant-majors, to continue the drive forward. And they did win the day. As they swept over the ridge, they found the bodies of over 250 dead Japanese.

The US transport fleet now remained in support of Fourteenth Army until the end of the battle, bringing in even more troops, including XXXIII Corps, to Dimapur under the command of Lieutenant-General Montagu Stopford. But while the airfield at Kangla was being saved by the heroics of 5th Division, by this time a further major battle had developed at Kohima, to the north. It was to be the fourth – and final – potential disaster to befall Fourteenth Army.

And the most serious threat of them all.

In the spring of 1944, Kohima was home to a small village of local Naga tribesmen and a handful of British buildings, not least the bungalow and tennis court of Charles Pawsey, the Deputy Commissioner for Nagaland, on Kohima Ridge. Lying on a low saddle amongst the hills, this lonely outpost between Dimapur and Imphal was defended by just 2,500 men, of whom 1,000 were non-combatants. And Sato's division was heading straight for them.

If Kohima fell quickly, General Mutaguchi intended to order Sato to drive straight on to Dimapur, which at the end of March was barely defended at all. General Montagu Stopford's XXXIII Corps was being hurried there, but until the divisions that were being flown in arrived in strength he had insufficient forces with which to defend both Dimapur and Kohima at once.

In fact, there was just 161st Brigade at Kohima, and Stopford worried that if the outpost were surrounded and defeated before the newly arriving 2nd Division reached this corner of the front, then there would be nothing with which to defend Dimapur. It was a dilemma, but Stopford feared the threat to Dimapur, lying clear of the hills and with its railhead and supply dumps, was the more serious and so ordered 161st Brigade to fall back. Slim supported his decision.

Although a logical course of action, it was the wrong one because 2nd Division was reaching Dimapur and now Kohima was terribly exposed. 'I have spent some uncomfortable hours at the beginning of battles,' Slim admitted, 'but few more anxious than those of the Kohima battle.' On 3 April, the decision was reversed and 161st Brigade turned back to Kohima. Two days later, 5 April, they had reached it, by which time some 13,000 Japanese troops were bearing down on Kohima Ridge.

Sangshak had given the defenders a crucial lifeline, however: because of the paratroopers' stand there,

General Sato's men had reached Kohima a week later than planned. The question now was whether the Royal West Kents and Assams – the two battalions of 161st Brigade at Kohima – could hold out against a force ten times bigger until reinforcements reached them.

Somehow, these few defenders doggedly managed to hold on to Garrison Hill. The fighting was bitter, bloody and at close quarter. It was also witness to a number of acts of breathtaking bravery, not least that by Lance-Corporal Jack Harman.

The son of the millionaire owner of Lundy Island off the north Devon coast, Harman had preferred the ranks to a commission. Eccentric and an unlikely soldier, he was also a man with scant regard for his own safety. On 9 April, he leapt out of his slit-trench on the ridge, charged across the open ground to a Japanese machine-gun nest and, with just rifle and bayonet, killed them all. He headed back, triumphantly brandishing the Japanese machine gun above his head, only to be shot in turn. For this action, he was posthumously awarded a Victoria Cross.

By 18 April, the defenders were struggling to hold a small perimeter on Kohima Ridge when the position was split by the Japanese. It looked as if all might be lost, but then, in the nick of time, Major-General John Grover's 2nd Division finally started to arrive from Dimapur. Overnight on 20 April, with the bloodied defenders just managing to cling on, the position was relieved.

By the time 2nd Division reached Kohima, the ridge had become a scene of indescribable devastation and filth. It had been the grimmest kind of fighting imaginable: close-quarter, often hand-to-hand, and with foul smoke and the appalling stench of rotting corpses ever present.

Despite the carnage, by the third week of April all four near-disasters facing Fourteenth Army had been averted. The enemy onslaught had been successfully checked.

Although Imphal remained besieged, Slim was not especially worried and now wanted to stick to his original plan: to grind down the Japanese at Kohima, on the Shenam Saddle, on the Tiddim Road and on the road north. Exploiting Japanese weaknesses, not strengths, had always been his plan; he knew they would not dare give up, but rather would keep fighting. Slim's supply lines, however, were now secure and reinforced, whereas Mutaguchi's were worsening daily. In the numbers game the battle had become, there could be only one winner.

At Kohima, the battle continued, despite the beginning of the monsoon adding to the misery. One of those arriving in the first week of May was Major Mike Lowry, commanding B Company, the Queen's Royal Regiment. He and his men had been at the Admin Box and had now been flown in to defend Kohima, reaching it amidst the scream of shells and pouring rain.

Lowry's men were flung into the battle on Jail Hill on 11 May, attacking in the cold early dawn behind a brief barrage. 'I started the ball rolling,' noted Lowry, 'by whistling over some grenades and then we all ran forward. But the terrain was not easy, there being many shell-holes, horizontal tree stumps and the odd trench to negotiate.'

Casualties swiftly rose and they soon became bogged down just yards from the Japanese positions. Both sides began sniping and hurling grenades. 'It was,' noted Lowry, 'the nearest approach to a snowball fight that could be imagined. The air became thick with grenades, both theirs and ours, and we were all scurrying about trying to avoid them as they burst.' They held their ground, but by nightfall Lowry had just 28 men left. He had begun the day with 79.

Opposite: Kohima Ridge.

The fighting around Imphal and Kohima was among the most brutal of the war, and especially so now the monsoon had arrived. 'We were soaked all the time,' Captain Robin Rowlands, an officer in the 7/2nd Punjab Regiment, said. 'And filthy. The mud was appalling.' So was the stench, as thousands of unburied dead soldiers lay strewn over the hillsides. Japanese troops were taught that being taken prisoner was dishonourable and would bring shame upon their families, so very often they fought to the death. Most British and Indian troops were short of their normal rations, but the Japanese were starving. Malnutrition and disease went hand in hand, yet Mutaguchi was still maniacally urging his men to keep fighting. 'If your hands are broken, fight with your feet,' he exhorted them, 'if there is no breath in your body, fight with your ghost. Lack of weapons is no excuse for defeat.'

Meanwhile, back in London and Washington, Allied war leaders were getting nervous and urging Mountbatten to instruct Slim to relieve the siege of Imphal urgently. Far away from the action, they were following lines on a map in which there was little movement but a continued maximum effort of air supply.

It was certainly slow, hard fighting, and it took the British a month just to push the Japanese 10 miles down the road south of Kohima. Bitter fighting also continued south and north of Imphal, and over the Shenam Saddle too, as the Japanese were prised from one hill after the other. Yet, by fighting for every yard, the enemy was playing into Slim's hands. He wanted to annihilate Fifteenth Japanese Army here in India rather than in Burma. Supported fully by Mountbatten, he stuck to his strategy. The gradual destruction of the Japanese Fifteenth Army would continue.

By the beginning of June, it was clear the Japanese were nearly finished. Yard by yard, mile by mile, 5th Division was pushing northwards from Imphal and 2nd Division was inching ever further southwards from Kohima. On 22 June 1944, the British forces met and, at last, after sixty-four days of ferocious fighting, the road was open. That same night, the first convoy in three months drove through to Imphal. The siege was over.

In the long month that followed, with the monsoon now in full swing, the shattered remnants of Mutaguchi's once-proud army began to fall back. At the end of the Imphal battle, the remnants of the Japanese 31st and 15th Divisions retreated back through the jungle and along the roads they had swiftly advanced over just a few months earlier when they had been so confident of victory.

Now they were beaten, exhausted, ill and emaciated. Robin Rowlands was among those sent in pursuit. Along the jungle tracks, he witnessed hundreds of dead Japanese soldiers lying where they had fallen, dead from starvation, disease and exhaustion. 'It was a terrible sight,' he said. Some had even resorted to cannibalism. The retreat became known as the 'Road of Bones'.

The shattered remnants of the Japanese Fifteenth Army crawled back into Burma utterly broken as a fighting force. On 20 July, General Mutaguchi finally gave orders for the survivors to fall back across the Chindwin River, his dreams of becoming the conqueror of India gone for ever. 'It is the most important defeat the Japs have ever suffered in their military career,' wrote Mountbatten on the day the siege was lifted, 'because the numbers involved are so much greater than any Pacific Island operation.'

Imphal was certainly a superb and also a decisive victory. Had Mutaguchi reached and captured Dimapur, then India really would have been vulnerable. Bengal had recently suffered an appalling

Opposite:
Lance-Corporal
Jack Harman
single-handedly
overpowers
a Japanese
machine-gun
nest.

*Left: B Company,
the Queen's
Royal Regiment
fight at Kohima.*

famine that had left millions dead and anti-British feeling in India was growing, especially in Bengal. The Bengalis were ripe for insurrection. If India had been lost, then the airfields from which China was being supplied would have been lost too.

Mutaguchi had been right – the battle had been the last chance for Japan to change the course of the war. It was the largest land battle the Japanese had fought up to this point in the entire war and the stakes had been enormous. At its end, the Japanese Fifteenth Army had been destroyed, just as Slim had planned.

Of the 65,000 fighting troops that had crossed into India back in March, 30,000 lay dead, rotting in the hills and jungle of Manipur and in the Naga Hills, while a further 23,000 had become casualties. Incredibly, only 600 had let themselves be taken prisoner. In all, so far in 1944, the Japanese had lost some 90,000 men fighting the British Indian Army and five entire divisions had been completely destroyed. Fourteenth Army had lost 24,000 casualties, many of whom recovered thanks to the improved medical care upon which Slim had insisted.

Hard fighting continued as Slim's forces pursued the Japanese into Burma. The long campaign of reconquest would continue into 1945, but by any judgement the year had witnessed an astonishing reversal of fortunes that could not have been remotely guessed at just twelve months before. Not only was Imphal a monumental victory for the British, it was also a complete vindication of Slim's strategy. Not for nothing has this been called Britain's greatest battle.

Right: Bill Slim. Master of War.

Opposite: It took a month to push the Japanese back just ten miles south of Kohima.

11: VICTORY IN EUROPE

Just a couple of weeks after the Allies had landed in Normandy on D-Day, the Soviet Red Army was poised to launch its biggest-ever offensive: Operation BAGRATION, named personally by Stalin, the Soviet leader, after the Russian field marshal mortally wounded at Borodino in 1812. Much of the Soviet Union lands lost to Germany had been retaken but the Baltic states were still in German hands and a huge bulge pressed into Belarus to the north of the giant Pripyet Marshes. BAGRATION aimed to push that giant salient back and smash the German Army Group Centre.

The Red Army had changed greatly since June 1941 when the Germans invaded. It was better trained, better organized and better led. Men like Marshal Constantin Rokossovsky, commanding the First Belorussian Front, were vastly experienced and supremely able. Rokossovsky even had the courage of his convictions to stand up to Stalin over the detailed planning of BAGRATION. Stalin conceded the point and allowed Rokossovsky to launch a two-fisted attack either side of the city of Bobruisk.

Partisans operating behind German lines but in touch with Stavka, the Soviet high command, were ordered to attack railways and other German communication lines. Some 143,000 partisans, organized into brigades and detachments, wreaked havoc. On 20 June alone, 147 trains were derailed.

At the front, the Red Army had amassed 2.4 million men against 1.2 million German troops, but the real difference lay in the arms they could bring to bear: 36,400 guns against 9,500; 5,200 tanks against 900; and 5,300 aircraft against 1,350. Red Army offensives began rather like a giant battering ram being swung into the enemy with immense force. BAGRATION began on 22 June, almost three years to the day from the German invasion of the Soviet Union.

With what little remained of the Luftwaffe busy battling the Allied bomber offensive or grounded through lack of fuel, Red Army Shturmoviks, robust ground-attack aircraft, pulverized German anti-tank guns and forward positions, and the huge concentration of force that followed on the ground was unstoppable. By 28 June, Rokossovsky's troops had destroyed the German Ninth Army, had forced Fourth Army into retreat and badly mauled Third Panzer. Bobruisk fell to the Red Army, then, on 3 July, so did Minsk. By the following day, Army Group Centre had lost a staggering 25 divisions. Such was the depth of Red Army logistics, the Soviet juggernaut rolled on beyond Minsk, something the Germans had not expected. It was what the Soviets called 'deep battle'.

Hitler demanded Vilnius in Lithuania be held to the last man, but it still fell on 13 July. Defying the terrain, the Red Army then used log roads to move 3,500 artillery pieces and over 30,000 vehicles through the Pripyet Marshes, allowing the First Belorussian Front to press on into Poland.

Opposite:
The Red Army
on the move
during Operation
BAGRATION.

Overwhelming force, deep-battle tactics and Hitler's insistence on no retreats destroyed Army Group Centre.

By the end of July, the Red Army had crossed the River Vistula but by then they were running out of steam. The Soviet way of war was very effective but incredibly costly to themselves too. By the time BAGRATION finally came to a halt on 19 August, the Germans had lost 771,000 men and most of their equipment, but the Red Army had lost 757,000 – almost as many – of which 178,507 were killed. These were staggering – and unsustainable – numbers, even for the Soviet Union.

Meanwhile, on 1 August the Warsaw Uprising began. The Polish Resistance aimed to push the Germans back out of the city but also to assert Polish sovereignty ahead of the Soviet advance.

The Warsaw Uprising was to prove one of the terrible tragedies of the war. Initially, the Germans were successfully driven out of the city, but the much-needed Soviet support was not forthcoming. Rather, the Red Army sat back while the Germans exacted swift and savage revenge. British Prime Minister Winston Churchill pleaded in vain with Stalin to allow the RAF to use Red Army airfields. Eventually, 200 supply drops were flown over from Allied bases in Italy, but it was not enough. German reinforcements were brought in under command of SS General Erich von dem Bach. Retribution was brutal with groups of soldiers moving door-to-door and street-to-street slaughtering inhabitants regardless of age or gender.

Short of supplies and with casualties mounting, the Uprising collapsed, although pockets of resistance continued until the end of September. In all, around 15,000 Polish Home Army troops were killed but a further 150,000–200,000 civilians were slaughtered and much of the rest of the civilian population cleared from the city. It was a terrible, merciless episode.

Meanwhile, on the Western Front, the Allies were able to capture huge swathes of land following the German collapse in Normandy. While the Canadian First Army moved up the Channel coast, British Second Army swept over the River Seine and pushed on into Belgium. Brussels was liberated on 3 September amidst cheering crowds, while to the south the US First and Third Armies made giant strides eastwards across most of France. More ground was retaken in fewer days than the Germans had achieved coming from the opposite direction back in May 1940.

France was also being liberated from the south. French and US troops had landed in Provence on 15 August and were now pushing up the Rhone Valley and meeting only weak resistance.

Right: The Warsaw Uprising.

Opposite: Soviet Il-2 Sturmoviks over the battlefield.

The Germans were pulling back on almost all fronts but Hitler now ordered his V-2 rockets to be launched. These were an astonishing technical achievement and the first man-made object to enter space. These ballistic supersonic missiles carried a warhead of nearly a ton of high explosive and were terrifying weapons for the civilians on the receiving end. The first landed on Paris and London on 8 September, but they were neither accurate enough nor plentiful enough to be remotely decisive. In fact, more slave labourers, many of them Soviet POWs and Jews, died manufacturing them in brutal conditions than were killed as a result of the explosions they caused.

The Luftwaffe also had pioneering new jet aircraft, but Hitler insisted these should be used as bombers rather than defensive fighters, the role for which they had been designed. Again, there were not enough of them to make a difference to the outcome of the war, nor were the engines strong enough to last more than about 20 hours of combat flying.

In contrast, the Allies now had enormous fleets of bombers equipped with ever-improving navigational and targeting aids. The differences between RAF night-time 'area' bombing and US daylight 'precision' bombing were blurring. On 10 September, for example, the US Eighth Air Force sent out 1,145 heavy bombers escorted by 705 fighters to nine different targets. The following night, Bomber Command sent out 226 aircraft to attack synthetic fuel plants at Darmstadt and a further 412 against oil targets during the day on the 12th, and a further 378 bombers on the night of 12/13 September. It was relentless and it was having a devastating effect on both German fuel supplies and cities.

While BAGRATION had been rolling through Belorussia, the Red Army had also launched a thrust through southern Ukraine, smashing the combined German and Romanian opposition, sweeping through Moldavia and prompting King Michael of Romania to mount a successful coup against the Fascist Marshal Antonescu. On 23 August, Romania declared war on Germany, its ally for much of the war, which meant the Nazi regime lost its last source of real oil. On 7 September, Bulgaria, which had allied with Germany through much of the war, also switched sides.

It was no wonder the Allies were hopeful of ending the war by Christmas. The Luftwaffe had retrenched to the Reich and was throwing increasingly poorly trained pilots to the slaughter. Germany's navy had been largely destroyed, while its army was suffering one devastating blow after another and, for the most part, was on the run. Despite the Nazis' possession of vengeance weapons like the V-2, it was strikingly clear the war was lost and almost any other leader than Hitler would have called an end to it. But the Führer was not like other leaders. Ideologically driven, he was determined to continue his annihilation of Europe's Jews and to fight to the bitter end. In Hitler's world view, there would be either a Thousand Year Reich or Armageddon. But there would be no surrender.

By the first week of September, the rapid Allied advances in the west were beginning to slow down as supply lines, running all the way back to Normandy, became overextended, and as the shattered German forces started to regain some order out of the chaos of defeat and retreat. On 7 September, however, a daring plan was agreed to use airborne troops to help win the war in 1944.

Despite the defeats the German Army had suffered, the Allied high command was aware the Germans might well want to fight on bitterly to defend the Reich itself. Much of Germany was bordered by a number of rivers, including the mighty Rhine, and dense forests, as well as the Siegfried Line, or Westwall – deep border defences of bunkers, mines, wire and gun emplacements.

Opposite: The V-2 rocket was the world's first long-range ballistic missile.

In northern Holland, however, the Westwall ended and the Rhine was narrower. If the Allies could break across the Rhine here, the route into Germany might be much easier – and once they had a firm foothold in Germany itself then total enemy collapse might follow and the war be over quickly.

Field Marshal Sir Bernard Montgomery, commander of the Anglo-Canadian 21st Army Group, argued to use the Allied Airborne Army to capture a series of bridges, the last of which, at the Dutch town of Arnhem, crossed the Rhine. While paratroopers and gliders secured and held the bridges, an armoured corps would go hell for leather down a single highway to reach each captured bridge in turn and help hold the ground while reinforcements were brought up. It would be a daring lightning strike that made use of the highly trained and motivated Airborne Army, and if successful offered tantalizing riches.

On the other hand, supply lines were so stretched that this operation would dominate Allied logistics, halt American drives to the south and would mean the task of clearing the long 30-mile River Scheldt that led to the vital Dutch port of Antwerp would have to be put on hold until it had run its course. And the only way it would succeed was if all the nine bridges were captured intact and the armoured thrust was able to get through to relieve the airborne troops holding them. It was high risk, to say the least.

Despite protests from General Omar Bradley, the US 2nd Army Group commander, and plenty of others besides, the Supreme Allied Commander, General Dwight D. Eisenhower, was persuaded Montgomery's plan was worth the attempt, partly for the chance of a route into Germany but also as a means of overrunning the V-2 rocket launch sites. Operation MARKET GARDEN was agreed on 10 September and launched just a week later on the 17th, by which time opposition had already stiffened considerably. One week was very little time to plan and execute such a complex operation – one that involved two American and one British airborne divisions, one Polish airborne brigade, the RAF and USAAF, and the British XXX Corps on the ground. There was no margin for error.

In the rush to get the operation ready, inevitably mistakes were made. At Arnhem itself, the British 1st Airborne Division was dropped too far from the bridge they had to capture, and because there were not enough aircraft to transport the entire airborne force in one go, half those landed had to remain at the landing zone to defend it before the next drop arrived. The bridge was captured by Major John Frost's 2nd Battalion, but there were not enough men there to hold it for long.

At Nijmegen, the US 82nd Airborne focused on securing the Groesbeek Heights, the high ground at the edge of the German border, rather than going all-out to capture the giant bridge across the River Waal. The armoured thrust of XXX Corps struggled to keep the pace along the one road they had been allocated but reached Nijmegen on time, only to find the bridge had not yet

Above left: The Siegfried Line.

Opposite: The bridge across the Rhine at Arnhem.

been secured. By the time it was in Allied hands, the British paratroopers still holding Arnhem Bridge were too few in number and too short of ammunition to hold out against growing enemy reinforcements.

On 21 September, the Germans recaptured the bridge at Arnhem and although leading troops of XXX Corps were across the bridge at Nijmegen and less than 10 miles away, they were too late to retake Arnhem and save the beleaguered paratroopers still holding out to the west of the town at Oosterbeek. On the night of 25 September, they withdrew back across the Rhine, MARKET GARDEN a failure. Although eight of the bridges had been captured intact, the one at Arnhem had proved a bridge too far.

Using the Airborne Army for a dramatic thrust was not in itself a bad idea, but the operation had been too complex with not enough time for preparation and planning. Its failure meant

Eisenhower reverted to a broad-front strategy of applying pressure along much of the German border, though only limited operations could be carried out until the supply situation improved. In the northern half of the front, that meant clearing the Scheldt estuary leading to Antwerp, which was now heavily defended even though the deep-water port had been liberated on 3 September. Clearing the Scheldt was left to the Canadian Second Army and became a bitter slog through October. Crossing rivers, canals and dykes and moving through flat, flooded polder country was extremely difficult. Not until 8 November was the Scheldt finally cleared, after which the Germans had lost around 12,000 killed and wounded and 41,000 captured, and the Canadian Army some 12,900 casualties.

Meanwhile, the US First Army spent much of October fighting in and around the German border city of Aachen. 'Aachen was terrible,' said Tom Bowles, an infantryman of the 1st Division. 'Worse than Normandy.' The city finally fell to the Americans on the 21st, by which time Charlemagne's ancient capital was a shattered wreck.

Although by the autumn most of the Channel ports – Dunkirk excepted – were liberated by the Canadians, the destruction of French bridges and railways before D-Day now worked against the Allies in their drive east towards Germany. There were also civilian needs – shattered towns and villages and a lack of basic food – that worked against the installation of rapid supply lines.

Even so, by German standards, the Allies were still awash with men, materiel and supplies, but mindful of mounting casualties and the probable need to invade Japan once Germany was defeated, Eisenhower and his commanders did not want to send their infantry and tanks to be slaughtered. By

Above: US troops fight in the Hürtgen Forest.

Opposite: Allied amphibious vehicles move through flooded polder country.

pressing hard against the length of the German border, Eisenhower hoped to overwhelm the enemy defence, which was why, at the beginning of October, General Courtney Hodges found his US First Army being thrown into the dense Hürtgen Forest to the east of the Belgian city of Liège.

The original idea was to draw German troops away from the battle raging to the north at Aachen but also to capture the Rur Dam on the far side before the Germans blew it up and swamped the borderland downstream to the north. US commanders tended to opt for the straightest line to a target – and to the Rurstausee, that was straight through the Hürtgen Forest.

The forest was a terrible place through which to attack, however. Dense, craggy and with few roads to the west, it was also laced with bunkers,

wire, mines and booby traps and every trail and track was overlooked by mortars, machine guns and gun positions. Allied air support was useless in such thick forest and the weather, terrible through the war-year winters, was closing in. The Hürtgen soon became a hellish battleground.

The initial attacks got nowhere but as October gave way to November, still more American units were flung into the meat grinder of the Hürtgen, which the Germans continued to reinforce through much easier lines of supply on their side of the border. A different option might have been to attack to the south-east of the forest, where the terrain was much easier, then cut up to the dam and bypass the Hürtgen entirely. But it wasn't to be.

To the south, General George S. Patton's Third Army crossed the River Moselle and attacked Metz in early November, a city he knew from his time there in the First World War, although the cut and dash of the summer was eroded by the rain, cold and mud and stiffening German defence. The city and most of its forts had fallen by 22 November. Even further south, the French and Americans of General Jake Devers's 12th Army Group also pressed eastwards. Casualties on both sides were high, but the Americans lost 118,698 casualties in November alone, and most of those were frontline troops.

With the Red Army in Bulgaria by early September, the Germans now struggled to extricate the 300,000 troops of Army Group E from Greece and the Western Balkans before Soviet forces trapped them there. With no naval strength and the Mediterranean closed to them, only streaming back overland would do.

Fortunately for Field Marshal Maximilian von Weichs, the Army Group E commander, the Red Army had its hands tied besieging Budapest in Hungary and so he was able to pull out his troops through Macedonia and Croatia even as Red Army troops were linking up with Tito's Yugoslavian partisans. The Soviet troops outraged Tito's Communists, however, by raping and pillaging the civilian population. This bought the Germans precious time.

Civil war, already simmering, now threatened to fully erupt throughout Greece. Determined that post-war Greece should not become a communist state and Soviet vassal, Churchill ordered British troops to be transferred from Italy to help disarm resistance groups and prevent a communist takeover. These were volatile, violent times, even away from the main battle fronts.

There was growing chaos within the Reich. Hitler's grip on power was as tight as ever, although he was by now a sick man, addled by a daily cocktail of drugs given by his doctor and increasingly paranoid about betrayal ever since the failed coup against the regime back in July. 'Honour' courts had been established to strip suspected officers of their titles. They would then be tried as civilians and invariably executed. Field Marshal Erwin Rommel, suspected of plotting against Hitler, was given the offer of suicide or public trial. On 14 October, he chose cyanide. Senior commanders were told to obey orders unconditionally and their families threatened if they failed to do so.

It was in this atmosphere of fear and paranoia that Hitler ordered a major German counter-thrust in the west. His plan was to smash through the Ardennes, the scene of his greatest triumph back in May 1940 and only lightly held by the Americans, and then drive a wedge between the British and Americans all the way to the key port of Antwerp. Incredibly, and in secret, the Germans managed to assemble a considerable force of two panzer armies without the Allies ever realizing what was going on. It was one of the reasons the Germans had fought so hard at the Hürtgen Forest: just behind it was one of the main assembly areas for Operation Wacht am Rhein – 'Watch on the Rhine'.

Snow lay thick on the ground in the hilly and wooded Ardennes that winter. In the early hours of 16 December, American troops, most recently arrived at the front and new to combat, were thinly holding the line when the skies opened and shells began screaming over. None of Hitler's generals thought the Führer's plan a good idea, as it had no realistic chance of success and every chance of depleting precious men, fuel and arms. But none dared show dissent.

And to begin with, the attack made progress. Speed was vital: they aimed to strike quickly and blaze a route to Antwerp before the Allies had a chance to offer any coordinated counter-attack. Two parallel offensives, the Sixth SS Panzer Army in the north and the Fifth Panzer Army in the south, burst through the American lines with a three-to-one manpower advantage and a two-to-one superiority in tanks and guns. Hitler had chosen December, when skies were leaden and the opportunities for the Allies to use their dominance in the air were fewer, but the falling snow made it harder for the attackers to stick to their strict timetable and slowed them down considerably.

Furthermore, the Americans in the area might have been green but they were not the French Army of 1940 and they quickly recovered their balance. As they fell back, they blew bridges, while determined stands were made at key crossroad towns like St Vith and at Bastogne, where the US 101st Airborne were hurriedly brought into the line. In the north, the rookie 99th Infantry Division held out on the Elsenborn Ridge, inflicting casualties on the Germans at a rate of eighteen to one, while behind them the 82nd Airborne helped halt Battlegroup Peiper, one of the main panzer thrusts. It was the actions of the 99th, above all, that were to prove decisive.

The German attack soon fell behind schedule. Capturing Allied fuel dumps had been a vital part of the plan, but the leading German units were unable to reach them; Battlegroup Peiper was forced to halt and then, on 23 December, pull back. Most of Peiper's tanks were abandoned as they ran out of fuel.

Opposite: The German counter-offensive through the Ardennes.

Overhead, the skies began to clear on the same day, and Allied aircraft thundered over in force, hammering German supply lines to the rear and shooting up troops on the roads. British forces were defending the River Meuse to the western edge of the Germans' furthest gains, while units from Patton's Third Army battled northwards to help relieve the situation around Bastogne. His troops reached the besieged town on Boxing Day, 26 December.

On the first day of 1945, the Luftwaffe, in a last-ditch effort, managed to launch Operation BODENPLATTE, a massed fighter attack of around 800 aircraft, which swept over the many Allied airfields now in Belgium and Holland. This attack caught the Allies by surprise, just as had the battle on the ground, and for the same reasons: because it was winter, because it made little tactical sense at this stage of the war, and because the Allies underestimated the Germans' ability to mount attacks on such a scale. In all, around 300 Allied aircraft were destroyed, mostly on the ground, and over 150 damaged, but few pilots or aircrew were among the casualties and the aircraft losses were made good in around a week. In contrast, 143 Luftwaffe pilots were killed and 70 captured. Among the casualties were 14 squadron commanders, an unrecoverable and devastating loss at this stage of the war. Rather like the attack on the ground, BODENPLATTE caused some short-term damage but in the longer term it was a terrible failure.

Officially, the Battle of the Bulge, as it became known, did not end until the third week of January, which was when almost all the Allied ground was recovered, but it had been lost to the Germans

within a matter of days and BODENPLATTE was very much the last roll of the dice. There was, though, still one last German attack in the west to be played out.

Operation NORDWIND was launched far to the south in Alsace and Lorraine on 31 December and aimed to split the US Seventh and French First Armies, destroy them and seize back the city of Strasbourg. Like the Ardennes offensive, it was insanely overambitious. The Americans used the Maginot Line to help them defend the attack and although the fighting was bitter for several weeks, the Germans managed to stamp only a small salient, the Colmar Pocket, and on 25 January, the attack was called off.

By this time, they had even bigger battles to fight in the east. Hitler had been warned about the scale of the Soviet build-up along the Eastern Front but refused to believe the strengths of the Red Army now along the River Vistula. The Soviet way of war was to conduct massive offensives of comparatively short duration – around ten weeks – then pause for several months and pull back the battering ram

Left: American troops made use of the Maginot Line defences.

Opposite: Operation BODENPLATTE.

for another swing. By 12 January, they were ready, with 4 million troops, nearly 10,000 tanks and some 40,000 guns and mortars.

Most German defences were swept aside. By 24 January, the Red Army had reached the Baltic, severing the historic city of Königsberg and East Prussia from the rest of the Reich. By the end of January, Red Army troops had reached the River Oder, 250 miles from their start point and less than 50 miles from Berlin.

As the Red Army swept through Poland, they liberated a number of extermination camps. Treblinka had been overrun the previous August, and Majdanek and Sobibor abandoned in the autumn, but the killing had continued at Chelmno and Auschwitz, which were finally liberated on 20 and 27 January. Around a million men, women and children, mostly Jews, had been murdered in the gas chambers at Auschwitz, and some 200,000 at Chelmno. The terrible depths of the Nazis' crimes were now laid bare.

The Germans were also starting to reap what they had sown with the vicious slaughter of Soviet troops and citizens during the years of occupation. Red Army troops now raped, murdered and pillaged tens of thousands of civilians as they swept into German territories. Many Germans preferred to take their own lives rather than succumb to the Russians. The orgy of violence in the east was set to continue.

Meanwhile, in February, President Roosevelt, Churchill and Stalin met at Yalta in the Crimea in southern Russia to discuss the post-war world. Britain was weary, its influence waning, and Roosevelt was in ill health, while Stalin was on home turf and in robust spirits; the outcome reflected the increased Soviet influence. By this time, the Americans especially were also increasingly concerned about the prospect of invading Japan in 1946 and anxious to preserve Allied lives and materiel in Europe as much as possible. At the end of the talks, among the points agreed was that Germany should be partitioned, east and west, Poland would be given new borders, shifting it west, and a communist government installed. Stalin agreed there should be democratic elections in Poland; he had no intention of sticking to this pledge, however. Yalta sowed the seeds of the future communist eastern bloc in Europe.

Right: Conditions during the winter of 1944/45 were brutal.

Opposite: Churchill, Roosevelt and Stalin at Yalta.

While the Red Army offensive halted in early February, on the Eastern Front, the Allies continued to push, amidst snow and freezing temperatures, through the Siegfried Line defences. While the Americans were busy pushing back the Bulge in the Ardennes, just to the north, the British XII Corps launched BLACKCOCK, an operation to push back the protruding Westwall around Heinsberg and to force the Germans back across the River Roer. It was part of a front-long attempt to straighten the line and close up further towards the River Rhine.

It is true that Allied armies had a longer logistical tail and fewer frontline troops than those in the Soviet or German Armies. In British Second Army, for example, 43 per cent were service troops while only 14 per cent were infantry and just 8 per cent were armoured units. However, for those in the infantry or in tanks, whether British, American or Canadian, the chances of getting through the fighting unscathed were statistically zero, as they were for German, Soviet and any other frontline troops. And whether one was lightly wounded, badly wounded or killed was really a matter of chance.

The conditions in the winter of 1944/45 were also terrible. In October and November, it rained almost endlessly, so that wherever fighting took place they were soon battling through quagmires of mud. Then, at the beginning of December, temperatures dropped and a blanket of snow fell across much of northern Europe. Life at the front line was relentless – there was none of the regular rotation of troops every few days as there had been on the Western Front in the First World War. Rather, troops could find themselves living in a foxhole in the ground, surrounded by mud or snow, for long weeks at a time. Everyone suffered. It was brutal.

The major Allied offensive for February 1945 focused on Montgomery's 21st Army Group part of the front to the north. Operation VERITABLE was to be led by the Canadian First Army, but with British XXX Corps attached. Also under Montgomery's command was the US Ninth Army, led by the very capable General William Simpson. The plan was for a two-fisted punch, with the Canadians with XXX Corps to strike first through the Reichswald, the mighty forest on the German border between Nijmegen and Cleve, then a little later, Simpson's Ninth Army would strike across the River Roer and link up with the British and Canadians. Together, they would then move up to the Rhine, clearing the Rhineland to the west. Then, in March, once the weather had started to improve, all along the front there would be a drive to cross the mighty river and make strides into the heart of the Reich.

VERITABLE began on 9 February, following the bombing of the medieval city of Cleve and the neighbouring town of Goch by the Allied heavies. This achieved very little except to destroy two historic towns, offer rubble defences for the defenders and block a huge number of roads, which needed to be cleared before the ground troops could push on through. For the most part, the Allied armies were, by this stage of the war, well equipped, well trained and well led, but despite the early lessons of Monte Cassino, Caen and St Lô, all of which were similarly pulverized with no appreciable benefit to the attackers, General Brian Horrocks, the XXX Corps commander, still ordered Goch and Cleve to be flattened before launching his attack.

To make matters worse, the Germans smashed the Rhine's dykes and so flooded the northern part of the battlefield as soon as the offensive had begun. The Allies faced two enemies: the Germans and the conditions.

None the less, by using amphibious DUKWs and other such vehicles, the British and Canadians were able to maintain their advance. The Reichswald was cleared, as were Cleve and Goch, and the forward units continued to push south-east and east towards the Rhine.

To the south, Simpson's Ninth Army was also lined up to cross the River Roer in what was intended to be the second part of the two-fisted punch. Unfortunately, the Roer was now also flooded, because although First Army had finally got through the Hürtgen and reached the dams

Opposite: As the German war machine fell apart, Allied armies remained well trained, well led and well equipped.

further south, the retreating Germans had destroyed the spillways and control machinery, so that a torrent had gushed downriver towards Ninth Army. Only on 21 February, with the floodwaters finally receding, was Simpson able to finally launch Operation GRENADE.

Despite the conditions, the combined attacks of VERITABLE and GRENADE hammered the German Fifteenth and First Parachute Armies. Field Marshal Walter Model, the German Army Group commander, pleaded with Hitler to withdraw back across the Rhine. Hitler refused permission.

On the Eastern Front, meanwhile, the Germans had counter-attacked in Pomerania, briefly gaining some ground, before Marshals Zhukov and Rokossovsky went on the offensive again, blasting their way across West Prussia and Pomerania until their armies were all lined up along the Oder. To the south, the Germans were still furiously defending Budapest, although increasingly desperately and hopelessly.

The Reich was imploding, however. In February, the Reichsbahn, the German railway, which had been the glue that kept the German war effort going, finally collapsed. Armageddon was approaching.

It was already upon many of those Germans stranded in the besieged city of Königsberg and the rest of East Prussia. A massive seaborne evacuation was launched in January and by the war's end an incredible 2 million had been rescued by the Kriegsmarine, the German navy, many in vessels barely fit to go to sea. Plenty did not make it, however, including some 9,500 crammed into the battered Baltic liner Wilhelm Gustloff when it was sunk by a Soviet submarine. It remains the largest number of lives lost on a single ship.

While the Red Army paused for breath along the Oder ahead of its final assault towards Berlin, the Allies were, by March, getting ready to cross the Rhine. All the bridges over the river were blown by the retreating Germans – except one, a railway bridge at the small town of Remagen. On 7 March, leading elements of the 9th Armored Division of the US First Army, using the newly arrived bigger Pershing tanks, neared the bridge. Suddenly, first one, then two explosions erupted as German engineers detonated charges to drop the bridge into the river below. To the amazement of American and German alike, however, when the smoke cleared, the bridge was still standing. Incredibly, the charges had lifted it up into the air only for it to land back down on its pillars.

Without waiting for orders, infantrymen, with covering fire from the Pershings, ran across it, driving the Germans back. By nightfall, tanks were across the river and within 24 hours the Americans had 8,000 men across. It was a bridgehead they were able to hold as more men, then divisions, crossed the bridge at Remagen.

Hitler's commanders had urged him to allow his beleaguered forces to fall back behind the huge barrier of the Rhine far earlier, but he had insisted they fight to the west of the river to the last man. As a result, around 300,000 men were killed, wounded or captured.

This meant there were fewer German forces to face the Allies on the eastern side of the Rhine. American generals have been criticized for not rapidly pushing beyond the Rhine at Remagen, but Eisenhower and Bradley wanted to continue with the strategy of piling immense pressure on the remaining German forces along a broad front. Germany might be imploding but there were still many prepared to fanatically fight on and the prospect of an invasion of Japan – one that was

Opposite:
The bridge at
Remagen.

expected to cost millions in casualties – loomed large. It was neither productive nor necessary to throw caution to the wind at this stage.

Rhine crossings were meticulously planned to the north and south in the third week of May and all were successful. Montgomery's crossing at Rees and Wesel was additionally supported by the most effective airborne drop of the war and huge artillery bombardment, as there were very good reasons for the exhausted British, now worryingly short of frontline manpower, not to take any chances either.

Even after the crossings, there were still a few stings in the Germans' tail – one US armoured column was destroyed as it tried to overrun an SS panzer training centre near Paderborn. Even so, Simpson's Ninth Army to the north and Hodges' First to the south swiftly encircled the Ruhr industrial heartland, capturing a further 317,000 enemy troops. It was clear the end of the war was near.

While the Allies crossed the Rhine, the Red Army continued its build-up for the latest swing of the battering ram. Three fronts – what the Soviets termed groups of armies – were now lined up along the Oder. In the north was Rokossovsky's 2nd Belorussian Front, directly east of Berlin was Georgy Zhukov's 1st Belorussian Front and to the south of Zhukov was Marshal Ivan Konev's 1st Ukrainian Front: in all, 2.4 million men, 41,600 guns, 6,250 tanks and 7,500 aircraft. Against them were some 750,000 troops, which included two understrength army groups. Not one division was full strength, and many units were made up of teenage boys and older men earlier excused duty due to their age. The German situation was desperate, to say the least.

Stalin deliberately egged on Zhukov and Konev to race against one another to the heart of Berlin. Zhukov, although closer, had to deal with the Oder crossings and the natural defences of the Seelow Heights, 35 miles west of Berlin, and although, when the storm broke on 14 April, his forces were so overwhelming they could hardly fail, it took him five days and horrific numbers of casualties to smash this first line of defence. German trenches on the Seelow Heights can still be seen to this day.

Further south, Vienna, the Austrian capital, was taken by the Red Army on 13 April, while over Berlin itself, RAF Bomber Command continued to pound the city by night. By the last raid, on 18/19 April, the Nazi capital was a wreck, a once great city reduced to rubble, its surviving citizens scavenging to survive in the cellars below. The following day, 20 April, was Hitler's birthday. From his bunker in the heart of Berlin, his twelve-year rule was now very near the end.

Right: The Red Army attack.

Opposite: The Battle of the Ruhr.

In the west, the Allies continued to find a mixture of willing surrender and fanatical resistance, although Patton's Third Army, especially, now hurtled eastwards into Bavaria and then Austria, capturing Linz, Hitler's home town. Prague was

Third Army's for the taking, but he was ordered to leave the Czechoslovakian capital for the Soviets.

It was now the Western Allies' turn to discover the horrific depths of the Nazis' warped ideology. Third Army overran slave labour camps around the V-2 rocket production site at Ohrdruf and at Nordhausen. 'Rows upon rows of skin-coloured skeletons,' wrote Charles MacDonald, an American veteran. 'One girl in particular I noticed; I would say she was about seventeen years old. She lay as she had fallen, gangrened and naked.' On 15 April, British troops liberated Belsen, a concentration rather than a death camp, but where overcrowding and inhuman treatment had led to catastrophic numbers of dead and dying. 'The living lay with their heads against the corpses and around them moved the awful, ghostly procession of emaciated, aimless people, with nothing and with no hope of life,' wrote the journalist Richard Dimbleby. 'This day at Belsen was the most horrible of my life.' There were plenty more camps besides, each with their share of tragedy, misery and suffering.

The fighting continued. Montgomery's forces were hurrying towards the Baltic. At any moment, though, German troops would pounce with *Panzerfausts*, short-range propelled charges, destroying another tank or vehicle. The end was so close, but it was still not over.

On 20 April, Rokossovsky launched his attack north of the city and up to the Baltic Coast. That same day, Zossen, to the south-east of Berlin and the German Army's underground bunker headquarters, was captured by Konev's men.

On 25 April, while the battle still raged in Berlin, Red Army troops from a guards rifle regiment in Konev's 1st Ukrainian Front met with Americans of the 69th Division, part of First Army, on the River Elbe at Torgau. A little way to the north, Simpson's Ninth Army swept through Hanover and then captured Brunswick and Magdeburg, three cities also ravaged by repeated Allied bombing. Simpson was all for pushing on to Potsdam and then Berlin, but he was ordered to hold where he was and leave it to the Soviets.

Eisenhower's decision not to fight all the way to Berlin certainly saved Allied lives. In contrast, Zhukov and Konev's forces were experiencing brutal casualty rates despite their overwhelming strength. To a certain extent, this was because Zhukov, especially, was pushing his men particularly hard in his efforts to win Berlin, but it was also because the Germans, depleted and beaten though they were, still fought on.

In his bunker beneath the Reichs Chancellory, Hitler had refused to flee as his inner circle had urged him to do. Rather, he had accepted his life would end there, in Berlin, with the final collapse of the Third Reich. It did not stop him from ranting at his generals' failings, however, or demanding yet more counter-attacks that could not possibly be mounted. Much of Berlin had been overrun by 30 April, the day on which he decided to take his life, shooting himself in the

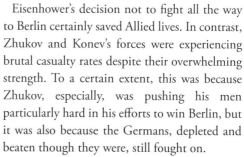

Left: Berlin falls.

Opposite: The Liberation of Belsen concentration camp.

temple at around 3.20 p.m. Afterwards, his body, and that of his wife of one day, Eva Braun, were burned just outside the bunker entrance. Later that day, the Soviet flag was raised above the Reichstag, the German parliament building, no more than a mile from the bunker.

German forces surrendered in Italy on 2 May, the same day that General Helmuth Weidling raised the white flag in Berlin. At 8 a.m. on the 5th, all German forces in Northern Germany and Denmark surrendered to Montgomery's 21st Army Group. Elsewhere, the fighting continued as Grand Admiral Karl Dönitz, who had taken over as Führer on Hitler's death, frantically tried to get as many troops – and civilians – into Western Allied-held territory as possible. The evacuation of Danzig and East Prussia also continued until the end, by which time a staggering 2 million people had escaped.

Finally, at 2.41 a.m. on 7 May, a German delegation led by General Alfred Jodl surrendered to Eisenhower at Supreme Headquarters in Reims in France. The Allies had demanded unconditional surrender – that is, no German terms at all – and had got it. The Soviet Union, however, wanted their own surrender ceremony and would not allow the announcement of the end of the war until theirs had been completed in Berlin.

It was a farcical situation, and inevitably the news got out, although via a German rather than Allied leak. The British and Americans declared 8 May to be VE Day – Victory in Europe Day. Celebrations were held around the free world – from London to Paris to Sydney and Toronto as millions cheered, drank and partied.

The Soviet surrender ceremony was finally conducted in an old barracks at Karlshorst in south-east Berlin, in the very first minutes of 9 May. As President Truman and Prime Minister Winston Churchill were both aware, however, and made clear in their victory speeches, the war was not over yet. There was still Imperial Japan to crush too. But the war in Europe was finally at an end and the Nazis, and all they stood for, crushed. A new, and very different, Europe would emerge from the ruins.

Opposite:
VE Day.

12: VICTORY AGAINST JAPAN

On 20 June 1943, the US submarine *Jack* was on its first operational patrol, moving south of the Japanese main islands, when its crew spotted a large enemy vessel. Manoeuvring the submarine into position, the skipper, Lieutenant-Commander Tommy Dykers, gave the order to fire. The first torpedo appeared to be running on a perfect course when suddenly it exploded early.

'Our worst fears about the magnetic exploders were realized,' noted Lieutenant Jim Calvert, the fourth officer. 'After all this training, after coming halfway around the world to get here, our first shot was a premature.'

Fortunately for *Jack* and her crew, they managed to safely escape a vigorous search for them by the Japanese, and later on that first patrol managed to hit and sink three other vessels. Despite this, for the US Navy's submarine fleet, the rest of the year was fraught with ongoing problems with their torpedoes. In all, the US submarines managed to sink 335 Japanese ships in 1943, amounting to 1.5 million tons, a sixth of what the Allies lost in the Atlantic that same year and not enough to cripple Japanese supplies.

It was a source of great frustration to the American crews but also to Admiral Ernest J. King, the Commander-in-Chief of the US Fleet and Chief of Naval Operations. King, one of the most senior commanders in the United States and the Allied Joint Chiefs of Staff, was not much interested in the war in Europe and had been doing his best to ensure the 'Germany first' strategy applied to as small a degree as possible. For Admiral King, there was only one mission in his life, and that was to beat the Japanese as quickly and completely as possible.

At Allied strategy conferences that year, King won backing for his plan to defeat Japan by focusing, above all, on the enemy's sea lanes. A glance at the map demonstrated the sense of this approach. Japan's empire covered a truly vast area: great tracts of China, Indochina, Singapore, Malaya, Burma, the Dutch East Indies, the Philippines, Borneo and New Guinea, as well as a raft of islands in the Central Pacific. All these places involved vast numbers of ant-lines of ships between Japan and their new empire and required manning with troops, arms and supplies. The entire empire was linked by these vital sea lanes. Without them, Japan would be finished.

There were, however, other, competing plans. General Douglas MacArthur, Supreme Commander of Allied Forces in the South-West Pacific, was anxious to retake the Philippines as soon as possible, a former US possession lost to the Japanese. 'I shall return,' he had promised when he left on 12 March 1942. Nothing that had happened since had made him waver from this vow. The British

Opposite: USS Jack on patrol in 1943.

were also trying to protect north-east India and retake Burma. Increasingly large numbers of British-Indian forces were strung out along the northern Burmese border.

What was troubling both American and British war leaders and planners, however, was that despite some successes, most notably in the South Pacific, the map had changed little since those first Japanese strikes nearly two years earlier. And time was marching on. The war needed to be won.

None the less, 1944 dawned with the US Navy, at any rate, in a strong position, with a huge numerical advantage in warships as well as naval supply ships. The torpedo problems had been resolved and US cryptanalysts had made big breakthroughs in cracking Japanese naval radio codes. Admiral King had reason to feel confident.

The war in Europe might have begun in September 1939 but Japan's war had begun two years earlier. Japanese forces had defeated the numerically superior Chinese Nationalists, taking first Shanghai and then Nanking, before capturing giant swathes of eastern China's seaboard and interior. Occupation did not bring the Japanese the riches they had hoped, however. Rather, it sucked up 45 per cent of the army and incurred immense costs, while in the mass of China where Japan had not ventured, the Nationalists under the command of the totalitarian General Chiang Kai-Shek, and the Communists in the north, continued to offer resistance. It was for this reason that Japan, war weary and running short of supplies, began looking elsewhere back in 1941. Indochina, Malaya, Burma and the Dutch East Indies were far richer in resources than the vast expanse of inland China.

Yet while the Nationalists managed to keep their war effort afloat from their new capital in Chongqing, they were in no position to fight back against the occupiers, who ruled the central eastern part of China with unremitting cruelty and savagery. The Japanese regarded themselves as racially and manifestly superior, employed millions of Chinese as slave labourers and beat and beheaded thousands for the slightest of misdemeanours. Displacement, massacres, starvation and

destruction on an unimaginable scale was the fate meted out to the Chinese people.

And although Chiang was the undisputed generalissimo, he was surrounded by sycophantic courtiers, corruption and a country racked by extreme poverty. In the north, meanwhile, were the growing number of Communists under Mao Zedung; only the Japanese prevented full-scale civil war. Organizing this unoccupied part of China, let alone even attempting to modernize it, was simply not possible at this time.

The British were already stretched in terms of men and materiel and also were deeply sceptical that bolstering Chiang's Nationalists would achieve much. However, the United States had high hopes that Chiang's China could become a major force and part of the Grand Alliance fighting the Imperial Japanese. Fired by the idea

Left: General Chiang Kai-Shek.

Opposite: A US Navy F4U Corsair on the flight deck.

that one day soon a properly trained, modernized and US-equipped army would begin the fightback against the occupiers, the Americans began sending in massive amounts of cash and supplies.

The Japanese conquest of Burma had severed any direct route into China; undeterred, the Americans began flying these supplies from British-controlled Assam in north-east India, over the Himalayas to Kunming, the nearest base in China. This was a dangerous air route at the mercy of rapidly changing weather conditions, soon renamed 'the Hump'. Even so, by 1944, some 18,000 tons a month were being brought into China by air – a considerable amount and an extraordinary logistical achievement.

By early 1944, however, the Americans had accepted it was unlikely the Chinese Army would ever be good for much. Many of the US funds and supplies had been stolen by Chiang and Chinese warlords, and, with the exception of a small number of troops hand-trained by General Joe Stilwell, the senior US commander at Chiang's court, the Chinese Army remained as poorly trained, ill-equipped and good for little as it had been when the Japanese had first invaded.

So instead, most of the US supplies were diverted to feed the needs of the US Air Force in China. Then, as if to underline the ineffectiveness of the Chinese Nationalist Army, the Japanese launched a new offensive in China for the first time in three years: Operation ICHI-GO.

Since September 1940, Boeing had been developing the B-29 bomber, known as the 'Superfortress'. It had cost a staggering $3 billion, making it the most expensive single weapons system ever built, and had incurred all manner of design problems and setbacks. In early 1944, though, it was almost ready for deployment in the Pacific theatre.

Capable of cruising at nearly 300 m.p.h., it was also the first combat aircraft to be fully pressurized, which meant it could fly higher. It carried ground-mapping radar and one in four had enemy radar detectors. This extraordinary leap into modernity could also comfortably carry 10 tons of bombs – its predecessor, the B-17, could take just two – and had a phenomenal range of 3,200 miles. The plan was to operate these against Japan from southern China.

The Japanese had learned about the Superfortress and quickly realized its significance and from where it was likely to operate. With this in mind, the Japanese high command found the will and arms to launch another offensive in China, driving south to link up with their territories in Indochina (later Vietnam).

Some half a million Japanese troops blazed their way across the mighty Yellow River and on into southern China on a 120-mile front. Despite the United States' two years of ceaseless supplies, the Chinese forces were brushed aside. Some forty Chinese troops were killed for every

one Japanese, while hundreds of thousands, if not millions more Chinese people were killed or faced famine and disease as a result of Japan's scorched earth policy.

By the time ICHI-GO finally ended in August 1944, Japan held more total landmass than at any point since the start of the war, despite recent losses elsewhere.

The breadth and depth of the Imperial Japanese Empire was something of an illusion, however. Japan was in fact in a terrible position. The larger the empire, the more men were required to hold that territory and the more supplies were needed, neither of which Japan could afford any longer. Both men and materiel were almost entirely delivered by sea, but by the end of 1943, the US Navy had fixed its problematic torpedoes and was beginning to sink huge numbers of ships. After seven long years of war, the Japanese economy was on its knees – some 80 per cent of its entire economy was devoted to the war effort, but precious few new weapons were arriving and both the civilian population and the armed forces were beginning to run short of everything, not least fuel.

Admiral King was determined that the destruction of Japanese naval power held the key to victory, and could very possibly avoid costly and attritional land campaigns. His priority in 1944 was to ravage Japanese merchant and supply shipping with his submarines and to use the overwhelming superiority in the scale of his surface fleets to try to force the Japanese navy to engage in a decisive battle at sea. To this end, he proposed attacking the islands of the Central Pacific: first the Gilberts, which had already been captured the previous November, and then the Marshalls and the Marianas. Capturing these outposts in the middle of the ocean would not only deny them to the Japanese, it would bring the Allied forces closer to Japan itself.

King found an ally for this strategy in General 'Hap' Arnold, the commander of the US Army Air Force. If China could not be used as a base for his B-29s when they finally became available, then Guam, Saipan and Tinian in the Marianas would do every bit as well.

In fact, capturing these island chains would be preferable, because although establishing airfields and bases in the middle of the Pacific was no easy task, it was nothing like as challenging as operating from China – either logistically or politically. By the spring of 1944, the Americans had finally accepted that Japan would not be defeated by a Chinese, American and Commonwealth coalition based in Asia. Rather, the priority for the Americans would be Admiral King's Pacific strategy. Gradually, the noose would be tightened around Japan until the country could barely breathe at all.

Above left: US Marines during the fighting for Tarawa, part of the Gilbert Islands.

Opposite: US Navy submarines devasted Japanese merchant shipping.

Capturing the Gilberts had proved that amphibious operations using the Navy, Marine Corps and Army needed much better coordination and planning – taking Tarawa had been particularly bruising. However, the United States repeatedly proved during the war just how quick it was at learning lessons. New vehicles, such as tracked, armoured carriers capable of swimming, known as Amtracs, not only delivered troops on to the beaches of Kwajalein in the Marshalls but also offered fire support; they were bristling with cannons, machine guns and flame-throwers. Kwajalein was captured after four days on 3 February 1944, for the loss of fewer than a thousand casualties and only 182 dead; Betio on the Gilberts had cost 1,000 American dead and 2,300 wounded. In contrast, almost all the 5,000 Japanese defenders on Kwajalein and the 3,000 on neighbouring Roi-Namur were killed.

In fact, the attack on the Marshalls had gone so well that Admiral Chester Nimitz, Pacific Commander-in-Chief, brought forward an assault on the Eniwetok Atoll, the last islands before the major Japanese naval base at Truk, in the Carolines, some 900 miles further west. Eniwetok was another stepping stone, swiftly captured in just five days.

On the same day Eniwetok was assaulted, 17 February, Nimitz also launched the aircraft from nine carriers against Truk in Operation HAILSTONE, attacking the Japanese fleet and installations there. Truk was an important forward base for the Japanese so they responded furiously, albeit largely in vain. US Navy aircraft had vastly improved over the past two years, as had the quality and experience of the pilots. By contrast, Japanese aircraft had barely improved at all, while because of the urgency of their current situation combined with the chronic shortage of fuel, the standard of Japanese Navy pilots had taken a nosedive.

Some 21 Japanese naval vessels were sunk, along with 32 vital merchant ships and more than 250 aircraft, catastrophic losses at this stage of the war. Also destroyed were 17,000 tons of precious fuel. The Americans lost around 40 men and 25 aircraft. Truk might have been a tiny dot in the ocean but it was a vital base the Imperial Japanese Navy were now forced to abandon. The US Navy had taken another leap closer to Japan.

The next US target in the Pacific was the Marianas. Here were Japanese airfields, and the islands were heavily defended by nearly 60,000 troops. US submarines had successfully stemmed the flow of supplies here – more than 30,000 troops had been killed en route by newly efficient American torpedoes – which meant that the defenders were effectively isolated. Their task – and they accepted it – was to defend the islands for as long as they possibly could.

Two Marine Corps Divisions – the 2nd and 4th – along with the Army's 27th Division were landed on Saipan from 15 June 1944. This time, the fighting quickly developed into an attritional bloodbath. The Americans were beginning to learn that the Japanese would mostly sooner die than surrender.

Both King and Nimitz expected – and hoped – that the Japanese Navy would mass their forces for a decisive battle and that was exactly what the new chief in Tokyo, Admiral Toyoda Soemu, ordered. Admiral Ozawa Jisaburo, commander of the First Mobile Fleet, had a reputation for aggressiveness and in the early summer began drawing his forces together from Singapore, Borneo and the Philippines. Just one major victory at sea, the Japanese believed, and perhaps the Americans and their Allies would sue for peace.

Opposite: Operation HAILSTONE forced the Japanese Navy out of their forward operating base at Truk.

Overleaf: A Corsair launches alongside an Iowa Class battleship of US Task Force 58.

The Japanese still had some state-of-the-art warships. Admiral Ozawa's flagship was the carrier *Taiho*, with its armoured flight deck, radar, pioneering engines and array of the latest anti-aircraft weaponry. It had been hustled into service early in 1944 without sufficient working-up by the crew, who, to make matters worse, had been rushed into service too and were undertrained. So sophisticated was the *Taiho* that only the engineering officer knew how to operate the ship. He was hastily made its captain.

The standard of seamanship, once so strong, was replicated throughout the First Mobile Fleet. By contrast, Nimitz's forces were both well trained and by now highly experienced. What's more, Nimitz had overwhelming numbers and three, not one, fleets available. The US Task Force 58 alone had 7 fast battleships, 15 carriers with 891 aircraft, 21 cruisers and 69 destroyers. Admiral Ozawa, by contrast, could amass only 6 battleships, 9 carriers with around 500 aircraft, 13 cruisers and 28 destroyers.

Despite the loss of 17 of 25 submarines before the fleets engaged, Ozawa still ordered carrier aircraft to take off on the morning of 19 June, hoping they might still reignite Japanese hopes.

In a mirror of the decline of the Luftwaffe and the growing strength of Allied air forces, the Japanese naval pilots were slaughtered. In what the Americans called the 'Marianas Turkey Shoot', the Japanese lost 293 aircraft at a cost of only 20 US Hellcats. Later that day, the brand-new *Taiho* was one of two carriers sunk by the increasingly dominant US submarines.

A further light carrier was sunk the following day and a further six warships were damaged before Ozawa ordered his fleet to hurriedly pull away. Although some 38 American pilots and crew were lost on 20 June, the Battle of the Philippine Sea was a resounding victory for the US Navy.

On Saipan, meanwhile, the slaughter continued, providing a grim taste of what was to come. Not only did the Japanese fight to the very last, many of the island's civilians were also caught in the crossfire of Japanese *banzai* charges. Nearing Marpi Point in the north of the island, American troops watched in horror as the surviving Japanese began beheading one another and blowing each other up rather than surrender. More than a thousand civilians also threw themselves off the cliffs and on to the rocks below. The surf turned blood red. If anyone had doubted the fanaticism of the Japanese, the terrible tragedy of Marpi Point and the loss of almost the entire 29,000-strong garrison on Saipan made crystal clear what could be expected until the war was finally over.

Guam and Tinian were the next to be assaulted. Guam had been a US territory before the war and was now home to a Japanese air base. Unsurprisingly, it was once again tenaciously held, with the majority of the 22,500-strong garrison fighting to the death.

All but 252 of the 8,000 troops in Tinian also lost their lives in a battle that took the Americans a week. Guam, more heavily defended, took them three to clear, finally falling to the Americans on 10 August, although the last Japanese troops, unaware of what had happened in the wider world, remained hidden in the hills until they were discovered nearly thirty years later, in 1972. Among the 2,000 American dead was Lieutenant-Colonel Douglas C. McNair, son of General Leslie J. McNair, one of the US Army's wartime architects, who had also been killed just two weeks earlier in Normandy.

While navy engineers, the 'Seabees', hastily began carving out bigger runways and airstrips for the arrival of the B-29s – now within range of Japan itself – the island-hopping continued, this time with a 1st Marine Division assault on tiny Peleliu in the Palau Islands. Although only 7 miles

Opposite:
US Navy Hellcats
dominated the
skies during the
Marianas Turkey
Shoot.

long by 3, Peleliu had an airfield at its southern end and its capture would not only deny its use to the Japanese but provide another base for the Americans. Even so, it was tiny and there was a good case for simply bypassing the island, which, thanks to the Battle of the Philippine Sea and the work of the US submarines, was now effectively isolated. The 14,000 Japanese troops of the 14th Infantry Division had been sent to Peleliu knowing theirs was a one-way ticket. Whether they were all eventually slaughtered by the Americans or starved to death was not clear, but Major-General William H. Rupertus, a man who had witnessed the Japanese attack on Shanghai in 1937 and had lost his children to disease while there, was determined to go ahead and persuaded his senior commanders. Rupertus reckoned Peleliu would be crushed in just four days.

In fact, although the airfield was swiftly secured, the Japanese, in a change of tactics, retreated to the ants' nest warren of tunnels and bunkers they had created in the Umurbrogol Mountain on the island's narrow northern strip. Almost every Japanese soldier had to be prised out, one by one, and

in brutal conditions: in steaming heat and on jagged dried coral. Rupertus lost half his division in this hellish battle before they were withdrawn and replaced by the Army's 81st Division. Peleliu finally fell on 27 November, some ten weeks after the initial assault.

It seemed that the more desperate Japan's situation became, the harder and more determinedly its troops fought. A nightmarish situation had evolved in which Japanese troops seemed hell-bent on fighting to the death rather than surrendering. Now, at Leyte Gulf, off the Philippines, the first *kamikaze* attacks had begun: young pilots, flying aircraft packed with explosives, simply crashed into their targets, killing themselves and taking with them as many Allied lives and ships as possible. Just a few months earlier, both in Europe and in the Pacific, there had been genuine hopes that the war might soon be over. The Japanese defence of Peleliu and the new suicide attacks from the air ensured such hopes were now completely dashed.

Right: US Navy 'Seabees' turned recaptured islands into airfields for the B-29s.

Opposite: Each victory in the Pacific was hard-won.

While Peleliu became its own self-contained bloody drama, out at sea another big naval battle was brewing. Admiral 'Bull' Halsey, commander of the US Third Fleet, had been launching carrier raids on the Philippines but also on Okinawa and Formosa (now Taiwan), both Japanese home territories. These were a reminder to the Japanese of just how close the Americans now were.

Meanwhile, the Philippines, not Formosa as Admiral King had originally urged, would be the next target for the Allies.

That General MacArthur would be allowed to fulfill his promise of returning to the islands he had left in March 1942 was in part down to Admiral Nimitz's backing. Ever the diplomat, Nimitz was eager to be as cooperative as possible and had assigned Halsey's Third Fleet, which included Australian and New Zealand and even Mexican naval forces, to support MacArthur's operations. And MacArthur was determined that the Philippines, previously his own fiefdom and an American imperial possession, should once more fly the Stars and Stripes without further delay. In this, the Allied Chiefs of Staff acquiesced.

Even Japanese intelligence, often badly flawed, realized this would be the Americans' next move. In Tokyo, Admiral Toyoda decided to throw his surviving warships into battle. With dwindling numbers of warships and drastic shortages of fuel and other supplies, he felt it was a last throw of the dice; a potential victory – however slight the chances – would offset the risk of losing a fleet that was otherwise doomed anyway.

The Americans, on the other hand, by now had vastly superior intelligence and soon had a clear picture of Japanese plans. MacArthur was able to land troops on the east coast of the island of Leyte, in the southern centre of the Philippine archipelago, with the support of Admiral Thomas C. Kinkaid's Seventh Fleet, while Halsey's Third Fleet hunted for the decisive engagement with the Japanese. The need to protect the invasion meant that in the Battle of Leyte Gulf, as it became known, the US Navy was not able to coordinate its actions or concentrate truly overwhelming force quite as well as it might have done. The Allied naval forces also suffered damage both from Japanese land-based aircraft on the Philippines as well as from the first *kamikazes*.

None the less, over four days from 23 to 26 October, the Japanese lost four carriers, three battleships, ten cruisers and nine destroyers, along with a further 10,000 sailors. After fifty years of dominance, the Imperial Japanese Navy was a spent force. There would be no more fleet actions against the Allies in this war. The sheer scale of the US Navy in the Pacific, now increased by the Royal Navy's Pacific Fleet and Commonwealth forces, was simply overwhelming.

US submarines continued to send more and more Japanese ships to the bottom of the sea. Some 3.8 million tons of Japanese supplies were sunk in 1944, of which submarines were responsible for 2.3 million tons. Half the entire Japanese merchant fleet was destroyed, while in all, some 197,000 Japanese troops were killed while in transit across the seas – some thirteen divisions, an entire army's worth. These were catastrophic losses. Japanese conquests in South-East Asia had given them what they needed: access to plentiful

Right:
The US Pacific Fleet in action.

Opposite:
US forces go ashore at Leyte.

supplies of oil, rubber, coal, cotton, timber and other precious resources. But they had not been able to get it to Japan and other places where it was needed. It was the tantalizing paradox of their imperial dream: they had gained the vast pan-Pacific empire of their dreams but were unable to milk its assets or keep it sustained. Its very scale was also its greatest flaw.

In contrast, the United States had shown what could be achieved with the kind of industrialization and exponential growth never before witnessed. It wasn't just the ever-enlargening naval fleets that were overwhelming the Japanese but the even bigger numbers of merchant ships keeping this astonishing effort going. Japanese naval ratings were almost starved while American sailors could drink Coca-Cola and eat ice cream.

After swiftly securing Leyte, MacArthur was determined to strike for Manila, the capital of the Philippines, with an assault on the island of Luzon. The numbers of Japanese troops defending the various atolls and outposts across the Pacific had been necessarily small, but on Luzon there was the entire Fourteenth Army commanded by General Yamashita Tomoyuki, known as the 'Tiger of Malaya' after his lightning victories back in 1942. Yamashita accepted that Luzon could not be held but, as with the defence of Peleliu, was determined to hold out for as long as possible, mainly by retreating into the mountains that ran down the eastern spine of Luzon.

MacArthur planned to attack with two armies of his own, the Sixth under the German-born General Walter Krueger, landing north of Manila, and the Eighth under General Robert L. Eichelberger. Both were extremely able and experienced commanders and their intelligence teams had a very clear picture of Yamashita's strengths and intentions. Despite receiving accurate estimates that Yamashita had more than 230,000 troops on Luzon, MacArthur insisted the figure was only 152,000. The Americans still had enough forces to win the battle – eventually – but MacArthur had willingly underestimated Japanese strength, which led to faulty presumptions and a battle that cost a lot more US blood than should have been necessary.

Even on the approach to Luzon, the US Navy was unprepared for the ferocity of the *kamikaze* attacks. 'At this late stage,' wrote a sailor on HMAS *Australia*, 'after all one had survived, the feeling was: "Not now – please not now!"' A *kamikaze* did hit *Australia*, killing 30 and wounding 64. Fortunately, though, the suicide fliers did not target the warships and the landings went off as planned on 9 January 1945.

Kamikazes had sunk 24 vessels since the middle of December and damaged many more, and the American admirals were beginning to worry about this cumulative toll. Then, suddenly, the attacks stopped. Unbeknown to the Allies, the Japanese had lost 600 aircraft in a month and there were only 50 left in the Philippines. These were hastily withdrawn, to be saved for the future defence of Okinawa and Formosa.

The fighting on Luzon was predictably grim. The all-important Clark Field air base was captured within a week but MacArthur's hopes of entering Manila in triumph on his birthday, 26 January, were thwarted, for although Yamashita saw no point in a senseless slaughter in Manila, Rear-Admiral Sanji Iwabuchi, who had 16,000 naval servicemen in the city, insisted on fighting to the last. The Imperial Japanese Army and Navy had never made good bedfellows.

The consequence was a bloodbath, in which Japanese troops furiously raped and executed thousands of civilians and in which the Americans were forced to fight for every house, street

and suburb. The beautiful old city was largely destroyed. 'Relaxing is impossible,' noted one American infantry officer, 'for uncontrollable muscles tighten and teeth are clenched. The blast of a heavy shell is unforgettable, as is the dud that goes bouncing overhead down a cobblestone street . . . Being bounced in the air and stung by blasted debris gets a trooper counting arms and legs and feeling for blood.'

Only on 3 March was Manila finally in American hands, but the Battle for Luzon still had weeks to run, marked by the dogged resistance of Yamashita's men. Even when starving, they fought on. Japanese troops had resorted to eating bats and cannibalizing the dead. More Japanese soldiers – as well as civilian Filipinos – died of starvation than from American guns.

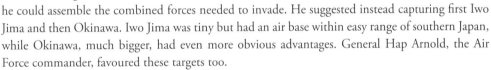

Admiral King still planned to invade Formosa, but it was a big island and Nimitz was not sure he could assemble the combined forces needed to invade. He suggested instead capturing first Iwo Jima and then Okinawa. Iwo Jima was tiny but had an air base within easy range of southern Japan, while Okinawa, much bigger, had even more obvious advantages. General Hap Arnold, the Air Force commander, favoured these targets too.

With the Americans now within touching distance, Imperial General Headquarters in Tokyo sent veteran units from China and Manchuria to prepare the two islands' defences. Some 21,000 troops were posted to Iwo Jima, a sulphurous island of just 8 square miles, 750 miles from Tokyo, and which was dominated by the dormant volcano, Mount Suribachi, at its southern tip. This peak came to house a warren of tunnels and bunkers and covered trenches. General Ushijima Mitsuru made it clear to his men that their task was to fight to the death.

Fifteen minutes after landing on the black gravel beaches on 19 February, murderous Japanese fire rained down on the invasion forces of the 4th and 5th Marine Divisions. Of the 24 marine infantry battalions landed, 17 lost their commanders, either killed or wounded, while one battalion after another was decimated. Marines managed to raise a Stars and Stripes on the summit of Mount Suribachi on 23 February – captured in a photograph that became one of the most iconic of the war – but three more brutal weeks of fighting followed, during which this tiny slab in the middle of the ocean was pounded by millions of shells, napalm, mortars, bullets and grenades. Both on- and offshore, the Americans, unusually, lost more casualties than the defenders. The difference was that only 216 Japanese were taken prisoner.

Above right:
US Marines raise
the flag over
Iwo Jima.

Opposite:
American troops
advance through
the Philippines

The war had not stopped in South-East Asia while the Americans were island-hopping and destroying the Japanese maritime power. After annihilating most of the Japanese Fifteenth Army at Imphal and Kohima in the summer of 1944, General Bill Slim's Fourteenth Army pursued the remnants out of North-East India in September. Despite the monsoon and appalling conditions, they kept going, into Burma and across the Chindwin River, one of the main natural obstacles in the north of the country.

In December, Indian troops of Fourteenth Army linked up with General Stilwell's US-trained Chinese troops. A few weeks later, the 'Burma Road' land-link to Kunming was reopened, allowing supplies to flow into China at long last. At this point, Chiang Kai-Shek promptly ordered his divisions back into China. If Slim was to retake Burma, Fourteenth Army would have to do it on its own.

Slim's aim was to destroy the Japanese Burma Area Army and, despite the difficulties of mounting an overland offensive in the remote and incredibly challenging terrain of northern Burma, he planned to confront the enemy in the Shwebo Plain, to the north-west of the mighty Irrawaddy River.

General Hoyotaro Kimura, however, the new Japanese commander in Burma, wanted to draw Slim's army deep into the country, where British lines of supply would become overstretched, and then counter-attack. It was an obvious ploy, but Slim soon came up with an inspired counter-plan. One corps, the 33rd, would cross the Irrawaddy and face the bulk of the Japanese forces near the key city of Mandalay. In secret, however, 4th Corps would advance in a wide loop through the jungle to Meiktila, Kimura's main logistics base, some 70 miles south of Mandalay. And catch the Japanese in a trap.

As a further distraction, a third British corps, including a Commando brigade and two West African divisions, would push south through the Arakan on the west coast. The Arakan operation began in January, part of a complex overall plan in which keeping 4th Corps' advance to Meiktila hidden from the Japanese was vital. Incredibly, through their command of the skies, both to keep enemy aircraft away and to drop supplies to General Frank Messervy's 4th Corps below, the Allies managed to pull off what, on paper at any rate, had seemed logistically impossible. The harnessing of land and air power had reached new levels of operational brilliance.

On 3 March, Meiktila fell in an attack that had achieved complete surprise. Kimura immediately ordered his troops to turn south and retake the town, but first the 17th Indian and then the 5th Indian Division managed to hold firm, whilst weakening Kimura's forces further. With Japanese, not British, supply lines severed, 33rd Corps attacked and took Mandalay on 21 March.

Once again, the Japanese had been decimated and now the road to Rangoon, the capital of Burma and a major port, lay open. Also operating behind Japanese lines were a growing number of Special Operations Executive (SOE) teams, working hand in glove with the Burmese National Army forces under resistance leader Aung San. Harassed by these guerillas and by the Fourteenth Army driving south, Kimura abandoned Rangoon, which was captured on 2 May, just as the monsoon began to fall and threatened to make the roads impassable. Victory had been snatched in the nick of time, and although fighting to the south continued, Slim's multinational force of Indians, Africans, Nepalese and British troops, with the help of the Burmese, had achieved what no one had thought possible.

Although the first B-29 raid had been flown the previous June, against Bangkok in Siam, and Japan first bombed a few weeks later, the full weight of the B-29 bombing campaign seemed to be a long time in coming. Air strips on Saipan and Guam had to be lengthened and asphalted, stores brought in, fuel and ammunition stocks established as well as ground crews and services. Really, it was a

Opposite:
RAF Beaufighters
flying in support
of Slim's forces
in Burma.

miracle that both islands were open for business by the second week of November 1944 and Tinian ready in December.

In the third week of January 1945, Brigadier-General Curtis LeMay, a veteran of the Eighth Air Force in England, arrived in the Marianas to take command of the B-29s. It had initially been planned that bombing would target industry only and be as 'precision' as possible. However,

Japanese industry was widely spread, the weather was variable and early B-29 raids had shown that high-altitude daylight raids were simply not very precise at all. Instead, LeMay chose to follow a 'just win' strategy, and relentlessly too. When weather conditions were fair, his bombers would attack from altitude during the day; when the weather was against them, they would attack at lower altitudes by night, when Japanese defences were at their weakest.

He also pursued a policy of using incendiaries filled with napalm and phosphorous, which were devastatingly effective against the densely placed, often wooden buildings in most of Japan's cities.

It was ruthless and brutal. The first mass night-time incendiary raid on Tokyo was on 9/10 March. In that terrible night, over 267,000 buildings burned to the ground and a staggering 83,000 were killed. Once again in this war, it was the civilians who were paying the harshest price.

The subsequent incendiary raids that followed, again on Tokyo but on other Japanese cities besides, reflected the Allies' anger and exasperation at the brutality of the Japanese armed forces and their stubborn insistence on continuing the fight. Americans were still battling on Luzon, for example, while the British were fighting in Burma and the Australians in New Guinea. It had been a very long war.

Meanwhile, in the Pacific, the Americans and their British and Commonwealth allies in the naval campaign launched their invasion of Okinawa, home to 450,000 native Okinawans and a Japanese territory since 1879. The island was the largest in the curling tail of the Ryuku archipelago and only some 320 miles south of Japan. By the spring of 1945, Okinawa was heaving with more than 76,000 Japanese troops of the Thirty-Second Army; it was unthinkable for the Land of the Rising Sun to concede such a jewel, no matter how badly the war was going.

Amassed for this battle was a joint US Army and Marine Corps landing force of around 182,000 troops of the Tenth Army and the US Tenth Fleet and Royal Navy's Pacific Fleet – some 1,457 warships and landing craft in all and a mighty armada.

Invasion day was 1 April 1945 – both Easter Sunday and April Fool's Day – and much to the surprise of many of those American troops coming ashore, they did so peacefully without a shot being fired by the Japanese defenders. If the Marines thought Okinawa was going to be a walkover,

Above left: US troops on Okinawa.

Opposite: Japanese kamikazes attack the US fleet during the Battle of Okinawa.

though, they were cruelly deceived. Rather, General Ushijima had decided not to contest the beaches, choosing instead to lure the Americans into a belt of well-prepared defences. The next 81 days were to prove the bloodiest single land-air-sea battle of the entire war.

To begin with, the Americans swiftly secured the centre of the island and then, after a tough fight, they cleared the north of the island too. Only then was all hell let loose. The Allied naval forces still off the coast, covering incoming supplies, came under repeated attack by *kamikazes*. In all, 1,500 suicide attacks were made for the Emperor in the seas around Okinawa. During the naval and air battle, 64 US Navy ships were sunk or severely damaged; 5,000 men were killed and a further 7,000 wounded – more casualties than had been suffered in the Pacific in the previous two years. The destroyer *Laffey* was hit by no less than six *kamikazes* and lost half her crew.

On land, the battle developed into a terrible bloody slaughter as the Americans, unimaginatively led by army commander General Simon Bolivar Buckner, ran into the series of defensive lines. Cactus Ridge, Sugar Loaf and Shuri Castle all became scenes of carnage. 'You know what it feels like when two nights in a row you don't get sleep?' said Dick Whitaker, a Marine on Okinawa. 'Put a hundred and one days of that back-to-back, and during that time you're sleeping in a hole every night and anything you do could get you killed, including absolutely nothing. That's what it felt like.'

Every yard of southern Okinawa had to be wrested from the Japanese, who used civilians as human shields for their own attacks. A staggering 200,000 Okinawans were killed – not far off half the population. Not until 22 June was the battle finally over. It was to prove the last battle of the war – and one of the bloodiest. Some 110,000 Japanese troops were killed, at a cost to the Americans of 7,613 dead, 32,000 wounded and a further 26,000 lost to accidents and disease.

The Japanese were beaten. They had lost the war. And yet they simply would not surrender; fighting was still going on in the Philippines and in Borneo, against the Australians. The B-29s continued to bomb Japan, US submarines continued to sink enemy ships, but still the Japanese kept going, fanatically to the death. The Allied planners were braced for an invasion of Japan – set for 1946 – in which they expected more than 2 million would be killed. War weariness and growing frustration at the senselessness of the slaughter was infecting the Allied high command.

But there would be no invasion and the war

Right: The mushroom cloud from the first atom bomb rises above Hiroshima.

Opposite: B-29 Superfortresses mounted relentless attacks against the Japanese mainland.

would not drag on into 1946. Instead, Emperor Hirohito agreed to unconditional surrender on 15 August, following the American decision to use a new and devastating weapon: the atomic bomb.

Britain and the United States had been working on such a weapon for several years, drawing on the pioneering work of nuclear physicists from an array of countries, including that of Germany: scientists who had escaped Nazi Germany and found homes in the US and Britain. While Germany had decided back in July 1942 not to prioritize atomic research, in the USA, the Manhattan Project had been given the green light – and immense funding – in 1943. At Los Alamos in New Mexico, some 120,000 men and women worked round the clock developing a weapon of unprecedented complexity and power.

When it would be ready was not entirely clear. By early 1945, they were close, but not close enough to affect the war against Nazi Germany. Then finally, on 16 July, the first atomic bomb was tested in the New Mexico desert, creating a huge mushroom fireball followed by blinding waves of light and crushing pressure. It was the kind of destructive might that could end the world, not just wars.

The decision to use the bomb on Japan was not taken lightly, but it was believed the Japanese would not readily surrender unconditionally as the Allies had demanded back in January 1943. The city of Hiroshima was chosen because it had some military value yet had remained largely untouched by bombers; there was no point flattening an already flattened city.

The first atomic bomb to be used in anger was dropped on 6 August, destroying much of the city and a significant proportion of the civilian population. Still Japan did not surrender, and so a second bomb was dropped, this time on Nagasaki, on 9 August – actually a secondary target, since bad weather prevented them dropping it on Kokura as planned. Nagasaki, a city of predominantly wooden buildings, was largely wiped from the face of the earth. It remains unclear how many died from the two bombs, but it was an enormous number: at least 130,000 and possibly as many as 225,000, although more had been killed by the B-29 bombing raids.

That same day, the Soviet Union declared war and invaded Japanese-held Manchuria. Still Japanese war leaders were split over whether they should fight on, but while they argued and the United States prepared to drop a third atomic bomb, Emperor Hirohito himself told his military chiefs the war had to end. His message of surrender reached Washington and London on the morning of 10 August. After feverish negotiations within Japan and with the Allies, the surrender was announced on 15 August and formally signed on 2 September. The bloodiest, most terrible war in the world's history was finally over. Some 60 million globally had lost their lives, entire countries had disappeared, a new nuclear age had emerged, and the world would never be the same again.

Opposite: The Japanese sign the formal surrender aboard the USS Missouri.

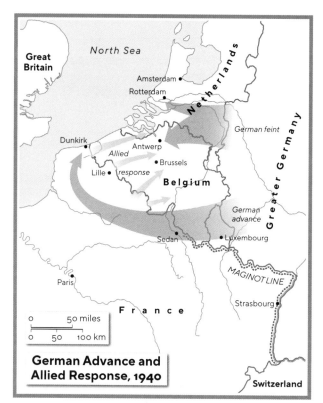

German Advance and Allied Response, 1940

Great Britain

North Sea

Amsterdam

Rotterdam

N e t h e r l a n d s

Dunkirk

Antwerp

Allied
response

Brussels

Lille

B e l g i u m

German feint

German advance

Sedan

Luxembourg

G r e a t e r G e r m a n y

MAGINOT LINE

Paris

F r a n c e

Strasbourg

0   50 miles
0   50   100 km

Switzerland

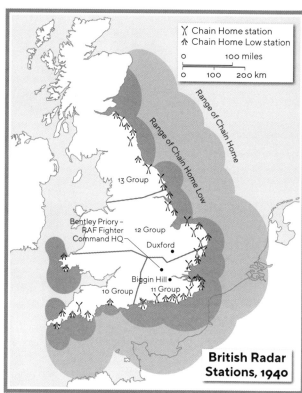

British Radar Stations, 1940

⋎ Chain Home station
⋏ Chain Home Low station

0   100 miles
0   100   200 km

Range of Chain Home

Range of Chain Home Low

13 Group

Bentley Priory –
RAF Fighter
Command HQ

12 Group

Duxford

Biggin Hill

10 Group

11 Group

Japanese Control in the Pacific

*Greatest extent
of Japanese
control*

Japan

Midway

Hawaii

Marshall Is.

Rabaul

Solomon Is.

Port Moresby

Samoa

Fiji

Tonga

Australia

Guadalcanal

New Zealand

0   750   1,500 miles
0   1,500   3,000 km

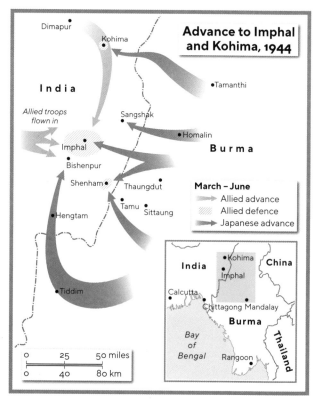

Advance to Imphal and Kohima, 1944

Dimapur

Kohima

I n d i a

•Tamanthi

*Allied troops
flown in*

Sangshak

Imphal

•Homalin

B u r m a

Bishenpur

Shenham

Thaungdut

March – June

→ Allied advance

Allied defence

→ Japanese advance

Tamu

Sittaung

Hengtam

Tiddim

India

•Kohima

China

•Imphal

Calcutta

Chittagong   Mandalay

Burma

*Bay
of
Bengal*

Rangoon

Thailand

0   25   50 miles
0   40   80 km

Front Lines

— 22 June 1941
— 25 August 1941
— 7 May 1942
······ 22 July 1942
--- 18 November 1942
--- 19 February 1943

Baltic Sea

Tallinn
Leningrad
Pskov
Riga
Danzig
Warsaw
Krakow
Minsk
Smolensk
Moscow
R. Volga
Bryansk
Orel
Kursk
Kiev
Kharkov
Voronezh
R. Volga
Stalingrad
Rostov
Astrakhan
Odessa
Maikop
Sebastopol
Grozny
Caspian Sea

Black Sea

Eastern Front

0   100   200 miles
0   200   400 km

INDEX

Illustration page numbers are in **bold**

PENGUIN MICHAEL JOSEPH

UK | USA | Canada | Ireland | Australia
India | New Zealand | South Africa

Penguin Michael Joseph is part of the Penguin Random House group of companies
whose addresses can be found at global.penguinrandomhouse.com

Penguin
Random House
UK

Previously published by Penguin Michael Joseph as individual books: 1. *Blitzkrieg*, 2018; 2. *The Battle of Britain*, 2017;
3. *The Battle of the Atlantic*, 2018; 4. *The Desert War*, 2018; 5. *The Eastern Front 1941–1943*, 2018; 6. *The Pacific War 1941–1943*, 2019;
7. *The Bomber War, 2020*; 8. *The War in Italy*, 2021, 9. *The Battle for Normandy 1944*, 2023; 10. *The War in Burma 1943–1944*, 2023;
11. *Victory in Europe 1944–1945*, 2023; 12. *Victory Against Japan 1944–1945*, 2023

This collected and amended edition first published 2023

001

The publisher would like to thank the following for the illustrative references for this book:
Admiral William F. Halsey Jr © Bettman/Bettman/Getty Images, p.149; AP Photo / Joe Rosenthal, p.315; Corbis via Getty Images, pp.2, 70, 277,
296, 298; Don Salvatore image – public domain (digital reproduction or scan of US Govt photo), John Godfrey and James Goodson – original
image reference courtesy of IWM collection, p.178; Getty Images/Tass, p.118; Hideki Tojo © World History Archive/Alamy Stock Photo;
Emperor Hirohito © Keystone-France/Gamma-Keystone/Getty Image, p.134; *Images of War: The Invasion of Sicily, 1943*, p.191, (soldiers in
the foreground), p.196; IWM (A 4545), p.52, (CH12283), p.164, (CH13020), p.165; Keystone/Getty Images, p.280; Major-General Spatz's
head – David E. Scherman/The LIFE Picture Collection via Getty Images, p.167; Pictorial Press Ltd/Alamy Stock Photo, p.293; Roger Viollet
Getty Images, p.vi; The US Army, photo – public domain, p.201; Universal History Archive/Getty Images, p.23 ; Wikimedia Commons, pp.11
(courtesy of Fallschirmjäger), 315 (AP Photo / Joe Rosenthal), 232, 243, 255

Every effort has been made to ensure images are correctly attributed; however, if any omission
or error has been made, please notify the Publisher for correction in future editions

Set in Adobe Garamond Pro 10/13pt and TT Norms Pro
Design and typeset by Nathan Burton
Printed in Italy by Printer Trento S.r.L.

The authorized representative in the EEA is Penguin Random House Ireland,
Morrison Chambers, 32 Nassau Street, Dublin D02 YH68

A CIP catalogue record for this book is available from the British Library

ISBN: 978–0–241–60132–7

www.greenpenguin.co.uk